LIVING LIKE A
RUNAWAY

LITA FORD

DEY ST.
AN *IMPRINT* OF
WILLIAM MORROW *PUBLISHERS*

In Loving Memory of

SANDY WEST

(July 10, 1959–October 21, 2006)

· · ·

DEY ST.

LIVING LIKE A RUNAWAY. Copyright © 2016 by Model T, Inc. All rights reserved. Printed in the United States of America. No part of this book may be used or reproduced in any manner whatsoever without written permission except in the case of brief quotations embodied in critical articles and reviews. For information address HarperCollins Publishers, 195 Broadway, New York, NY 10007.

HarperCollins books may be purchased for educational, business, or sales promotional use. For information please e-mail the Special Markets Department at SPsales@harpercollins.com.

A hardcover edition of this book was published in 2016 by Dey Street, an imprint of HarperCollins Publishers.

FIRST DEY STREET PAPERBACK EDITION PUBLISHED IN 2016.

Designed by Paula Russell Szafranski
Endpaper photograph by Dustin Jack
Title page and chapter opener image (silhouette of Lita Ford) by Dustin Jack

Library of Congress Cataloging-in-Publication Data has been applied for.

ISBN 978-0-06-227065-8

23 24 25 26 27 LBC 9 8 7 6 5

CONTENTS

Dancin' on the Edge. Having never gotten to see the Runaways live, I was truly impressed not only by Lita's performing but also by her guitar playing. *Here was a girl who could really play!* And I'm not talking playing good "for a girl," I'm talking playing good for *anybody.* Lita Ford could wail, and night after night she rocked the house. Let's face it, up to that point, with rare exception, a "female rocker" was pretty much viewed as an oxymoron. Lita Ford was standing flat-footed on the stage each night, wearing denim and leather, shredding on her guitar, and daring anyone to deny her right to be there. *And nobody could.* Lita Ford was just what the women's movement in the rock-and-roll world needed.

Not being a hanging-out-and-partying kind of guy, I really didn't get to spend much time with Lita during that tour, but we both came to respect and appreciate each other. And while my band Twisted Sister's career crashed and burned after one big record (my bad!), Lita's continued on. Culminating with a platinum album and number one single, Lita Ford had become an iconic female rocker. The Queen of Metal!

I FELL INTO obscurity for more than a few years and lost touch with and track of Lita Ford. At some point I heard rumors about her getting married (again) and retiring to some tropical island, but that was all I knew. I was having enough of my own troubles trying to reinvent myself and take care of my family without worrying about who was doing what in the world of 1980s rock. In fact, '80s rock and rockers had both died a horrible (yet much needed) death at the hands of grunge. Every band I had known was dealing with its own crisis.

By the early 2000s, I had finally pulled out of my personal slump, having found new careers in radio, voice-over, and filmmaking. To celebrate my return from the dead, I took my family on our first real vacation in years, to a resort in Turks and Caicos.

A couple of days after getting there, we returned to our room to find the phone-message light flashing. I figured it was the hotel management checking to see if we were finally happy with our room, having moved three times since we had arrived. (Hey, once a rock star, always a rock star.) I hit the message button and a voice from my past started speaking to me.

"Hey, Dee. It's Lita Ford. I live on the island and would love to have my family get together with yours."

Lita Ford? She lives here? Wait—*how did she even know I was here?*

When I called Lita back, she quickly pointed out that it was a small island, and when an iconic '80s rocker shows up, the island's resident iconic '80s rocker is quickly informed.

Lita had retired from the music business, with her husband and family (she now had two young boys, James and Rocco), to a quiet life in the tropics, and while she had deliberately disconnected from her past to find her future, the one rocker she'd met during her years in the business who she wanted to reconnect with was me. Lita Ford the rocker/family woman knew she could hang with Dee Snider the rocker/family man. She knew I didn't party, drink, or get high, had been with the same woman (Suzette) since I'd met her in 1976, and that we had four children of our own. This fit perfectly with the post-rock-and-roll life Lita had built for herself.

Visiting Lita and her family for the first time at her home in the tropics, I was taken by (and a bit surprised at) how domestic she was. Lita had approached her new life with the same intensity and dedication that she had used to attack her career in rock and roll: she gave it everything she had. A loving wife and mother, she doted on her family, giving them all (especially her children) the kind of love and attention they needed and then some. Cooking (even baking bread each day from scratch!), gardening (growing fresh fruits and vegetables), cleaning, homeschooling her boys, and everything else in between, Lita was definitely a rock-star mom.

That afternoon, Lita and her family took my family to see the beautiful home they were building on an island off the coast of Turks and Caicos, accessible only by boat. I couldn't help but notice how removed this property, an oceanfront paradise, would make Lita and her children. While her husband was clearly excited about the prospect of further disconnecting from civilization, I could see that Lita was less than ecstatic. While she loved her family deeply, I know she worried about the effect that social isolation might have on her children . . . *and herself.* And what about her music?

Later, after a delicious dinner back on the mainland at Lita's house, I asked her that very question: *What about your career?* Did she miss it? Was it over? Would she ever come out of retirement to kiss us deadly again? Lita assured me that her rock-and-roll days were far behind her, and she had absolutely no interest in ever going back.

Since that reunion dinner in the early 2000s Lita and I have remained friends, spending a lot of time together. Hell, our tribes have even gone on vacation together. And since that fateful night, Lita has come blazing out of retirement to rock the world once more. She blames me for her return (you're welcome, everybody!), but Lita's not fooling anyone. The girl was born to rock, and whether she's in a band, performing solo, or just being an amazing, dedicated mom, nothing can ever change that. And why would we want to?

The rock-and-roll world needs Lita Ford!

PART I

FROM THE CRADLE TO THE STAGE

CHAPTER 1

SWEET SIXTEEN

I had a dream that I was sweet sixteen

And could play in a rock and roll band

I saw some guys that played guitar

They said, "Come on if you think you can."

—"ROCK AND ROLL MADE ME WHAT I AM TODAY"
(WRITTEN BY LITA FORD)

I GUESS I COULD START WITH WHEN I WAS BORN OR MY FIRST CONCERT OR the first time I picked up a guitar or something like that. We'll get there. But if you want to know the moment when everything started to shift for me, it was my sixteenth birthday party.

It was a Saturday night in September 1974. I was going to turn sixteen in a few days, and my mom wanted to throw me a party at our house. I wasn't really the type to have a Sweet Sixteen, but I told my mom I would invite some friends from school and we'd keep it small. My mother had my aunt Rose and uncle Wyman over; they were planning to play cards inside and keep an eye on the party in the backyard. My dad was on a fishing trip in Oregon and due back the following night.

We lived in Lakewood Village, the "safe part" of Long Beach, California. My parents chose the area because the schools were better than the ones in downtown Long Beach, though not in my opinion. They were too white-bread for me. By the time I got to the ninth grade, I begged my parents not to send me to Lakewood High. It was full of football players and cheerleaders, and I knew I wouldn't fit in. I wanted to go to Long Beach Poly. Long Beach Poly was rivals with Compton High and a war zone. Behind wrought-iron walls that were approximately forty feet high, we would be searched for guns or knives with metal detectors. It was more like a prison yard than a high school. A thirty-minute bus ride across town for me, Long Beach Poly was full of Crips and gang fights, drugs, guns, drive-by shootings, and riots. Violence was a common occurrence, and then school administrators would shut down both schools for days. If they felt the schools were ready to rumble, or that a riot was about to start, we'd all be on high alert.

Poly was where I met three guys who liked to play rock music as much as I did: Marc Seawright, Anthony Bledsoe, and Kent Taylor. These were the guys who taught me you had to have dynamite in your soul to have dynamite in your guitar playing. We often would ditch school to go to somebody's house to jam.

Mark Seawright, who played bass and sang, was a tall, intelligent, and handsome black guy who was a star football player. He wore a rainbow-colored wool hat with a little ball on top and reminded me of Jimi Hendrix. Anthony Bledsoe played guitar. He was a badass. He played with his thumb, never a pick, which I thought was so weird. The school was majority black; me and my friend Kent Taylor, who was our drummer, were minorities. Kent was tall and as skinny as a string bean, with long brown hair. At the time, he lived mostly in his car. We all met in this program called School of Educational Alternatives, or SEA for short. It was for kids with high IQs but low grade-point averages. Teachers said we "weren't applying ourselves." The truth was school just didn't interest us in the least. Basically, we didn't fit in the box. A few years later, one of my schoolteachers saw me in the rock magazines at Queen parties, or with Kiss, Alice Cooper, or Rod Stewart. He knew I would amount to something someday. So he let me slide and gave me the credits I needed to graduate.

I'd write notes for me, Mark, and Anthony and give them to the nurse's office, which would then excuse us from school for the day. Why the nurse's office bought my bullshit is beyond me. The hard part was trying to come up with a different illness for all of us. I also had to change my handwriting and the pens and paper I would use. Marc, Anthony, Kent, and I would go to the first few classes, sometimes just first period, then we would head to Norm's Coffee Shop, where we would talk about what we were going to do when we were rich and famous rock stars. We would end up at someone's house where we could jam. It didn't matter whose house it was as long as we could rock out as loud as we wanted. Jimi Hendrix was a huge influence for all of us. We'd also play tons of Sabbath and Deep Purple. We knew it all by heart, and those were the songs on the set list for my birthday party that night.

At about eight P.M. on the night of my sixteenth birthday, the guys and I were in my driveway setting up to rock. A handful of friends had already arrived. As I mentioned, my mother had invited my father's sister, Aunt Rose, and her husband, Uncle Wyman. They were playing cards inside. More people started to show up outside. My mother started making sandwiches for everybody. I said, "Mom, what are you doing?"

She said in her thick Italian accent, "Oh, Lita, the kids are drinking. I don't want to see anyone get drunk." What she didn't know was that it was about to become a block party. Suddenly, more and more people were arriving. She finally gave up when she realized she didn't have nearly enough bread. I went outside and started jamming with my band. My mother was getting a little nervous about the volume. We were playing so loud that they couldn't hear or talk in the kitchen and the whole house was shaking. My relatives had to scream back and forth to each other to play cards.

"You got a nine of hearts?"

"No, Isa! You got a six of clubs?"

Our front and back yards were both full of kids. People kept coming with their own supplies of alcohol.

The party began spilling into the street and down the block. It was pandemonium. We kept playing. Police helicopters were starting to circle. Sirens blared from a distance in between songs. It took the cops a while to figure out where the chaos was coming from, because the streets were too full of kids and cars for them to get through easily. My mother was passing through the backyard looking for me. When she finally found me she said, "Lita, I was walking through the crowd and I noticed one of the kids was wearing a badge. Then I realized it was Officer Steve."

My mother worked at St. Mary's Medical Center, and the police officer knew her from there. Almost everyone in Long Beach knew my mother. Officer Steve screamed to her, "Lisa, this is your house?" (My mother's name was Isabella, or Isa, but people here called her Lisa.)

"Yeah, this is my daughter's sixteenth birthday party!" she screamed back.

"Since it's your house, it's okay. Just make sure you quit by midnight." It was ten P.M. at that time. That's when my father showed up a day earlier than expected. He wanted to surprise me for my birthday. I thought I was in big trouble, but instead he cracked open a beer and stood in the crowd to watch us play. My dad was the greatest. We shut down at midnight, as promised, and then we spent the next couple of hours cleaning up the entire neighborhood. There were soda cans, beer bottles, wine bottles, trash, and cigarette butts in the street, in the gutters, on the neighbors' cars and lawns for several blocks. What a mess!

After the party, word got out about the girl in Long Beach who could play guitar. The following weekend some local band was doing a show at a party. I didn't know who the musicians were—they were friends of a friend—and at the last minute their bass player pulled out. They called me and said, "We know you don't know us, but would you play bass for us?"

"I don't play bass," I told them. "I play guitar."

"You can figure it out."

I guess I couldn't argue with that. After all, I figured out how to play guitar by ear. *How hard could it be?* I thought to myself, and I said, "Okay."

I ended up doing that show at some little club in Long Beach. Little did I know that people were there scouting for musicians. Back then, the LA music scene was a small world that thrived on word of mouth and people vouching for your talent. Word started to spread through Los Angeles that there was a girl who played bass. People were shocked that a female was playing hard rock. At that time it was unheard of.

I WAS TEN years old when I asked my mother for my first guitar. She bought me a Spanish-style acoustic guitar with nylon strings for my eleventh birthday. She also signed me up for lessons from a guy in a little studio around the corner. He taught me my first chords. Although I liked Creedence Clearwater Revival, it just wasn't riffy enough for me. I wanted to play heavier stuff like Black Sabbath, Deep Purple, or Led Zeppelin. I quit going for lessons after two weeks and decided I could teach myself instead.

I liked playing, but I didn't like that guitar. That kind of guitar was mostly for classical-style playing; it didn't make the right kinds of sounds. I was looking for a rock-and-roll sound. The power and the grit that come out of heavy metal music and the way it makes people feel and act attracted me, and ever since I can remember I've been drawn to it. It's more or less the attitude that I loved, and that attitude is a part of me, so I was able to relate to it more than to any other attitude in music. I wanted something with balls, with some aggression, and hard rock offered that. Seeing Black Sabbath in concert a few years later would confirm all my feelings about this music I loved. It's just something that's in my blood. It's natural to me—like what color my eyes or my skin are. It's a part of who I am.

I finally said to my mom, "I like playing guitar. And I want one with steel strings." So, God bless my mom, she got me an acoustic guitar with steel strings for Christmas. Of course, that's not what I wanted either, but I didn't have the heart to tell her. I played that guitar for two more years until I was able to get a job and make enough money to buy my own electric guitar.

When I was learning to play, I found out that by listening to the records quietly you could hear the notes and mistakes better. At the time, my mom and dad had an old stereo system. It was this huge thing where the dials were in the top of the right side, the TV screen was in the middle, and the turntable was on the left. The entire system was bigger than I was! I would sneak back into our apartment and put on whatever solo I wanted to learn that day. I would quietly start dissecting the song. I love Jimmy Page, but I gotta say, he had the most mistakes. I learned his solos note for note. If it went by too fast for me, I would gently slide the needle on the turntable back in the grooves of the record, over and over and over, until I had pieced together an entire solo or song. By the time I was thirteen I had mastered them all.

Neighborhood friends would come over just to sit around and watch me play. I never grasped what the big deal was. They couldn't understand why they couldn't do it but I could. Never mind being a female. It didn't occur to me while I was growing up that I was doing anything out of the ordinary by liking the type of music I did. No one told me that girls can't do this. That never entered anyone's mind at that time. Even though I had no female role models, it didn't dawn on me that I was doing anything that hadn't been done before.

I WOULD HAVE been excited that all these people were talking about my musical ability, but soon I was dealing with something I could not yet comprehend. I had gone out a few times with a guy named Davy, a guitar player who was a couple years older than I was. He was a cool guy with long hair and crooked teeth. We would play guitar together. He was more advanced than me, so he really taught me a lot. He was the one who taught me my vibrato. However, the consequences were bad news. I found out I was pregnant. I was only sixteen! Davy was a gentleman, but I didn't want to tell him for fear he would try to talk me into marrying him and keeping the baby. I was just too young to deal with that. There was no chance of me raising a child at that point in my life: I wouldn't have made a good mother at the age of sixteen. I had a friend, Karen, who had had an abortion not too long before this.

I asked Karen what to do. She directed me to a medical facility where the doctors would give underage girls abortions. I couldn't believe they would do it without any parental consent, but they agreed. I started making the arrangements.

I told my parents I was going hiking up to the mountains for the day. I said that I would be home later that night. It was horrible. I was a petrified little girl, alone, with a baby inside of me. I had so many questions, but nobody to answer them. *What do I wear? What if the doctors are quacks? What if they destroy my insides? How long is the recovery and how do I excuse myself from school?* The funny thing was there weren't any mountains around where we lived. My parents never questioned me, though. They had complete faith and trust in me. But I had to do what I had to do. I had to betray my parents. I think they would have helped me and understood, but I didn't want the drama or concern, so I just took it upon myself to go and get it done.

At this time many people were trying to outlaw abortions. They were picketing abortion clinics and chanting, "Stop killing babies." It was all over the news. I felt like a murderer. But I knew that if I kept the baby, it would have to be raised by my parents, who both worked full-time. It wasn't possible for us to have a child at that time. So I toughened up and went through with the abortion. All alone. I stayed away from Davy after that.

No one knew. The doctors were great, and everything went smoothly, thank God. But after the abortion, I was so upset. I never wanted to get pregnant again, so I told my mother that I was putting myself on birth-control pills. She didn't argue. I was becoming sexually active and she knew it. It was the right thing to do.

Soon after that I went to a Halloween party where there was a palm-reading woman. I told her about the abortion. Karen and the palm reader were the only people who knew about it. I always wondered if the baby was a boy or a girl and I wanted to know. She told me it was a boy. I guess I was really meant to be with the boys. My instincts had already told me it was a boy: I still love him today, and sometimes wish I had never had that abortion. But I was a wild child.

When I saw Black Sabbath as a thirteen-year-old, I knew I wanted to be a rock star. It became my dream, and I knew I was going to fulfill it. I saw the light at the end of the tunnel, guiding me toward that dream, and I knew it was real. My fantasy was to become the queen of rock and heavy metal: the one and only female guitar player of my stature. All the hurdles I was going to have to jump to make that dream come true weren't going to be possible with a child to care for.

LET'S BACK UP a little before I get into the madness of the Runaways.

I was born in London to a British father, Harry Lenard Ford, whom everyone called Len, and an Italian mother, Isabella Benvenuto. At the age of twenty, my father found himself serving in the British army. Hitler's Nazi Party had driven Britain and France to declare war on Germany, and that set the stage for what would become one of the most violent and largest armed conflicts in world history: World War II. Four years into the war, my father was stationed at Anzio beach in Italy, and as a result his battalion was one of more than twenty that took part in the Battle of Anzio, otherwise known as Operation Shingle. Of the thousand men in his troop at Anzio, my father was one of the nine who survived.

However, during the battle a stick grenade was launched toward him. A stick grenade is exactly what it sounds like: a stick that's about fourteen inches long with a grenade at the end of it. It has a time-delay fuse of four to five seconds and an effective blast of about twelve to fourteen yards. My dad put up his hand to shield himself from the blast, and it blew off his middle and ring fingers. Ironically, his hand was left in the shape of the heavy metal horns. For the rest of his life, my father picked shrapnel out of his body when it would rise to the surface of his skin. He kept the pieces in a little jar in the medicine cabinet.

When he was hit, he was taken to the nearest medical facility, and while he was recovering in the hospital in Italy, he met my mother, Isabella Benvenuto. *Benvenuto* means "welcome" in Italian. My mother was a very loving and caring person. This is one reason why she was a nurse's assistant during the war, and I think had I not been a musician, I would have been a nurse myself, because I like to care for and help people just like she did. She had volunteered her time tending to wounded soldiers at the hospital, and my father was one of the soldiers she helped.

My father had picked up on the Italian language and started to fall in love with her deep, passionate, and alluring Italian voice while he was still recovering. He learned to speak Italian fluently and became enamored of the entire Italian culture: their language, food, even Italian opera. My father would often say that the Italian people were the most passionate and caring he had ever met. What first attracted my mom to my father was the fact that he needed her help. He was also a survivor, and she was drawn to him for that reason. He was a lover and a gentleman who liked guns and motorcycles: a little on the James Dean side, but with a British accent. They were both in the war, going through hell at the same time. They were there to save and help each other, and they lived to tell about it. That bond became the foundation for the love they had for each other. He was discharged from combat with two missing fingers and a wounded face, but he had fallen in love with my mother and asked for her hand in marriage. They were married on January 19, 1945, in Trieste, Italy, where the mountains meet the sea.

After they honeymooned in Trieste, they moved to England. Shortly after they got married, my mother suffered a miscarriage in a train station. This was a traumatic experience for my parents, so they decided to wait before trying to have another child. My mother became pregnant again and gave birth to a baby boy, who would have been my older brother. At the age of nine months, however, he caught pneumonia. They took him to the hospital, but the doctors were not able to help him and so my parents were faced with the death of their firstborn child. My mother hardly ever spoke about this—I think it was too painful a memory for her.

About two years later, my mother became pregnant again. On September 19, 1958, Lita Rossana Ford was born. My father was one of eleven kids, nine of whom were girls. He was probably hoping for a boy, but no, he got me instead.

Until I was four years old, we lived in Streatham, a working-class neighborhood in South London. We didn't have a lot of money and rented a little flat where the walls were all covered in different-colored but equally faded paper. My mother would invite some friends over for birthday parties or play dates, and I can recall waiting for my father to come home from work. I would ride my red tricycle with white fringe coming out of the handlebars down the street to meet him. It was an everyday ritual.

I remember watching my favorite television shows, which included the Disney movie of the week every Sunday night and *The Ed Sullivan Show*. I loved how he would pronounce *show* as *shoe* when he said, "It's going to be a really great *shoe* tonight," but the best part about his show was the Italian mouse Topo Gigio, whom I referred to as "Popogigio." He captured my childhood heart while declaring his love to everyone. There has never been a children's cartoon character as cool as Topo Gigio! I also remember taking drives to the English Channel, which was a full-day adventure. Running on the beach, climbing the rocks, and going fishing meant I was exhausted by the end of the day. On the way home we would stop and pick fresh strawberries at a nearby farm.

My mother, however, wasn't quite as fond of England. She grew up on the beaches of the Mediterranean and couldn't stand the cold, gray English weather. She longed for a place with more sunshine and beaches. Her younger sister, Livia, lived in Boston, and we moved there when I was four, thinking it might be better weather. It was nice and warm in the summer, but the winters were brutally cold with tons of snow. It was actually ten times worse than England! My father had to shovel his truck out of the driveway almost every morning because the snow would block it in. Needless to say, we didn't stay there more than one winter. When I was in kindergarten, we moved to Dallas, where my aunt Flo lived. She was one of my father's nine sisters. We were only there for about a year before my mother was able to convince my father to move to Southern California, where two more of my father's sisters lived—and where there were warm, sunny beaches. By then I was in second grade.

Once we moved to California, my mother was in heaven. She grew up on the beaches of Italy and was a sun worshipper, so she loved being near the ocean. As a child, I remember my mother picking me up from school every day and heading straight for the beach. We'd be there until sundown, and when I got older, if my mom was working the later shift and couldn't go with me, I'd ride my bike to the beach and spend the day there by myself.

My father became a mechanic for the Ford Motor Company. He eventually went into real estate and worked for Century 21 in one of those snazzy mustard-colored blazers. I still have his jacket. At first we lived in a little apartment in Long Beach, but my father did quite well at work and was able to buy a three-bedroom home in Lakewood Village, a suburb about five miles outside of North Long Beach, thinking that I would go to Lakewood High, which was a safer school than Long Beach Poly. It was a little ranch-style house, and my parents decorated it Italian style. Every room was different—one room was all plaid, one all mirrors, one all horses, one all brick. My father was really handy and built a faux-brick arch in the kitchen and planted 280 rosebushes in the garden for my mother. Those rosebushes were her pride. They lined the entire perimeter of the front and back yards. My father also turned the garage into a back house with a bathroom, shower, and little kitchenette. He drywalled it and painted it, and my parents put a bedroom set in it along with my father's Sony reel-to-reel tape recorder. It became a mini-apartment, which I took over and used to continue learning the guitar. That is the home where I grew up, and years later it was the home I would return to every time the music scene beat me down.

My parents were always filling the house with music when I was little, usually Italian opera by Pavarotti, or Mario Lanza and Dean Martin. It was a wonderful thing. I would bring my parents into the back house to play them the latest lick I'd learned and they always loved it. "Oh, Lita, play the Black Sabbath again," my mother would say in her great Italian accent. "Play me the Santana."

MY PARENTS WEREN'T the only ones who encouraged my love of music. My cousin Paul, who was six years older than me and the oldest of my Long Beach cousins, also knew about my fascination with heavy metal and had been to plenty of rock concerts. He invited me to see Black Sabbath with him at the Long Beach Auditorium. It was September 25, 1971. Only six days after my thirteenth birthday.

Paul picked me up in his '54 Ford. The Long Beach Municipal Auditorium was an eight-thousand-seat hall that opened during the Depression next to the Pike, an amusement park built over the ocean. It must have been beautiful back then, but by 1971 the Pike was seedy and nearly abandoned. Used syringes littered the beach, and the roller coaster probably should have been shut down years before. When we entered the auditorium, I looked around, taking in the big, echoing barn with a balcony that ran all the way around. To some it probably looked like the place had seen better days. To me, it was a wonderland.

The Long Beach Arena, as we called it, was thick with smoke. At that point I didn't even know what marijuana was, but the funky smell and haze that hung over the crowd made me feel like I was part of a scene I wanted to know more about. Paul bought cheap tickets in the balcony, but we didn't stay there long. We snuck down to the floor where there weren't any seats. Instead, everyone was standing around, packed together under a cloud of pot and cigarette smoke. We made our way toward the stage.

There were crazy fans in the crowd who were hanging off the balcony and dropping onto the stage below. The dark hall was carefully lit to make the guys onstage seem like silhouettes—part men, part shadow. All you could really see were these massive piles of thick, black hair, and, every so often, a glint of light would bounce off the crosses they wore around their necks.

My life flashed before me as I focused on the guitar player, Tony Iommi. He seemed superhuman, almost godlike. I had never been to anything quite like that concert before. It seemed like I had crossed over into a whole new world, and I never wanted to return to the old one.

I walked out of the arena knowing what I wanted to do for the rest of my life. I wanted to make people feel the way Black Sabbath had just made me feel. It didn't occur to me that I was a girl. Nothing went off in my head that said girls couldn't do what Black Sabbath did.

SOON I'D MADE up my mind that I needed a chocolate Gibson SG like the one Tony Iommi played that night. I wanted to earn it with my own money, though, so the next year I decided that I would get a job at the St. Mary Medical Center in Long Beach, where my mother worked in the dietary department. There was an opening for a food administrator. I was only fourteen, so I was too young to get a job. In the interview I lied about my age. I had big boobs and my mother helped me play that up by giving me a padded bra. The supervisor, Jaylee, asked me how old I was, and before my mother could say a word, I answered, "I'm sixteen," which meant I was old enough to work. I got the job.

It was a full-time job every day after school. I pushed a food service tray from room to room and served everybody their meals. These people were very ill—some were dying—and they each had a different diet. It was very important not to screw up. Certain patients could only have fluids. Others got baked chicken and mashed potatoes that I had to heat and serve. It wasn't all that easy for me, since my heart went out to some of the patients who were so ill.

I saved all the money I made until I could afford the SG. I went to a local guitar store and picked it out. I knew exactly what I wanted. I paid $375, which was cheap for a Gibson SG. I took it home and plugged it into my father's Sony reel-to-reel tape player. I slapped on the echo and it sounded like God.

IN APRIL 1974 I saw an ad for the Cal Jam on TV. A few of my favorite bands were playing, and one of them was Deep Purple. I had never seen Deep Purple play live, but their lead guitarist, Ritchie Blackmore, was another one of my idols, with his double-picking guitar solos. I decided

I had to get there no matter what. My friend Patti wanted to go too, but there were a few obstacles. First of all, our parents wouldn't allow it. Second, it was fifty miles away in Ontario, California. We were only fifteen and could not drive. Our only option was to lie.

Patti told her parents she was spending the weekend at my house, and I said I was staying over at her house. She was a beautiful Indian girl with long black hair that went to her waist. We were both dressed in faded Levi's and T-shirts and carried the camping gear we needed to stay the night in Ontario. We met at the corner bus stop early in the morning because it was a good place to start hitchhiking.

We knew we could get into huge trouble, but screw it—it was worth whatever shit we were getting ourselves into. We stuck out our thumbs and waited for a car to stop. After a while, a pickup truck pulled to the side of the road and a weird guy rolled down his window.

"Where you headed?"

"Ontario," I told him. "You?"

"Alaska. But I can stop off in Ontario. Hop in, girls."

Alaska? Really? I questioned myself, but we got in anyway. I was a little older than Patty so I made her sit in the backseat. She was scared. The guy driving had never seen California before. Back in 1974 it was really beautiful. Strip malls had not overtaken the landscape yet. Instead there was a lot of wide-open space and mountains and palm trees as far as you could see. The man decided he had to get it all on film, so as he was driving he started looking for his home movie camera. He was digging in his bag, reaching into the backseat. He let go of the wheel and Patty freaked. I grabbed the wheel and held the truck steady as he found his camera. I held the wheel for the next few miles while he filmed. Patty was in the back, sure we were going to wreck, but I refused to die until I saw Ritchie Blackmore play guitar in the flesh.

Finally, we made it to the Ontario Motor Speedway. We just had to face the final obstacle: we were not old enough to get into the show. Now what? We snuck in through an opening in the fence and found a spot to set up our camping gear. We were surrounded by people making out, getting stoned, pissing in beer bottles, and talking music. Awesome!

The stage at Cal Jam was built for eight major bands. It was enormous, made of five hundred sections of scaffolding and twenty-three thousand square feet of plywood. There were four towers that held fifty-four thousand watts of sound and a million-watt lighting system that lit up everything from the stage to the parking lot. A quarter million people filled the grandstands and the vast grounds inside the racetrack. Patti and I fought our way into the infield.

The bands were the best of the best: Seals & Crofts; Earth, Wind & Fire; Rare Earth; the Eagles; Black Oak Arkansas; Black Sabbath; Deep Purple; and Emerson, Lake & Palmer. We liked Black Oak Arkansas because their lead singer, Jim Dandy, was hot.

Black Sabbath came on when it was still daylight. Once again, I was so infatuated with every move Tony Iommi made. Deep Purple came on next, and by this time it was dark. The entire vibe of the festival changed. The stage lights came on, and they were breathtaking. The way the light hit Ritchie Blackmore was captivating. It captured how he held his guitar so gracefully, how he stood, and how his fingers moved. There was a battle between Jon Lord on keyboards and Ritchie on guitar. I just stood there with my mouth open watching these two guys. The cameraman seemed to be getting in Ritchie's space and I think it pissed him off, because at the end of Deep Purple's set, Ritchie threw his guitar up in the air and smashed it to the ground, sending pieces flying. Then he took the guitar neck and shoved it right through the cameraman's very expensive television camera lens. Ritchie had obviously had enough of him by that point and it was payback time. I thought it was the coolest thing I'd ever seen. Blackmore mesmerized the audience that night. Nobody could follow that act. Nobody could match that rage. Not even Emerson, Lake & Palmer, who came on last with Keith Emerson's revolving keyboards.

During the weekend we made friends with some guys who gave us a ride back the next day so we didn't have to hitch again. The whole way home I kept thinking about how great both Ritchie Blackmore and Tony Iommi were. If I had known the Sunset Strip existed, I would have set my sights on those lights that same day.

BUT LONG BEACH would not let me leave for Hollywood before I learned to fight, to be tough, to take no shit. I didn't know it then, but it was great training for a life in rock and roll. I was sixteen years old when I got into my first big fight in 1975. My mom and I were going to Boston to visit my cousins and my aunt Livia. We had to catch a plane. My mother said, "Lita, we don't have time to cook dinner before we go. Why don't you run up the street with Daddy's car and get some sandwiches from Arby's?"

There was a big mall a few blocks away from our house with a couple of fast-food joints. I drove to Arby's and went in to order some food. There were only four other people in the restaurant—two girls and two guys. They had on tons of gang markings and wore headbands, and the girls had on these big false eyelashes. They had a look to them that said: *Do not mess with us.* I, on the other hand, was wearing my bathing-suit top, cutoff jean shorts, and flip-flops. Once I got my food, one of the guys said to me, "Hey, baby, let me pinch your chi-chis."

I looked at him and said, "You're fucking crazy. Your girlfriend is right next to you. How could you talk like that in front of her?" And I walked out of the restaurant.

And then, of all things, his girlfriend got mad at *me!* She followed me into the parking lot and picked a fight. We were yelling at each other. She was screaming, "Don't talk to me that way."

"I didn't say shit to you. Your boyfriend is the one with the big mouth. I was talking to him."

"Well, don't talk to him that way!"

I walked away from her, thinking she wasn't worth my time. The next thing I knew, she grabbed the Coke from my tray and threw it inside my father's car. That really pissed me off, but I didn't let it show. I put my food in the car very calmly and drove off without saying a word to her. But instead of going home, I went to my girlfriend Peggy's house and told her, "Peggy, there are four of them and one of me. I need your help."

She didn't ask for any details. Her only question was "What do you need me to do?"

"I just want you to drive."

She hopped in her mom's car and we went to a drive-through McDonald's and bought a large Coke. Then we drove back to the Arby's, but they were gone, so we drove around the mall looking for them. We cruised around the parking lot looking in between cars and down the sidewalks. Finally, I saw them outside of JCPenney. I told Peggy, "Pull over to the curb. There they are." She stayed in the car and I approached them with the Coke in my hand. The girl had her back to me so she didn't see me coming. I tapped her on the shoulder. She turned around and we made eye contact for a split second before I threw the Coke in her face. We immediately started throwing punches. Her girlfriend jumped on top of me and grabbed my hair, trying to get me off her friend. I was sitting on the girl's chest, holding her down. Her fake eyelashes were starting to fall off because of the Coke I had thrown in her face. After a few minutes, I was just trying to get her to stop hitting me. One of the guys hauled me off her. My knees were bloody from kneeling on the concrete. I said to the girl, "I'm leaving. We're done. This is over." I started walking quickly back to Peggy. She had left the car door open for me. Just as I got one leg in the car door, I felt the bitch coming up behind me. She had taken off her belt and wrapped it around my face. The buckle caught on my nose and I felt it crack in half. That fucking cunt! Even though I never hit her once, she still took her belt off and hit me in the face! I kept my face down so she didn't see the blood coming out of my nose. I somehow managed to get in the car and close the door. "Move," I told Peggy. "Get out of here." Blood was dripping down between my boobs. "I think I need to go to the hospital," I said.

Peggy took one look at me and said, "Ah, yeah, Lita, I think so."

She took me to the ER, but they wouldn't work on me because I was underage. I called my parents, who were wondering where the hell I was with their roast beef sandwiches at this point. I told them what happened. They gave the hospital approval to work on me and then got in the car to come meet me. I had a broken nose and needed stitches on the side of my nose. I found it funny that I needed parental approval to get my busted face fixed but not to have an abortion. I'd never known how painful it was to have a broken nose. The right side of my face was black and blue, and my eyelid was swollen shut. One side of my neck was completely bruised. I still had a deep scar on my nose, together with seven stitches, and the white part of my right eye was bloodred when I auditioned for the Runaways that same September—the first of many battle scars yet to come.

CHAPTER 2

THE AUDITION

Hello Daddy, hello Mom,

I'm your ch-ch-ch-ch-cherry bomb!

—"CHERRY BOMB"
(WRITTEN BY KIM FOWLEY AND JOAN JETT)

SOON AFTER THE STREET FIGHT, I RECEIVED AN UNEXPECTED PHONE CALL.

"Is this the girl who plays bass?" a man said.

I was frustrated that everyone thought I was a bass player so I told him, "No! I'm not a bass player!"

"Well, I have a proposition for you, young woman. It requires being able to play an instrument. Do you play an instrument?"

"I play guitar."

"Well, we need one of those too."

"Who is 'we'?" I wanted to know.

"The Runaways. An all-girl teenage band of rebellious jailbait rock-and-roll bitches. Have you heard of them?"

"No." Everything about the voice on the other line told me that this dude was as strange as they come. But for some reason I was intrigued. "What's your name?" I asked him.

"KKKKIIIIMMMM! My name is KIIIIMMMM FOOOWWWLEY! I'm a mastermind producer-songwriter and I can make you into one of the biggest rock stars in the world. You will fuck the best rock stars. You will tour the biggest arenas. You will be on the cover of every magazine. You will become a legend."

"Ah, yeah. Okay. That all sounds good. But what do I have to do?"

"Do you have a car? Do you have an instrument?"

"Yeah, I have a chocolate Gibson SG. I drive too."

"Will your mummy and daddy let you get out for a few hours? If you could find your way up to the rehearsal facility, we'd want to see you play. We want you to audition."

"Where are you located?"

"Hollywood."

"Shit. That's far from me. I don't know how to get there."

The conversation went on and on. We went through my entire life story in about an hour. We talked about Black Sabbath and Deep Purple, and how he knew Ritchie Blackmore personally. We talked about high school and guitars. He really sucked me in. I hung up not only knowing where Hollywood was but also seeing a light I always knew existed. I just didn't know how to get there. But Kim Fowley had described that light and given me directions toward it.

I told my parents about it. They immediately told me, "Get in the car and go down there."

My parents helped me pack up my gear in the back of a brown 1972 Monte Carlo that they had bought for me from my aunt Rose as a birthday gift. With my bloodred eye and my still-bruised face, I looked a little possessed. After placing my chocolate Gibson SG in the backseat, I pulled out of the driveway and headed for the freeway. I had never been to Hollywood before. It seemed far from Long Beach—an entire planet away.

THE AUDITION WAS in the heart of West Hollywood, on San Vicente and Santa Monica Boulevards. It was upstairs above a drugstore that has long since gone out of business. It was a little shithole with walls that were covered up with thick, old, dusty brown curtains to keep the sound from leaking through, brown carpeting to dampen some of the noise, and no stage. There were amps and a drum kit in the room. When I got there, Kim Fowley came up to me. He started doing his sales pitch again, but all the while I knew he was checking me out from head to toe. He was tall, skeleton-like, and looked a bit like Frankenstein, but with blue eyes, wavy brown hair, and a weird overbite. He was wearing an orange-brown suit. He spent the first five minutes telling me what a big deal he was and how he was going to make us all stars. As he was talking I kept thinking, *I was right. He is some Hollywood freak.*

He introduced me to the two girls in the band so far: Sandy Pesavento, the drummer, who had not yet adopted the name Sandy West, and Joan Jett, the rhythm guitar player. Sandy was pretty and athletic, with a great personality and a real excitement for playing music. She was far more outgoing than Joan. Joan was a small, shy teen with light-brown hair wearing a T-shirt and jeans. She stood in the shadows behind Kim.

Kim broke the awkward silence by slapping his hands together and saying, "Okay, play something." I wanted to make their jaws drop, so I started to play "Highway Star" by Deep Purple, which has an amazing guitar solo. Sandy was a big Deep Purple fan, and, much to my surprise, she kept up with me on the drums. I was so thrilled to hear another girl playing one of my favorite songs. She was excited too. Meeting Sandy was a breath of fresh air. When we locked in musically, we locked in as friends too. We both came from a hard-rock influence, and we jelled right away. We were musically equal. We kept throwing riffs at each other. She asked me, "Do you know Led Zep? Do you know Hendrix?" I knew them all.

Joan's musical tastes weren't as heavy as what Sandy and I liked. Her idol was Suzi Quatro, whom I'd never heard of, and Joan liked more glitter-rock stuff. I looked over at Joan and Kim, and their mouths were both wide open. She stood there looking at us, and I could tell that what Sandy and I were playing was a style of music she wasn't familiar with. The audition was a success. I was in the band after that and was told to come to rehearsals later that week.

After watching Joan play a few days into the rehearsals, I realized she wasn't playing barre chords. I asked her if she wanted me to teach her how, and she said yes. Joan was a fast learner. During those first rehearsals there was a bass player named Micki Steele, who wasn't there when I first auditioned because Kim wasn't sure whether I played bass or guitar, and he wanted to leave his options open. We went through bass players like we went through toilet rolls. Micki wasn't happy with the band, and the feelings were apparently mutual. She couldn't stand Kim, and she didn't like the style of music we were playing. She didn't want to be part of a teenage rock band, which was fair enough because she was already twenty-two.

Kim had just finished reading a book called *Blondes in the Cinema*, and he was fixated on the way that light reflected on blond hair. "We have to find a blond girl to sing," he kept saying. "We need a blond Mick Jagger," I said, and Kim agreed. The Sugar Shack was a popular teen club in North Hollywood that I wasn't familiar with. Apparently, you weren't allowed in unless you were under eighteen, but of course they let thirty-six-year-old Kim Fowley in because he was Kim Fowley. "Teen bitches will be there," he said. There was a buzz in the Sugar Shack that night because people had heard of the Runaways, and word had gotten out that Kim and Joan had gone there to look for the lead singer. Kim Fowley created the buzz. He was the king of hype. That's all the Runaways were in the beginning—Hollywood hype. And now it was time to get serious.

THE FOLLOWING DAY we all met at the rehearsal space above the drugstore. We were sitting around in the room, jamming, waiting for this girl Kim had found at the Sugar Shack. Finally she arrived—Cherie was thin and pretty, with platinum-blond hair cut exactly like David Bowie's in his Ziggy Stardust days. She was nervous as hell. She looked like a little lost girl to me. I thought she was way too young, but I suppose Kim wanted someone cute. And that she was. Especially when she lit up a cigarette.

Kim shut the door and said, "What Suzi Quatro song did you learn?"

"'Fever.'"

I stood up and said, "'Fever'? You learned 'Fever'? Why?!"

"Well, it's kind of a sultry song," she stammered. "I thought you could hear my voice."

"I'm not playing 'Fever,'" I told everyone. "I want to play some rock and roll, goddammit." Cherie and I hadn't exactly hit it off. Sandy wasn't too happy with her, either.

Kim Fowley said, "Okay, hold on. We'll write a song. What sounds like Cherie? Cherry! We'll write a song called 'Cherry Bomb.'"

Kim took Joan into the other room as the rest of us stood in the room twiddling our thumbs. Twenty-five minutes later they came back out and Kim pointed at Joan and said, "Play this. Doo-doo-doo-doo-doo-doo-doo-doo." Joan started mimicking Kim on the guitar. Kim started to sing the lyrics to "Cherry Bomb."

Cherie auditioned for the band singing that song. I was skeptical about her singing abilities. She was so young and undeveloped. Plus, finding her at a nightclub freaked me out. What parent allows their child to go out in Hollywood at night without an adult? She was only fifteen. But she was a kid hungry for rock-and-roll fame.

I was pacing. I wasn't thrilled, but I didn't really have any input. None of us did when it came down to it. It was up to Kim. Obviously with Cherie it was about her looks and her blond hair. Kim was set on her being our front person, and that was that.

After making her wait a little bit longer, Sandy said, "Okay, welcome to the Runaways."

Cherie sighed with relief. Everyone shook her hand, even Kim, as he looked at her like she was a piece of meat. He was relieved that his search for a lead singer was over. I still was not convinced. I had hoped for more after learning such complicated guitar solos.

Now we needed someone to play bass. Rodney Bingenheimer, a legendary player on the Sunset Strip and owner of Rodney's English Disco, told Kim about a young Kiss fan named Jackie Fuchs who he met in the parking lot of the Starwood. Rodney seemed to know how to find the pretty girls. He was smitten with Jackie and her love for Kiss. "I'm a bass player," she told Rodney. Kim thought he'd ask her to come audition, not knowing what to expect. How could she refuse? It was the chance of a lifetime.

The next thing we knew, Jackie Fuchs showed up to audition and the only song she knew was a Kiss song, of course: "Strutter." To be honest, I was not in love with Jackie's playing. Sandy was against her joining too. She just was not cut from rock-and-roll cloth. "She looks like the girl next door, there's nothing rock and roll about her," I said. Sandy agreed and said that she looked like a "Valley princess."

Kim said, "Hey, listen to me, you pieces of dogshit," pointing his finger in our faces. "All the kids next door might find comfort with her. You should thank her for being her or you'll never get signed. She's good enough to make this what Mercury Records wants," which meant that we would get signed if we let Jackie into the band. As Runaways legend has it, shortly before Jimi Hendrix died, Jimi told Denny Rosencrantz, who would be the A&R man for Mercury Records in 1975, "Denny, someday girls with guitars are going to play rock and roll. And they'll be before their time. They're going to be like aliens when they show up in the rock-and-roll climate. Whenever they show up, no one will know what it is. If you're still around when an all-girl band comes along, remember this moment." But Denny Rosencrantz didn't sign us based on Jimi Hendrix's word.

It seemed to me that everyone said yes to Jackie because they didn't want to look any further. I felt like she didn't belong in a rock band. I did change my no into a yes, but only for the sake of getting signed. Jackie improved with time, as we all did.

FOR THE NEXT few months, we rehearsed in an uncomfortable trailer on the corner of Cahuenga and Barham in the San Fernando Valley. It was actually a trailer that you could pull by hooking it onto the back of a truck. It was parked in a lot right next to the Hollywood 101 freeway and belonged to a guy named Bud who was about a hundred years old and had no teeth. Kim leased it from him for probably twenty-five cents an hour. There was nothing in it but a filthy multicolored shag rug that had all kinds of stains on it. It was really disgusting and in a dirty location, but I didn't care. To me it was a place where we could play as loud as we wanted and nobody would bother us. One day, Bud's Saint Bernard came into the rehearsal room and was ready to give birth. She produced a litter of puppies right there while we were rehearsing. Oh my dear God! There was afterbirth and fluids all over the freakin' carpet. Somebody ran outside to tell Bud what had happened while the rest of us just kept right on rehearsing. It was a little distracting to say the least. Bud called it a day. Kim let us go home while Bud had the mess cleaned up.

We would all get to the trailer around 4:30 P.M., right after school. We were always starving once we got to Bud's trailer. One good thing about that location was the deli around the corner. I would get an avocado-provolone-and-tomato sandwich on egg bread almost every day. Sandy would get a cheeseburger. Sandy and I would scarf our food down and then get straight to work on music. We had the longest commute, so we got there later. I would leave school early and drive from Long Beach to her house in Huntington Beach. On a good day that would take at least thirty minutes. Then I'd turn the car around and drive to the Valley. We would take the 405 to the 101; that was a good hour-and-a-half drive. Jackie, Joan, and Cherie would already be there because they lived much closer.

Sandy and I would talk the whole drive. She would tell me about her family and her sisters. She was the total black sheep of the family, and her mother wasn't very supportive of her decision to be in a rock band. It seemed like no matter what Sandy did, she could not make her mother happy. To me, she was the best one out of all her sisters and it was a shame her mother didn't see it. On one of our long commutes, Sandy came up with a song we called "The Nipple Song." We had to find some way to keep ourselves occupied, so why not a song? The lyrics overlapped like they do in "Row, Row, Row Your Boat," and it started off with Sandy singing, "Are your nipples getting hard?"

And I would answer, "Yes, my nipples getting hard!"

Sandy: "Getting hard!"

Me: "Getting hard!"

Sandy: "Are your nipples getting hard?"

Me: "Yes, my nipples getting hard!"

And then we'd both sing "*Wooooooooooooh!*" and we'd start all over again in unison. A lovely tune.

It was hysterical and we'd have a blast. It was becoming the Runaways' theme song. We also had another song we came up with called "Cinema." The lyrics were simple: "Cinema, cinema, cinema face." Another groundbreaking tune.

A lot of early Runaways shit got hammered out around those rehearsals. One day we sat around thinking about what we could change our names to so they would sound more rock and roll. Joan had already changed her name from Joan Larkin to Joan Jett. We all decided we should do something similar. Sandra Pesavento became Sandy West, and Jackie Fuchs became Jackie Fox. I sat there for a while thinking, *What the hell am I going to change my name to? Lita Paris? Lita London?* I tried everything but nothing seemed right. I finally said, "To hell with it. If they don't like me for my name, fuck 'em anyway." Cherie's name was already made for Hollywood since she had a mother who was an actress and she knew how to name an LA kid. Cherie Currie. You couldn't beat that.

One time a few of us rehearsed naked. Just for fun. We threw the crew and the roadies out and locked the door behind them. Then we took off all our clothes and we played in the nude. We started off with "The Nipple Song."

Sandy and I sang out to the girls on the other side of the trailer:

"Are your nipples getting hard?"

Joan and Cherie: "Yes, my nipples getting hard!"

Sandy and me: "Getting hard!"

Joan and Cherie: "Getting hard!"

Everyone: "*Wooooooooooooh!*"

At age sixteen, my body had already developed. I was a 36C bust,

26-inch waist, 36-inch hips. I was really the only one with a figure, so it made me feel fat. I hated that. Although it was considered a perfect figure, it made me feel awkward. They had to airbrush some cleavage onto Cherie's chest on the first album cover because she had her blouse open and there was nothing there. I didn't realize until later that curves were a good thing.

I would get home around midnight and crawl into bed. In the morning I would beg my father to let me stay home from school. I would say I was sick or was going to vomit. He never bought my bullshit. If I wanted to be in a rock band, that was fine with him, but I also needed to graduate from high school, so I dragged my ass to Long Beach Poly every morning and then got out of there as soon as possible so I could pick up Sandy and get to the rehearsals.

ONE AFTERNOON DURING rehearsal, I had a realization. It was about October 1975 and we were two weeks into the Runaways at this point. I thought it was strange that none of my bandmates ever talked about boys. We were teenage girls—boys were supposed to be a favorite topic, but they were always giggling about other girls. At the same moment, it dawned on me that Joan and Cherie were always together and chummy, not in a friendly way, but in a romantic way. Joan went everywhere with Cherie and followed her like a shadow. I just thought they were becoming best friends, but then it hit me: *they were all into girls*. All of them except for Jackie. Jackie was straight and she also didn't do drugs.

Before then, I didn't even have a name for being gay or bisexual. I had never been around an openly gay person in my life. I know it sounds crazy now, but back then my parents never talked about it with me. Why didn't anybody discuss it? If not my parents, then my teachers? Kim? It was 1975. Being gay or bisexual was considered "wrong" by mainstream society. Period. I'm sorry to say that it fucked with my head. If someone would have taught me that men sometimes slept with men and women sometimes slept with women,

I wouldn't have been so shocked. Instead, I was left to figure it out for myself.

First I found out that Sandy, the one I had bonded with the most, was a lesbian. Then I found out that Cherie was messing around with Joan. I was so freaked out that I quit the band. I blamed it on Kim. I said I couldn't take his weird behavior anymore. But that was bullshit. I understood someone being a foulmouthed lunatic. But I did not understand lesbianism or bisexuality. I thought one of the girls might make a move on me, and before that could happen I packed up all my gear and went home. I told my mom and dad I had a fight with Kim and quit. My parents were upset. They really thought we were going to achieve something as a band.

About a month went by, and I kept having nightmares that the Runaways would go on to achieve superstar status while I got left behind. One day in mid-December 1975 I got a phone call from Joan, Cherie, and Sandy. I knew Kim put them up to it. At this point they were in the studio recording the first album, but they had not yet been signed to a label. They said, "Lita, please come back. We can't find anyone to replace you. Nobody can play like you." I was stoked. By this point I had come to terms with their behavior, and it was no big deal. I knew they wouldn't make a move on me because I didn't play that way and they respected that. That phone call also let me know that I was really good, because they'd obviously been auditioning girls, but none of them had made the cut.

I said to Kent Taylor, "Will you go with me and tell me what you think?" I needed a second opinion from someone I trusted. We loaded my gear into my Monte Carlo and drove to West Hollywood's Cherokee Studios. When we got there, Sandy was in the drum booth getting the sound dialed in and Joan was tuning up. The entire band and Kim greeted me and thanked me for coming back.

As soon as we walked in, Kent started looking at this huge mixing board and microphones. He turned to me and said, "If you don't get on board with this, you're fucking crazy." Kent knew Sandy West somehow.

He said to her, "Holy shit, it's you. I told you about Lita when you were trying to get a band together. Remember?"

Kim was still kind of getting sounds together. We all jammed a bit and Kim kept stopping the tape to tell us, "You gotta think with your crotch. You guys are going to open up for the Tubes in three weeks and you have to think with your pussy." Kent looked at me like, *What is this guy's deal?* He hadn't seen anything yet. That was the tame side of Kim Fowley. It wasn't long before he was calling us dog meat, dog bitches, dog cunts, dog pucks. But I learned from the "gay episode" to stop trying to figure people out, to tune people out, and to focus on my own six strings.

THE BAND HAD been together for a little while, and we thought it would be a great idea to see *The Rocky Horror Picture Show* as a band. Everyone but Jackie went to the theater that night to watch it. I had started to develop a fixation with transsexuals, and although I never had sex with one, I liked them. I always felt that Tim Curry dressed up as a transvestite was an awesome sexual fantasy of mine. I also think it may have been the inspiration for Cherie's corset. With some of the girls experimenting with their sexual identities, I thought this was the perfect transsexual/rock-and-roll movie to go see. We all took a liking to the movie and we would do the entire "Time Warp" song together, complete with every dance move. We would line up and do it at rehearsals, restaurants, live shows, radio stations, parties, everywhere. When we did line up in front of the drum kit to do the "Time Warp" at rehearsal, Kim would say, "Hey, you filthy bitches, cut that shit out!" But we kept right on dancing, middle finger in the air, directed toward Kim. And yes, even when we rehearsed naked that day, the "Time Warp" dance made it into our "set list," along with "The "Nipple Song."

CHAPTER 3

BORN TO BE BAD

I called my mother from Hollywood the other day

And I said, "Mom, I just called to tell ya I joined a rock and roll band.

And I won't be comin' home no more."

—"BORN TO BE BAD"
(WRITTEN BY NIKKI WILLIAMS, MATTHEW WEST, AND SAM MIZELL)

WE SIGNED A CONTRACT WITH KIM FOWLEY IN DECEMBER 1975. EACH OF US HAD TO bring a parent to the signing because we were all underage, so I drove there with both my parents. The contract stated that Kim Fowley would act as our agent in signing us to a label. We didn't know anything about publishing or royalties at the time. We were just happy to be getting a record deal at all; nobody wanted to question anything and look like the asshole of the bunch. Instead, we signed on the line: like a bunch of assholes.

One of our first shows was in Nick St. Nicholas's living room in Malibu. Kim didn't give us many details before we showed up, so when he opened the door and we saw the Steppenwolf bassist, I just about fainted. Steppenwolf was one of my favorite bands. The place was dark, dingy, and full of famous faces or faces I knew I should have known. There was no stage, so we set up by the brick fireplace in the living room. I was a little nervous, but once we started playing that all went away. We had written some Runaways songs, but we did covers too so people would hear something they were familiar with.

We did several shows where we opened for the Tubes. They started their show with the lead singer, Fee Waybill, driving onto the stage in a motorcycle with one girl on the back of the bike, all S&Med out. It was a hot way to begin a show, used by many other artists (Mötley Crüe and Judas Priest are two examples) in the years to follow.

I thought the girls in the Tubes were so hot: ripped-to-shreds muscular, sexual, beautiful vampirettes. They were sexy to me. I asked them how they stayed so fit and trim, because I was still trying to lose my "baby fat." They said they swam in the pools in the different hotels they stayed at on tour. I tried it a few times, but it didn't stick. The wet bathing suits were too hard to travel with in my suitcase.

Fee was sexy with his huge platform boots à la Elton John and an exposed six-pack stomach, sometimes wearing only a G-string during the show. He had an intimidating sexuality that was erotic to watch and was a lot of fun to be around. The Tubes were a turn-on. They combined quasi-pornographic antics while poking fun at media, consumerism, and politics. Can you imagine being a teenager opening for these guys?

Whenever we did shows with the Tubes, it meant we played bigger and better venues. The Runaways were paired with a band like theirs because they were erotic and unusual. Sexual, yet rock and roll. Great songs with great riffs. Between the Runaways and the Tubes, you were sure to be in for a great show that you'd most likely go home and masturbate to, whether you were male or female. Ha!

But the Tubes were serious workers; they didn't party and stay up all night like us. That was another thing I liked about them—they worked hard and it showed.

We could play our songs onstage, but we kind of just stood there, not doing much. This frustrated Kim, and he tried to show us how to act onstage. He told us to look at him while he acted like a female Mick Jagger doing a striptease. He stuck his ass in the air, twisted his shoulders, wet his lips with his tongue, and said, "Mmmm, look at me, I'm Cherie Currie." We all stared at him, thinking, *No, you're not.*

"Hey, you bitches!" he yelled. "This isn't funny! I'm trying to show you how to move onstage so you don't stand there like a bunch of dummies!"

Kim realized he wasn't getting anywhere and brought in Kenny Ortega, who had choreographed the Tubes, to help with the Runaways' stage show. Kenny is now one of Hollywood's biggest names: his choreography credits include Michael Jackson's world tours and films like *Flashdance*, *Dirty Dancing*, and *High School Musical*, but the Runaways were one of the first bands he ever worked with. He put a few simple, synchronized steps into our act and showed us how not to run into each other. He taught me a lot about how to move onstage. In fact, years later when I started the Lita Ford Band, I won *Metal Edge* magazine's award for Best Female Rock Performer every year for ten years in a row, and I think a lot of it had to do with many of the things Kenny taught me early in my career.

OUR FIRST HEADLINE gig was at the Starwood, in Hollywood. We played there on January 28 and 29, 1976, to a packed house both nights. We all wore jeans and T-shirts that said THE RUNAWAYS with our names written underneath. Our parents came too and they wore shirts that said LITA'S DAD, JACKIE'S MOM, et cetera. Those two nights were really the gigs when we all jelled as a band, mostly because it was the first time we saw the crowd go crazy. They witnessed the magic of Kim Fowley's vision: an all-girl jailbait rock band. And everybody wondered why they hadn't thought of it first.

After the show, we were surrounded by the celebrities Kim had invited. Half the time we didn't know who they were, even though we should have, but that night I recognized two of them quite well: Robert Plant and Jimmy Page. I guess they had a night off and wanted to see this girl band everyone was talking about. Kim really knew how to create a buzz. He gave Plant a Runaways T-shirt, which he wore when he posed for photos with us. I was speechless to be standing next to Jimmy Page, one of my guitar heroes. But it was Plant who talked to me. Jimmy Page was very quiet. Plant took me aside, looked me in the eyes, and asked me if I could play bass. Again with the fucking bass playing! Why did everyone think I played bass?

"For who?" I asked.

"Led Zep."

He might have been drinking or pulling my leg, but he seemed to be dead serious in that moment. I wondered what their bass player, John Paul Jones, did to piss them off. That guy was one of my bass-playing idols. There is no way they're going to replace him, I thought. Especially with a teenage girl. Not surprisingly, I never heard about it again.

JUST DAYS AFTER that Starwood show, on February 4, 1976, we signed another contract, this time with Mercury Records. Soon after, Kim hired his assistant, Scott Anderson, to be our manager because Kim didn't like going to shows and he didn't want to go on tour with us. He gave those responsibilities to Scott. "He's going to handle the day-to-day operations," Kim told us. Scott was about twenty-five. He was a nerdy-looking preppy guy with a big nose and an eye for Cherie. Right away I knew he was full of shit and bound to be trouble.

Immediately after that signing, we finished recording the first album, which didn't take us long. Maybe a few weeks. I don't know if it's because we didn't have any money, or because Kim pocketed most of it. He later claimed that he was trying to make a real teen-age record with all the mistakes still in it. Kim had a way of making everything sound like it was part of a grand plan, but I had questions from the beginning, like: Where's the money? How much would we get? How much was the studio? How much would we get paid at each live show? None of us saw a dime from that first album, but I guess we assumed that's how the music business worked. But surely we would make money from touring, or so I thought. We would all soon learn that Kim was a master at getting people to do what he wanted, which would work both to our benefit and our detriment.

We were becoming quite the hometown heroes. This meant that

the pressures were getting more intense, and some of the girls in the band started to dabble in drugs. Sandy had a friend named Toni who used to hang around all the time. She had big boobs and bright-red lips. She was hot!

Toni had been in a bad accident when she was sixteen. She had been a champion dirt-bike motorcyclist, ranked third in the world, when she was hit by a drunk driver while riding her motorcycle. She died twice on the operating table and had fifty-seven surgeries to repair the damage done to the leg that had broken in seven different places. She got to keep her leg, thank God, but it was now part titanium. She was like the bionic bitch. Because of this, she always had a lot of prescription drugs on her, but she never took them. One night before a show I saw her trying to give Joan and Sandy pills in the dressing room. I grabbed her, spun her around, and threw her out on her ass. I was pissed, but soon I realized that I could not control anybody else's drug habits. If they didn't get the drugs from Toni, they could get them from somebody else. A lot of people were drawn to Toni because she was hot or because she always had a bag full of drugs. I was drawn to her because she was fearless. There was nothing Toni couldn't conquer, and because of that she became my hero and, eventually, my best friend.

MEANWHILE THE RUNAWAYS were being profiled in a lot of rock magazines. One magazine sent a reporting team to my house in Long Beach to do an interview in my room. They took a picture of me sitting on my bed under a poster of Ritchie Blackmore. Soon after that magazine hit the newsstand, I got a phone call from Ritchie. Ritchie fucking Blackmore! I nearly went into cardiac arrest just hearing his voice. Kim Fowley had given him my number. We talked for a bit about music and then he said, "Would you like to come to my house for a visit?" You can guess my answer.

He lived in a nice, one-level home up in the hills under the Hollywood sign. I drove there in my Monte Carlo. I had a photograph in a manila envelope on the dashboard. When I got out of the car, I was shaking and my palms were sweaty. I had to climb up a rickety flight of stairs to the house, which was hidden away so you couldn't see it from the street. Ritchie answered the front door and the first thing he said to me when I set foot in the house was "That's a very interesting photograph."

"What photograph?" I asked.

"The photograph on the dashboard of your car."

My face went white. How did he know that was there? You couldn't see the car from the house. I was already nervous, but that really freaked me out. I wondered what else he could see. That afternoon we talked about guitar and rock and roll and what it was like to be in the business as long as he had been. That was the first of many visits to his house.

Ritchie and I became friends. He was a really interesting, super-talented guy, but he had just gone through a divorce and seemed to be lonely. We had sex once or twice (long after I'd turned eighteen), and I could tell that he missed his ex-wife and probably still loved her. I could feel it. I don't know why they separated. I never asked. I would soon find out that fame and loneliness went hand in hand.

Ritchie would play the cello for me. He took lessons from Hugh McDowell of Electric Light Orchestra and said it was "refreshing" to learn a new instrument. We also played guitar together. He taught me to play in minor keys and his famous Blackmore "Snake Charmer" scale. I sucked up every bit of it. He would play me these heavy, sexy guitar runs, and I would go home and practice them. I listened to everything he told me and immediately used it with the Runaways. Ritchie told me that he actually took ballet. I said, "You take ballet? That's a weird thing for somebody like you to do." He told me it gave him strong legs and it made him graceful onstage. He would bend one leg and lean in a lunge for the whole concert; everything worked around that one stance. I started to do that too. I fell into my own style eventually, but for a while I imitated him. All the Runaways imitated our idols in the beginning.

After every visit I left in a trance, intoxicated by his presence and all the information he would lay in front of me. He gave me a gold ring that was shaped in an owl's face with rubies for eyes. Owls were his thing. He collected them. He loved them for their intelligence, and he almost looked like one with his heavy black eyebrows. That ring was my pride and joy. Ritchie also gave me one of his special guitar picks, a five-sided home-plate-design pick with a pointy head made out of tortoiseshell. I used that one pick through the entire three-month tour, which is kind of unheard of. I kept it in my mouth like chewing tobacco when I wasn't playing so I would never lose it. I wore it down to nothing. I continued using the home-plate-shaped picks and I still do. Aside from Ritchie and a couple of others, virtually no one uses this very obscure pick shape. I can't use any other shape comfortably. I find that the very sharp tip on it allows me to double-pick my notes in a more articulated way, and it also makes it easier to make all the squealing and screaming sounds with the harmonics that I use in my playing.

One day, when I was leaving Ritchie's house, I drove down the hill from his place and I crossed the center dividing line. The Hollywood Hills are not easy to drive in to begin with—the roads are narrow, cramped, and full of twists and turns. But add to that the fact that I was driving a car as big as a boat and I was flying high from playing guitar all afternoon with one of my heroes, and I was not paying as much attention to the road as I should have been. Before I knew what was happening, I crossed the double yellow line and I slammed into a guy on his motorcycle with his girlfriend on the back. They fell off the bike and slid down the hill, away from my Monte Carlo. I was horrified. I thought I had killed them. I rushed out of the car, and miraculously they were both okay. We were all shaken up but could not have been luckier. The driver was furious with me, rightfully so, and the girlfriend was complaining that she got oil on her jeans, and I thought, *Okay, they're fine if that's her biggest complaint.* I told them to have the bike fixed and send me the bill. I had convinced them not to call the police, but I sure learned my lesson about crossing a double yellow line! As I drove off I was so embarrassed and wondered if Ritchie had already seen a "vision" of the whole thing. He never said anything about it. Thirty-five years later, I ran into the driver of the motorcycle backstage at a Mötley Crüe–Poison concert in Fort Lauderdale, Florida. He said, "Lita, do you remember me?" I said, "No, sorry, who are you?"

"I'm the driver of the motorcycle you hit on Kings Road."

I freaked out! I told him how badly I felt and how it had affected my life—and my driving!—and that I was still very sorry. No one had been hurt so I figured we could laugh about it now, thirty-five years later, but he *still* seemed to be angry about it! He didn't smile and looked at me like I was filth. I continued to smile and tried to shake his hand, but he declined. This was a backstage party at a rock concert—people are supposed to be happy at parties. I said, "Good-bye. Have a nice life," and I walked off.

Although I still lived at home, during this time my parents helped me rent an apartment in Hollywood, on Larrabee Street. It was right around the corner from the Whisky A Go Go. I got the apartment on a side street off the Sunset Strip because driving through traffic between Long Beach and Hollywood was so horrific. It was easier to stay in my apartment most of the time, but I didn't really move out of my parents' house. I would go back and forth between the two places.

My apartment in Hollywood was on the fourth floor over a street where people could park their cars. If anyone left their sunroof open, my friends and I would empty my refrigerator through the window into the open sunroof of a guy's Porsche parked below on the street. Cantaloupes, chocolates, Filet-O-Fish, whatever we weren't going to eat. We thought it was hilarious until the day the police showed up at my door asking if I knew anything about a Filet-O-Fish they found hanging from some guy's steering wheel. We cooled it after that.

IT WAS 1976 and we were about to start a tour of the United States in support of the album *The Runaways*. Despite all my conversations with Ritchie about the grind of touring, I never really understood what he was talking about until we hit the road ourselves. None of us were mentally ready for that first tour. How do you prepare a bunch of teenage girls for that kind of chaos, scrutiny, and instability?

The Runaways were scheduled to do coast-to-coast radio and press. We did interviews with all the top rock magazines, including *Creem* and *Circus*, and visited all the top radio stations in every major city: St. Louis, Detroit, Cleveland, New York, Los Angeles. We would walk into radio stations and destroy the place with fire extinguishers and use the fruit platters in dressing rooms to see if they'd stick on the walls or the ceiling. The deli trays were good for ceiling decor, especially the cheese. Our local radio stations in Los Angeles, KLOS and KNAC, were the most understanding, but because they were locals, we would cut them some slack. Hey, we had to live up to our reputation. I was good with handcuffs, so I would usually handcuff the disc jockey to something, maybe the radiator pipes or some sort of plumbing. Then we would just leave him to figure out for himself how to get uncuffed. Nine times out of ten they seemed to like it.

Our first few shows on that tour were in Ohio. We didn't exactly travel there in style. Kim bought a brown station wagon with wood paneling that served as a lame excuse for a tour bus. A roadie drove us, and along the way he did tons of coke and uppers to stay awake for all twenty-four hundred miles. We sat three people in front, three people in back. I had to teach myself to sleep in that station wagon with my butt scooted down and hanging off the seat, my knees up on the back of the seat in front of me. When I was lucky enough to get the window seat, I would stare out at the night sky. I always looked for my star, wishing upon it that God would guide me and make me a better guitar player. I'd look for the brightest star in the night sky—the one that seemed to be calling out to me the most—and I would fix my gaze on that star until I fell asleep.

I had graduated from high school, but my father went to pick up my diploma since I couldn't make the ceremony. I was onstage, opening for the Ramones. The second show of the tour took place at Cleveland's famed Agora, and that's when we really saw the pandemonium that an all-girl rock band could cause. The Agora fits a thousand people and the concert was completely sold out, but that didn't stop another five hundred teenagers from breaking in or conning their way inside. The audience was nearly all guys and they were going crazy. We were waiting in the back room, blasting music before the show. Each time the song changed there would be enough of a lull that we could hear the crowd roaring and stomping and calling for us. My adrenaline starting pumping. We walked out onstage and looked out into a sea of teenage guys beating the shit out of one another to get closer to the front of the stage. They were screaming our names. They were there for the fucking fantasy, just as Kim Fowley had said. I stared back in their faces and showed them the truth: a chick who could shred.

We toured with the Ramones for quite a while, all throughout the USA. One night, at the end of the tour, I wandered off with Dee Dee Ramone to get some drinks. Dee Dee was a full-blown junkie at the time. He was the better-looking one of the band and would have been the lead vocalist if not for Joey, but Dee Dee had trouble playing and singing at the same time. Their music was fast, so the band members had to either play their instrument or sing, but never both. So Joey became the lead vocalist.

Dee Dee was very intelligent and his bass playing was precise, two things that I have always found attractive. After a few drinks we made our way back to the hotel and had sex. I think it was more of a curiosity thing than sexual desire. Dee Dee and I talked about the adventures of the tour, the different states and the different shows. I guess it was our way of saying good-bye to each other. The next morning the tour was over. He went back to New York and I went back to LA.

Two days later, I was sitting on the toilet in my apartment and my crotch felt really itchy. I didn't know what was going on, so I shaved off all my pubic hair. I saw these little things crawling on my skin. What the fuck! I freaked out. I called Toni because her mother is a nurse and I thought she'd know what to do about those little buggers. She showed up dressed in a nurse's uniform, with a little nurse's cap on her head, stethoscope around her neck, and bright red lipstick. Her top was unzipped, showing her cleavage. She had enough to spare. She found me sitting on a sheet in the middle of my living room floor, naked, trying to pick these little bastards out of my crotch with a pair of tweezers. Even though I was freaking out, I had to laugh at her in that nurse's uniform. She took one look at what was happening and said, "I think we have to go to a real doctor." Fucking Dee Dee Ramone had given me crabs. The shyest Ramone of the bunch. My one and only STD. Judging by the amount of sex I had with rock and rollers throughout my career, I'd say that's not so bad. Anyway, thank God for Kwell lotion.

CHAPTER 4

QUEENS OF NOISE

We're the queens of noise,

Come and get it boys.

—"QUEENS OF NOISE"
(WRITTEN BY BILLY BIZEAU)

"AREN'T YOU HOMESICK?" CHERIE ASKED ME AS WE DROVE THROUGH THE
Midwest to our next gig.

"Of course I am," I told her. "But when I get home, I want to be somebody."

I understood the road was part of the deal, but I'm not saying I liked it. That first tour was rough on all of us, but especially Cherie. Cherie had never been outside of California before, and now we were crisscrossing the United States. Our itinerary saw us drive from LA to Ohio to Illinois and then back to Ohio, New York to Missouri, then back to Illinois and Michigan, then back to Ohio, Tennessee, and Texas, then back to New York, then Illinois, and end in Wisconsin. If that doesn't sound like a drag to you, get out a map and run that route with your finger. Now picture doing it in a cramped station wagon with a driver on uppers, in the heat of the summer, with little to no sleep, and only stopping to pee, eat, or play a gig. Everywhere we went it felt like we had to prove ourselves again and again. Nobody had seen an all-girl rock band before. We knew that they were coming out because they had heard the buzz and they wanted to see if we could live up to it.

The most important gig was at CBGB in New York City: we were opening for the Ramones. Sure, we had proved ourselves to the LA fans, but we were hometown girls in LA. This was New York City. This was CBGB, the rock-and-roll institution in the city that has always defined what was cool. I knew that this was the real test. CBGB truly was one of America's all-time rock-and-roll shitholes: a place that was full of fans, media, sweat, cockroaches, sex, drugs, puke, graffiti, and great rock and roll. Man, if those walls could talk. The ceiling was so low you could hit it with the headstock of your guitar while standing onstage. The plumbing ran across the entire length of the ceiling through the outside, so you could actually hang on it or swing from the pipes. You could never really get a good sound in CBGB, no matter what you played through, because it was shaped like a shoebox. It was a place that you would just get in, play, vomit, get the T-shirt, and get the fuck out of as soon as possible. Still, to play there is a great honor and everyone who ever got on that stage should consider themselves lucky. It was a piece of rock and roll—or should I say raunch and roll—history. The next day all of New York City would read about it, and if New York said you were cool, you *were* cool. The Runaways had the honor of playing there three different times, and every time we packed it and we rocked it hard!

When we were driving up to the entrance to the club, we looked out the windows and saw that the line went down the block. We knew that most of the people waiting were never going to get in. I started to get really pumped up. As soon as I stepped out of the car a bum puked at my feet. *Welcome to New York Fucking City,* I thought. The reviews from that show were mixed. The male reviewers mostly praised us, while it seemed the female reviewers didn't know what to make of us yet. One female reviewer said we were "girls trying to act like boys." She got it wrong. We were girls trying to be better than the boys. And I was determined to let everyone know it.

One night, after a show in Chicago, we stayed at the Lake Shore

Holiday Inn across from Lake Michigan. After the gig, I decided to go to bed for a change instead of going out. I was rooming with Sandy, who had left to go to the bar for a couple of drinks. When she returned to the room, she quickly climbed into bed and fell asleep.

A few minutes later, a noise woke me up. I opened my eyes, thinking it was Sandy, but Sandy was passed out cold in the next bed. That's when I realized there was a guy standing in our room! He had tripped over my suitcase, which was in the middle of the hotel room floor. I didn't panic, but rolled over to act like I was just tossing and turning. He came over to my bedside table, which I was facing, and he went through my purse. He was no more than two feet away from me. I watched him with my eyes half open as he took all the cash I had out of my wallet.

I let him take whatever he wanted from our room. I was afraid he was going to rape us or try to kill us.

After he walked out of the room, I woke Sandy up and told her what had happened. I don't know how this guy got into the room. Maybe Sandy didn't close the door right. She said she was drunk, so maybe she forgot to lock it. Maybe the intruder was one of the people who worked in the hotel. He probably saw Sandy was drunk in the bar and followed her back to her room. Who knows? All I know is we were scared and we called the police right away. We looked around the room to see what else he took and that's when I realized he stole all the jewelry I had left on the bathroom sink, including the owl ring that Ritchie Blackmore had given me. I was devastated. "Shit! My ring!" I yelled. "The bastard!" Well, at least he didn't shoot us. When the police came, they took down as much info as possible and then said, "Sorry, girls, we most likely won't find your jewelry, but can we have your autographs?" *Autographs?* Were these cops for real?

We had three more shows to go, all in Wisconsin. Our last gig was in Milwaukee on August 29, 1976, a full month and a half after we left California. After playing Milwaukee, I was so excited to fly home to LA instead of having to sit in that horrible station wagon again. When we landed at LAX, my father was waiting for me. My parents were always a cornerstone in my life. No matter what, they were there for me. I had never been away from them for that long, and as soon as I saw my father I ran to him, threw my arms around him, and started to cry. He laughed. I think he was relieved to know that I still needed him. Six weeks on the road wouldn't change that. Truly, nothing would.

KIM HAD A two-bedroom apartment a few blocks from me on Palm, right below the Sunset Strip. It was just a few blocks from mine, and Joan lived with him. He had one bedroom and she had another. It was nothing more than a roommate relationship. Kim and Joan had this arrangement that if Joan met a cute straight girl, she would get her number for Kim. It worked out just fine until Joan's partying spun out of control.

Eventually, Kim called her mother and said, "Joan has drug issues. I can't have her dying here. You need to deal with her." Joan realized Kim was trying to put her back at home with her mother, so she moved out of Kim's apartment and into a place a couple of streets over in a little greenish building off the Sunset Strip. I used to go there, but Joan never once came over to my place. She had a roommate named Lisa, a beautiful blond who would later end up with our roadie, Kent Smythe. Joan seemed to be in love with Lisa and was devastated by her relationship with Kent. I couldn't understand being that much in love at our age, with another girl.

Shortly after Joan moved out, Kim said to me, "Hey, I have an extra bedroom. Why don't you move in?" I left my little apartment on Larrabee and took Kim's spare room. That was the beginning of quite an education for me. There were many times when I would come home and Kim would be fucking a girl on the dining room table. I was more discreet when I brought a guy home. I became an expert at sneaking a guy into my bedroom without Kim knowing. Not that Kim would care. But I didn't want to subject the guy to the weirdness of Kim Fowley.

The other part of my education would happen in the mornings

when I was eating my cereal and Kim would be on the phone talking business. I listened to how he worked, heard him sell these people the rap of a lifetime just as he sold me when he called me a year before. He promised them that the Runaways were the greatest thing to happen to music in a long time, that we were going to save rock and roll and would be international superstars. And because he said it over and over again, he truly believed it and he made everyone else believe it too. Then, because everyone believed it, it started to come true.

WE LEFT FOR Europe about a month after getting back from that first US tour. Jackie's mom came along as the chaperone because British immigration required we have a parent with us since most of us were underage. We all felt comfortable around her because she would never question or reprimand us. She was sweet and easygoing, and we felt like we could say anything to her. Jackie's mom didn't get in anybody's way, although she kept a close eye on everything, and there was a lot to keep an eye on in the UK because those boys went crazy as soon as the Runaways touched down.

Our photos were on the cover of British music magazines such as *New Musical Express* and *Melody Maker*. Our single "Cherry Bomb" was on Capital Radio. We played *Top of the Pops*. We did shows in Glasgow, Birmingham, and London. Everywhere we played was a sea of guys in denim and leather, screaming, crazy, and drunk. Every so often we'd see a girl or two. The Runaways headlined two sold-out shows at the Roundhouse in London, an old train station where rock bands had been appearing since the 1960s. In the audience were musicians from all the new punk-rock bands—Siouxsie Sioux, Billy Idol, and members of the Ramones, Blondie, the Sex Pistols, the Clash, and the Damned, among others. In England we really started to feel we were part of a movement like never before.

The Runaways played a gig at Sheffield University during that first UK tour, and I remember it being absolutely packed with young guys. As it would turn out, Joe Elliott of Def Leppard was one of the dudes at that show; years later he came up to me and handed over a Polaroid photograph of me that his friend had taken that night. He remembered there being some sort of huge commotion in front of the stage— almost as though there was a fight going on or something. Then the crowd parted and he noticed that a guy in the front row was jerking off. "Lita, he was there having a wank in the front row! It was like a Jethro Tull album cover or something! I don't know if that happened at all of your gigs, but it certainly happened at the gig I was at!" It definitely wasn't the only time something like that happened at one of our shows. The guys were going nuts, turning over our cars, throwing knives and condoms onto the stage, breaking down the barricades. Sometimes they'd jerk off into a rubber, add some bizarre ingredients like cooked noodles, and throw it onstage. It was both terrifying and thrilling. But through it all, legit outlets like *Sound Magazine* were covering our shows and word was spreading about the crowds we were drawing, and about how we were "liberating" women in Japan. People were coming to see what the fuss was all about. They didn't know what to expect, but a lot of them ended up thinking the same thing Joe Elliott did: *Fuck, these girls can really play!*

At some point Robert Plant had told Cherie a story about collecting hotel room keys and framing them. So Cherie, Joan, and Sandy decided to collect the keys while we were in Europe. Then Cherie took a hair dryer from the hotel because the plugs were different and hers would not work in Europe. The hotel called the police about the hair dryer, and just as we were getting on a boat to cross the English Channel to head to Brussels, they stopped us.

When they searched us, they found that Sandy, Cherie, and Joan had keys from six different hotels. The police thought they were taking the keys to go back and steal out of the rooms. They were not buying the Robert Plant story, and all three girls got arrested. They did not arrest me because I had a British passport and was, and still am, a British citizen. Jackie and I waited with Scott, Kent, and the rest of the crew. They kept them overnight, but eventually released them the next day. We missed our next show, though. All this over a hair dryer and hotel room keys. I was pissed, and that one delay wasn't the only reason why.

While we were in Europe we started to notice that Cherie, Joan, and Scott Anderson would disappear together. There were times when Jackie, Sandy, and I were getting ready to do scheduled press and TV interviews and we didn't even know where they were. We would wind up sitting by ourselves, waiting for everyone else to show up. There was no support or meals, nor did I see any money. I was sick of it and getting pissed off.

In fact, I was so fed up, when we were back in the States, I lost it with Cherie one day. Cherie was always late for everything: interviews, photo shoots, rehearsals, sound checks. You name it, she was late for it. I was sick of waiting around for her. I pushed my way into her hotel room and I said to her, "What are you fucking doing? Why are you always late? You are probably fucking Scott." I said it to rile her up. I went on: "You're probably pregnant! For all I know you could be." She didn't say anything, but she burst into tears. I said, "Are you? You're pregnant?" She just cried. I walked out of the hotel room and slammed the door, not sure what to do or say. I was pissed. And confused. I couldn't even imagine how Cherie was going to deal with this kind of pressure.

According to Cherie, during the break in the tour, her father scraped together every last dime he had to give to Cherie for an abortion. Scott refused to acknowledge that he had gotten an underage girl pregnant. Cherie never spoke about it to me. She never spoke to me about anything anyway, and honestly I didn't give a fuck because I wanted to get on with the band.

Cherie was also distracted by the relationship she had with Joan. When Cherie wasn't with Scott, she was running around with Joan. Meanwhile I'm wondering, *Doesn't anybody want to play any fucking music?* Sometimes while we were on tour I would go to the hotel exit stairwell with a bottle of Johnnie Walker Black Label and my guitar. I would sit there and think or try to figure things out. Why didn't we have any money? Why wouldn't the girls listen to me when I brought it up? I would try to make sense of the other girls' sexual identities or wonder why Cherie was always with Scott and then with Joan. I felt like those stairwells were my sanctuary. Nobody knew where I was. They could search the whole hotel and they wouldn't find me. Who would look in the stairwell? I wasn't in the bar. I wasn't in the restaurant, I wasn't in the parking lot, I wasn't at the park across the street. I was hidden in a place where no one could find me.

WE WENT BACK in the studio almost as soon as we came home from our 1976 tour of Europe to record our second album, *Queens of Noise*. We had been fighting so much with Fowley, we decided to work with another producer, Earle Mankey, an engineer who worked at the Beach Boys' Brother Studios in Santa Monica. He was also a guitarist who played on the Sparks records. He was a long-haired, hip Hollywood rocker who knew how to make an album carefully, not slapping it together like Fowley did on our first album. He was the one who came up with "Queens of Noise" from a songwriter in another band he managed called the Quick. Cherie missed a few days of the sessions, for one reason or another. When she returned, she threw a shit fit about Joan singing lead on the "Queens of Noise" track, but Joan sang it well, so we didn't change it.

I loved being in the studio. We didn't have to fly or stay in hotels. We could go home every night and sleep in our own beds. But best of all, we could get creative, and if we made musical mistakes, we could fix them. Sandy and I stuck together in the studio, and we jammed a lot in between breaks. She loved it. It was something that Jackie would never do with Sandy. For the *Queens of Noise* album I wrote a song called "Johnny Guitar." It wasn't meant to be a Top 40 type of song. The producer had an idea to show off the Runaways' musical strengths, which were Sandy on drums and me on guitar.

There were a lot of disagreements during the production of *Queens of Noise*. Cherie and Joan in particular had arguments, mostly because Joan sang on a few of the lead tracks. I liked Joan's voice on those songs; I thought it gave the album more diversity, but I tried to stay out of the drama. Jackie took her frustrations out on all of us. She complained everything was making her sick, and she was becoming a hypochondriac. She needed to go home, in my opinion. So did Scott Anderson, for that matter. The fact that he was still creeping out Cherie made it very uncomfortable and it wasn't exactly ideal for the rest of us, either.

On that album it is apparent that we were all developing our own musical styles and becoming more confident in our abilities, which was huge! We were becoming our own people instead of trying to mimic our idols, but the majority of the public was still in denial, because the Runaways were *way* before our time. That's how it is when you're the first to do something: you get shit on. Inside the music scene, though, people recognized our ability, and we were hanging out with the big dogs: Queen, Kiss, Alice Cooper, Deep Purple, Rush, Led Zeppelin. We knew them all by the time we did *Queens of Noise*. We were interesting, original, musically talented bad girls, and everyone wanted to meet us.

After we recorded the album, we went back on the road for another US tour that took us everywhere from New York to Michigan, Ohio to Texas. We did a couple of dates opening for Rush at big halls in the Midwest. They didn't seem to want to have anything to do with us, though, and the feeling was mutual. We sat at a table together and took a picture for the tour. That was it. We never really spoke to each other. March 1977, we went out on another extended tour, this time as headliners.

We played the Royal Oak Theatre in Detroit with Cheap Trick. Some of the Runaways' fans didn't like Cheap Trick, and they started charging the stage with knives. Detroit was a rough town. Our hotel even had bulletproof windows. Detroit was also a heavy rock-and-roll town. If the fans loved you, they treated you like gods. If they didn't, they treated you like shit. They loved us, thank God. When we got to the Agora in Cleveland, Tom Petty and the Heartbreakers were added to the bill. The Runaways headlined. It was a small venue and everything was so cramped. We threw both of those bands out of the tiny dressing room and made them change in a trailer in the alley behind the venue. There were no hard feelings. Cheap Trick was one of my favorite bands at the time, and it was the beginning of a career-long relationship with the guys. They're like my big brothers.

When we got back to Los Angeles, we celebrated the official release of *Queens of Noise* with a sold-out concert at the Santa Monica Civic and a sold-out four-night run at the Whisky. The lines at the Whisky wrapped around the block every single night. We still hold the record for the most sold-out shows in a row there. That was when I figured out who was really the boss. We were! I was sick of our managers not paying us, playing with us, and hurting us. One of those nights I put my foot down and said, "Hey, dickheads, guess what? I'm not going onstage."

It was really only a test to see what would happen if I didn't do what management said. Scott Anderson started to beg me. "Oh, sweetie, honey. You can't do this."

"Oh, yes I can," I snapped back.

Too bad the other girls didn't back me on this. Instead they all looked at me like I was nuts.

"Come on, Lita. Don't do this," Cherie said to me.

Sandy was in shock. "What do you mean you aren't going onstage?"

The only one who seemed to be on my side was Jackie. One time she actually tried to call an attorney to help us, but when you're a kid, attorneys don't always jump when you tell them to.

The managers all begged and pleaded with me. I knew right then and there what to do to have the upper hand with these guys. I still played the show, but I was happy to know that I had a foolproof plan in my back pocket.

After that, we went back to New York to play two more shows at CBGB, but this time we were veterans and New York did not intimidate us anymore. The first time we played there a lot of the reviewers weren't so sure about us, but this time they started to praise us.

After the last CBGB show, I handcuffed Scott Anderson to his briefcase while he was asleep. Sandy was with me. We stripped off all his clothes, then took Sharpies and drew obscenities all over his ugly, naked body for what he had done to Cherie. It was unforgivable. He deserved something in return. We left him in the New York City hotel and caught a flight to the next show. He never talked about it. The Runaways were riding high. He wouldn't dare go up against any of us.

As much success as we were having in England, Hollywood, and New York, nothing prepared us for what was about to happen in Japan.

CHAPTER 5

JAPAN

I said, Mama but weer all crazee now.

—"Mama Weer All Crazee Now"
(Written by Jim Lea and Noddy Holder)

IN THE SUMMER OF 1977, MERCURY RECORDS SENT THE HEAD OF WEST COAST
publicity, Eileen Bradley, to watch over us in Japan. "Anything happens
to these girls and it's your neck," the executives told her. Eileen was only
twenty-eight, with a thick New York accent, a huge Afro wig, and a cigarette always dangling from her mouth. We all took a liking to her immediately. Her one job was to keep us out of trouble. The poor woman.

By this time Scott Anderson was gone, probably because he was
afraid of going to jail for getting an underage girl pregnant, so Kim sent
Kent Smythe to Japan with us. I was not sure sending Kent was a wise
idea because he was a bit of a shit stirrer. Still, the seven of us boarded
the flight, waving good-bye to our parents and Kim, as we set off for the
other side of the world.

We had a four-hour layover in Hawaii. When we got back on the
plane the stewardesses gave us floral leis, and we all took our seats in
coach. Nobody recognized us or had any clue that we were even a band.
When we landed in Japan, Eileen gathered us together before we got

off the plane. "Look," she said, "if anything happens over here, it's an international incident. I'm the first one to go down and you're all coming with me. So don't do anything stupid."

After the brutal seventeen hours of traveling, I wanted nothing more than to get to the hotel, take a shower, get out of my clothes, and stretch out. The Japanese had other plans. We stepped off the plane and were greeted by pandemonium.

All we could see and hear were thousands of Japanese, all in the process of losing their minds. Runaways fans! There were so many of them and they were going so crazy that the security guards had to form a human barrier with their arms latched together to hold them back. We barreled down the path they created through the sea of people. They showered us with gifts, shoved autograph books in front of us to sign, screamed our names, and even cried. It was like Beatlemania—or Runawaymania, I should say. We had no warning that this would happen, probably because we never saw any details about our record sales. I'm sure Kim knew exactly where our record charted in Japan; he just chose not to tell us. He never felt it was important to tell us anything, especially where business was concerned and money might be a factor. If we had known how huge we were in Japan, maybe someone else besides me and Jackie would have started asking questions, and Kim didn't want that.

We were also greeted at the airport by the promoter, Mr. Udo, and his team.

They took us straight to a press conference. No rest for the weary. We still had the floral leis around our necks and the clothes we had been in for way too long. No time to change, refresh, shit, shower, or eat. Mr. Udo was going to get his money's worth out of us.

I was walking in front of Cherie. An arm reached out through the line of security guards. The hand was going for my long, silky, hair, which apparently some Japanese found exotic. Cherie grabbed the arm at the wrist, and as she did that another arm came out and pulled her hair. We both got scalped of a good section of our hair, which hurt like hell. These fans really wanted a piece of us!

We were directed by security to run toward our waiting limo. As the limo tried to drive off, all the fans piled on top and crowded around. The car couldn't move. We didn't know what was happening. We couldn't see out the window, and neither could the driver. The reception took us all by surprise, and it was a little scary, but we also thought it was awesome! We didn't know if this was what Japan was like with every band or if it was just us. As it turned out, the Runaways, Queen, Kiss, Deep Purple, and Led Zeppelin were the most popular rock bands in Japan, and the appearance of one of those bands on Japanese soil was cause for collective insanity.

At the press conference, they presented us with sake. "What the hell is this stuff?" I whispered to Eileen.

"It's wine."

"But it's hot!" I whispered to her. I was grossed out by it, but I tried not to show it. The Japanese were so full of respect and class. I didn't want to hurt anyone's feelings, so instead I threw it into a plant the first chance I got.

The Japanese press seemed happy and friendly, and it was obvious that the reporters had done their research. They already knew who our musical idols were and asked us questions about them as well as typical questions like "What is your favorite food?," "How did you learn to play?," "How do you like Japan so far?," and "Are you glad to be here?" They spoke brilliant English, and they were all very impressed with how good a drummer Sandy was and how great a guitar player I was, mainly because we were very young and female. Cherie's blond hair and blue eyes intrigued them. We were like creatures from a different planet. I felt like we were being dissected under a microscope. And with no shower!

Mr. Udo gave us the five-star treatment, including gifts on that first day: a tape recorder/cassette player, real ivory earrings, roses, and beautiful pearl necklaces that came wrapped in purple satin pouches, packaged in another satin pouch with Japanese writing on it. Each girl got a different-colored pouch. It was all so overwhelming and incredible because we were used to being treated like shit. We actually felt like rock stars for the first time.

When we finally did get to the hotel, we found out that we each had our own room. For the first time, we didn't have to share, and this was no Motel 6 kind of place. It was a beautiful luxury hotel called the Tokyo Prince. They tried to give Eileen the presidential suite a few floors up and she said, "No, just give me a regular room right near the girls at the end of the hall." Every night she would put her ears to our doors to make sure nothing suspicious was going on. We were actually really good for the most part, largely because we were afraid of being thrown in a Japanese jail. They were so strict and proper wherever we went, and so jail in Japan sounded frightening. Another reason was that the drug laws were very harsh.

Japan was very puzzling for all of us in terms of the food, culture, and language. We would walk into a restaurant and see these menus featuring seaweed with octopus and crazy stuff like that. We tried to be polite, but none of us wanted to eat it. I eventually gave sake a second try. I guess I just had to get used to it, although I still stuck to my usual diet of whiskey and McDonald's for most of the trip. Eileen had the hotel employees deliver Quarter Pounders to our rooms every night so when we got there we would actually have something to eat.

The Japanese tour organizers assigned us our own guitar techs, who had their act so together that they didn't need any direction from me or the other girls. We just had to plug our guitars into the Marshall amps, tune up, and play; we didn't use any pedals or effects at that time anyway. It seemed like all the techs were named Hiro. I asked Joan, "What's your tech's name?"

"Hiro," she told me.

"No, that's my tech's name."

We couldn't go anywhere without causing a huge scene. We went to do an in-store appearance where the street outside was so crowded, the mob crushed the limousine roof as the car slowly inched its way through the crowd. It was difficult making it into the store, but we made it.

Everywhere I went, there were people behind me, people in front of me, people sticking their heads out of windows and yelling, "Rita,

Rita!" We would turn around and there were sixteen people following us, whispering to each other, giggling, and one person would walk up and hand me a gift. Whether it was a necklace they were wearing or the ring they had on, they would take it off and give it to you. By the end of the tour, I had so many gifts given to me, I had to buy another suitcase to get them home.

Our tour of Japan lasted six weeks and we played large auditorium shows in big cities like Osaka and Nagoya. We went by bullet train from city to city, and since these trains traveled through people's farms, it was really interesting to see the rice fields. It was a hell of a lot more educational than being in high school.

For all the chaos that followed us outside, the audiences in the venue were very conservative. No one was allowed to stand up and shout, and after each song they would applaud politely. As they waited for the next song to start, it was so silent you could hear a pin drop. It was a strange feeling being onstage with that kind of audience reaction, especially since we had dealt with such crazy crowds in the US and the UK.

Soon we only had two more shows to do, including the big show at the Budokan in Tokyo, and we had to finish the recording of the *Live in Japan* album. In one week we would be heading home. The night before the Budokan show, we were doing a sound check and somehow Jackie's favorite bass, her Gibson Thunderbird, got tipped over. It was sitting on an old guitar stand that was not very sturdy. It was almost like it happened in slow motion. Jackie tried to grab it before it hit the ground, but she didn't make it in time. It snapped the headstock clean off as it hit the wooden stage. Oh shit! We all stood still looking at the broken bass. Thunderbirds are known for skinny necks that are easy to snap. Of course we had a backup bass, but this gave Jackie a reason to throw a hissy fit at Cherie. None of us would have intentionally knocked it over, but Jackie thought Cherie had done it on purpose because she was standing near it when it fell over. Someone most likely tripped on the cable and pulled it over. Who knows. Either way, Jackie blamed Cherie. Eileen tried to calm the girls down, and I just walked off. We were so close to the end of the tour, but things were starting to unravel.

Then, for some reason, the record company sent Eileen home.

"I really think I should stay," she said.

"No, they only have a few more shows. It will be fine," the executives told her.

Eileen knew in her heart that she shouldn't leave, but the record company needed her back in the States. So Eileen left . . . and that's when all hell broke loose.

ONE DAY CHERIE said she couldn't do the press conference because she was feeling sick. She went back to the hotel and we all went out and did the appearance. When we came back, we saw Cherie sitting on the floor in the lobby in a kimono that was spread out like someone was getting married. She was signing autographs and taking pictures. Jackie went crazy. "This is too much! She thinks she's the only star!" Jackie was unhappy about a lot of things. She never really was cut out for rock and roll. She hated that she couldn't grow her nails long and play bass, and that the cords onstage kept wrapping around her high heels so she couldn't wear them while performing. I used to tell her to wear boots, but she liked these delicate little slip-on sandals with heels that you couldn't wear and still move around with onstage. She couldn't eat certain foods, and all kinds of smells—food, deodorant, hairspray, my Noxzema—made her nauseous. If it had any fragrance, it would make her sick. Jesus Christ! She was hard to be around, and she was starting to lose it. In Japan, she had some female medical problems and went to the hospital. It turned out she had a yeast infection, which was something that could have been taken care of very easily. According to Jackie, she couldn't communicate with the doctors. They handed her a doll and asked her to point to what was wrong. By the time she got back to the hotel, Jackie was more upset than before she had left for the hospital.

Kent, who liked to antagonize people, saw this as an opportunity to wind her up even more. If he saw a reason to irritate someone, he would. When Jackie came back to the hotel, Kent was messing around with his cassette recorder. Being the dog that he was, he went into her room and at first he acted sympathetic, but then he said something to get her riled again. Without her knowing it, Kent was recording the conversation. He had the tape recorder hidden in his coat pocket. She was screaming at him. "I'm sick of being sick. I want to go home. I want to see my own doctor. I'm sick of being sick."

The entire meltdown was recorded. Kent was so pleased with himself and he made his way to my room to play me what he had captured on tape. When I heard Jackie screaming, "I'm sick of being sick!" over and over again, hysterically screaming, I said, "That's nothing new," and I slammed the door in his face. What I didn't know was that when Kent had left the room, Jackie ordered room service, broke the plates, and had cut a jagged slice down her arm, from her forearm to her wrist. Someone called for help and Jackie was taken to the hospital again, where they taped her arm shut. I didn't know, but just like that, Jackie had quit the band. Much to my surprise, she left for the United States on a flight the next morning.

Now what?

We only had one show left, but it was the biggest concert of the tour—the Budokan in Tokyo. It was the most important and well-known rock arena in Japan, where all the biggest bands played. All the press, TV, and radio interviews we had been doing were leading up to this show. There was no way we could cancel or back out, and we were in a panic. We had a meeting and decided that Joan should take over playing bass because we figured she could get by with what she knew from playing guitar, and I could cover all the guitar parts. It worked out all right, and I was proud of Joan and the rest of the girls for pulling it off.

This was the only show where the audience could not be contained by the security guards. They went nuts. Runawaymania was in full effect, and it was awesome. After the show, as we left the dressing room, I caught my boot heel in the rolled-up cuff of my pants and fell down a flight of stairs. I was hurt, but I didn't need to go to the hospital or anything like that, so I brushed it off and went back to the hotel.

My back ached. I had twisted my ribs and legs in my fall down the stairs. I went to the hotel bar to get a couple shots of whiskey to kill the pain. The tour was over and the Budokan show was done: what a relief. Time to celebrate! Sitting at the bar was the first American guy I had seen in a long time, so I moved closer to him. I asked him where he was from, and he said he was from Texas. I think he may have been with the crew from one of the bands at the Tokyo Music Festival. I don't know if I ever knew his name.

He pulled these oval-shaped pills out of his pocket, explaining they were some kind of downers, called footballs. Pills like that simply were not available in Japan. I was impressed. "Do you want a couple?" he said.

I thought, *Holy shit! Downers. How cool!*

"Yes!" I replied. The tour is over, let's have a fucking football.

Not only did I have a few shots of whiskey, I had a couple of those footballs too. Before long, we went up to my hotel room and wound up in bed together. We had a great time, and I forgot all about tumbling down the stairs. He was fun and the sex was hot. He was gentle with me, and afterward we both fell asleep, probably because of the footballs.

I woke up and had to pee. I looked in the toilet after I went and it was full of blood. Immediately I thought, *Okay, it's just a really heavy period,* so I went back to bed. I fell asleep for another thirty minutes or so, then got up to sit on the toilet seat to see if the bleeding had stopped, but it had actually gotten worse. I looked a little closer and realized that there was more blood than any normal period: way more blood! I was full-on hemorrhaging. The toilet was filled with clotted blood. I sat back down on the bed as the Texan just lay there. The bed was covered in blood—it looked like a murder scene. The weird thing was, I wasn't in any pain, and I didn't think he had done anything to me. With that much blood, you would think I'd be in tremendous pain.

I didn't accuse him of hurting me, so I told the Texan, "Get out!"

He acted confused. "What? Why?"

I said, "I don't know if you did or didn't do anything. Just get the fuck out. Now!" I pointed to the door.

He looked innocent, he truly did, but how does a person hemorrhage the way I was hemorrhaging unless someone hurt you? I didn't care what his story was, I just wanted him gone.

I didn't know what to do or who to call. Definitely not Kent! Eileen had left already. I tried Cherie, who was, of course, with Joan. I asked them to come to my room. When they got there I was lying on the bed. I asked Cherie and Joan if they could see something. "No, Lita," they told me. "It's just a bunch of blood."

Really? No shit! I didn't need them to tell me that.

Cherie told me that the night before she got with some American guy. When he found out she was underage, he filled a Coke bottle with warm water and used that to fuck her. Gross!

"Did he use that on you? Maybe it broke?" she asked.

"Fuck no! I wouldn't let anyone fuck me with a Coke bottle, Cherie! Boy, I feel much better now," I said sarcastically.

They were no help at all, and eventually they left my room. I lay there contemplating dialing 911. But how do I dial 911 in Japan? Just dial 911, I guess? If I didn't hurry, I would for sure bleed to death at the rate I was losing blood.

I cracked open my hotel door to peek into the hallway. A man walked by. An American! In desperation I said, "Excuse me, sir. Please help me. Please!"

He walked over a little closer, then peeked through the hotel door and saw the blood on the bed. Shocked, he told me to lie down. "Don't move. I'm dialing 911." It turns out he was the tour manager for Deep Purple. Of all people, it had to be Ritchie Blackmore's tour manager? I listened to him anyway since he seemed to have a level head on his shoulders. At the time I definitely did not. I was scared to death. I could hear the ambulance screaming in the distance, getting closer. They finally arrived. When they got to my room, they strapped me down to a gurney and took me to a Tokyo hospital.

The medical staff in admitting didn't know what was wrong with me, so they put me in the labor ward. I could hear a woman screaming in the next room. I didn't know if they understood what I was saying. There wasn't a lot of communication. I held the sheet tight against my face as the woman in the next bed kept screaming. When the doctor finally came to work on me, I asked, "Why is she screaming?"

"She's having a baby."

"I'm in the labor ward?"

"Yes." They told me I was cut open as if I'd had an episiotomy, so that was the logical place to take me.

"Make sure you stitch me up tight," I said. "Make sure everything's tight down there."

The doctor understood perfectly well what I meant. He smiled. With a giggle he said, "Oh, okay!"

He gave me fourteen stitches. Because of the language barrier, I couldn't find out if it was a cut or a tear or what it was. To this day I have no idea what happened to me. Because of the number of stitches, I assume the Texan had cut me. I didn't feel him tearing me or hurting me, and if he had something like a cock ring, some sort of sex toy, or even a knife, I have no clue, because I didn't feel any sort of pain while we were having sex.

I woke up in the hospital room and saw Joan asleep in a chair next to my bed. None of the other girls had come to see me. I asked Sandy to come, but she said hospitals freaked her out. It was weird because Joan and I never really hung out together, but the instant I saw her sitting at my bedside table in the hospital, I felt a tremendous respect for her. The Runaways were never a team, but that said a lot to me. She brought me the cassette player that Mr. Udo had given us so I could play some music in the hospital, since I was stuck there for three days while they finished mixing and mastering the *Live in Japan* record.

I listened to various Black Sabbath tapes, with "Sabbath Bloody Sabbath," "Children of the Grave," and all these nasty, heavy-duty songs. The nurse asked me if I could turn off Black Sabbath because the lady in the next room was dying. I turned it down, because I figured it wasn't really music for someone to die to, but I didn't turn it off. I had to have my Black Sabbath.

About twelve years later, the Texan called me. He wanted to talk about the incident in Japan. I didn't know whether he wanted to explain himself or ask me what happened. I said, "Don't ever fucking call me again," and put the phone down. It freaked me out. Obviously, he had been thinking about it all these years, but at this point I wasn't going to believe anything he said anyway; it didn't matter, and I didn't want to know.

On the flight back from Japan we all sat there silent, stunned, and shell-shocked. We created Runawaymania, but what had just happened? Jackie was completely gone, the others were wrecked, worn-out, and exhausted, and I had fourteen stitches because of some dude whose name I didn't even know. I was eighteen and felt like I had lived an entire lifetime of adventures in six weeks.

CHAPTER 6

GOOD-BYE, CHERIE

Shades of gray don't fade away,

They're waiting for the night.

—"Waitin' for the Night"
(Written by Lita Ford, Kari Krome, and Kim Fowley)

WHEN WE CAME BACK FROM JAPAN, KIM DID HIS USUAL BITCHING ABOUT
expenses. Mercury Records released *Live in Japan,* which was certified
gold in Japan. On the night that the album was supposed to be turned
in, Kent and the engineer were the only two left in the studio. Me and
the rest of the girls were long gone because we were finished recording
the album. This is when the engineer accidentally erased Joan's rhythm
guitar part off the song "Queens of Noise." Oh shit! Kent flipped out. It
was the wee hours of the morning and there was no time to find Joan to
rerecord her part, so Kent ran up a few flights of stairs to another apartment, where he had previously met a guy who owned a Stratocaster. He
woke him up and begged him to borrow the Strat. Kent used that Stratocaster to replace Joan's parts on "Queens of Noise." Eureka! It worked!
Thank God nobody noticed. *Live in Japan* was meant to be a Japanese-
only release, but it worked its way into other markets and became a huge
success for the Runaways. Literally a lot of blood, sweat, and tears went
into it.

Now, back home, we had to deal with the loss of Jackie. We needed a bass player: again! An eighteen-year-old girl from Newport Beach named Vicki Tischler was next to audition for the Runaways. Vicki and Kim had connected and she went to see him at Larrabee Studios. He thought she would be a good fit, so two days later we all went to the Studio Instrument Rentals (SIR) rehearsal studio on Sunset Boulevard, a proper rehearsal facility with pool tables and places to hang out. Joan, Sandy, Cherie, and I were lounging on the sofas when Vicki walked in. Nobody said anything at first. We could tell that it was going to take a little bit of work to get her up to par with the rest of the band. She needed to transform into a rock star instantly.

Vicki was joining the band at a bad time, and my heart went out to her. There was a lot of drug abuse and tension between band members, and she had her own issues to work through. One of them was the fact that she was epileptic, which meant she needed to be on medication for her condition, and that medication made her lethargic. This gave Kent a chance to antagonize her during live performances. She was insecure, frightened, and intimidated. Anyone would be at that point. Kent would her with rubber bands and spit wads to get her to move onstage. This really pissed me off. It bothered me that Kent treated her that way. He always found humor in wreaking havoc and causing trouble. Vicki was mild-mannered, and being new to the band, she never said anything to Kent. She would have major epileptic seizures and bite almost clean through her tongue. They were wicked attacks. She needed a stable environment, and the Runaways were everything but stable.

No one in the band wanted to take the time to help Vicki. Joan was completely off in another world. Sandy, being the drummer, was getting sick of all the changes to the rhythm section and had no patience for another bass player. No one else wanted to deal with it, but I wasn't going to let that girl or the band suffer anymore. We had already been through hell. I roomed with her and took her under my wing. She clung to me because she knew I cared and was willing to help protect her. I worked with Vicki, trying to help her change her style, lose weight, and change her whole approach. I got Kent to stop picking on her, and Vicki started to blossom. She looked and sounded better and started to fit into the band quite well by the time we were ready to shoot the album cover for *Waitin' for the Night*.

ONE DAY WE were all sitting around waiting for Cherie. Nobody knew where the hell she was, *once again*. Two hours later, she finally came strolling in. She looked tired and haggard. I took one look at her and said, "Get yourself together," as I pointed toward the dressing room, which was behind a frosted-glass door. I was sick of her always being late or completely absent. When Cherie said, "I have to leave early to take my sister to acting class," after arriving two hours late, that was the straw that broke the camel's back. I lost it. In my mind, I'm thinking, *Why can't someone else give her a ride? A roadie? Doesn't she have any other friends? Parents? She couldn't take a taxi or a bus?* A lot of prep goes into the photo shoot of an album cover—for the band, the studio, and the photographer.

She went into the dressing room and closed the door. I followed her into the dressing room and was so angry that I didn't notice the top window above the door was open, so everyone could hear us. When I started yelling at her, she started to cry and be her usual dramatic self. I blew up in her face. I was finished with her fucking off: "You have to choose between your family and this band." I meant for that day. Cherie thought I meant forever.

She said, "I can't do this anymore. I've had enough." Looking back, I understand now that Cherie had a lot of pressure on her. She had to deal with Scott Anderson getting her pregnant, Joan Jett being in love with her and taking over on some of the lead vocals, and Kim Fowley's demands on her to be the front person that he had envisioned for the Runaways. There were always people clinging to her, and I think that had a lot to do with why she left too. She was young and it was overwhelming for her, and even though I think she wanted me to give her my approval, I was always angry at her. There was demand for her to be at autograph signings, interviews, and other media events, and while she thought that she was doing her best, applying herself 100 percent, she didn't realize all these other things were getting in her way. She was always late or absent, and it all came to a head that one day at Barry Levine's studio. I think all of the pressures built up and finally got to her. We were all exhausted, and I didn't want to fuck around anymore. We went ahead and shot some photos with Barry anyway, without her, and later on one of those photos became the album cover for *Waitin' for the Night*. When she left that day, we didn't know she was going to quit, but that's exactly what she did.

Now we were out a lead singer. We had two choices. The Runaways could break up right then, or we could keep going. When Cherie walked out, she didn't realize that she had left her burden on Joan's shoulders. She had dropped a bomb on Joan. This would change the face of the band. Could Joan fill those shoes? Could she wear a corset? She didn't have blond hair and bright blue eyes, and she wasn't as feminine as Cherie. We all looked at Joan and asked her if she thought she could handle taking over as the lead vocalist. She was hesitant at first, but she agreed because for her, breaking up the Runaways at that time was not an option. The rest of us had to step up too.

Joan took over the vocals on *Waitin' for the Night*. Even though Joan did a beautiful job on the vocals, I was never credited for cowriting the title track, which was typical Runaways bullshit. This was the first time I had really paid attention to Joan's voice. She had come into her own as a lead singer. She was under the gun and had to prove herself as a front person. It seemed natural for her, but soon the pressures of being the lead singer of the Runaways would take their toll on Joan too.

AFTER WE FINISHED *Waitin' for the Night*, we went to Europe in late 1977. Our first stop was Northern Ireland, during the Belfast bombings. We had a tour bus, and military tanks would stop the bus, come inside, and check for bombs and weapons. After they were done checking our bus, they'd ask for autographs. Bomb-sniffing dogs would check the venues before the audience was allowed in. It was really nerve-racking and we weren't used to it. One of the hotels we stayed at had been bombed already, so we were staying in the part of the hotel that had been deemed safe. We played for a sea of denim and leather. It was all rowdy, drunken dudes, snow, and alcohol. This was when my consumption of hard liquor increased. It was so cold, and that made it difficult to play guitar. The guitars were cold so the strings wouldn't bend and you couldn't feel your fingers. It was so cold at some of the outdoor festivals that I needed to do something to loosen myself up and warm my bones so I could move my fingers on the guitar. Coming from an Italian and British household, liquor was not a foreign substance to me. It was never seen as something that was forbidden. At first I liked shots of the blackberry brandy my mother had given to me before I left for Europe. From there I moved on to Johnnie Walker Black Label, which became my drink of choice.

Up to that point in my life, my alcohol consumption had increased or decreased depending on the company I kept; it came and went depending on the men I was with too. While we were in Ireland, I had a drink with Captain Dirty, who was the head of the Belfast Hells Angels. He really took a liking to us. The Hells Angels literally stood onstage with us while we played and no one, including us, was going to tell them to move, so they became our security guards. They turned out to be really cool guys. Because of them, whatever we wanted, we would have. Vicki saw a belt some young boy was wearing and was eyeing it from the stage. Captain Dirty saw that and ripped it off the young boy and laid it on the stage in front of Vicki.

That night I came into my hotel room that I was sharing with Vicki. It was late so I was trying to be careful and quiet. I went into the restroom and noticed black curly hairs on my hairbrush. *Gross,* I thought. *Who's been using my hairbrush?* As I walked to my bed, I looked around and found two people were rolling around on the floor next to my bed. It was Vicki and, much to my surprise, she was with a guy! But how could anyone refuse the black Irishman she was with: the one and only

Phil Lynott from Thin Lizzy. Lucky bitch! I loved Phil! I guess that explained the kinky hair in my brush. I crawled into my own bed and went to sleep. The next morning they were both gone.

That European tour lasted about a month, and then we returned home to start another American tour in early 1978, which we were all excited about because we were going on the road with the Ramones again. It was during that short break that I met the Who's John Entwistle. He was between wives. We met backstage at a Cars concert. The one thing John Entwistle and I had in common was spiders: we both loved them. We hit it off that first night and we headed over to the Rainbow after the concert, then we ended up at the Riot House. He had about a quarter gram of blow and we were going to snort it, but we dropped it down the side of the pullout couch and never found it again. Things got hot pretty quickly after that, and before I knew it I had stripped out of my clothes and we were on the bed. All of a sudden John looked a little freaked out and he stopped and pointed at my thighs. "What happened to you?"

I had no idea what he was talking about. I looked down and noticed that my legs and inner thighs were black and blue! I was wearing a new pair of jeans and I had been horseback riding earlier that day. My jeans were really tight and it helped cause the bruises. Needless to say, John was looking at me like I was into sadomasochism or something. I tried to explain my horseback-riding story, but he wouldn't have it. We ended up having sex anyway, so he couldn't have been that freaked out.

AT THE START of the American tour, Kim Fowley basically bailed on us. I think he was disappointed that Cherie had left the band: he had never envisioned Joan as the lead singer. At the beginning of the Runaways, Kim had wanted Kari Krome to play guitar and be the lead singer of the band. He was more fond of Kari's looks than of Joan's, but Kari didn't have Joan's talent. Kari was the one who pushed Joan forward. By this point he didn't care for Vicki, Sandy was a drummer and always in the background, and he was afraid of me. I think we had started to lose some of our audience because with Cherie leaving, we had lost the more feminine front person, and Kim didn't like that. Kim brought in Toby Mamis to take his place, and I was really confused. I'm not really sure where he came from, but I thought he was ten times worse than Kim in his ability to manage us. He was a very short, round guy with an Afro and Coke-bottle glasses. He lived off the old diet soda Tab. Somehow he never lost weight, though. Everything about him annoyed me. Even the way he drank his Tab. Toby was clueless about us girls. He was an outsider and not creative or fatherly, as even Kim had eventually become in his own weird way. Toby just didn't fit the group, and nobody really paid much attention to him.

Our first show of the tour with the Ramones was on January 7, 1978, at the Palladium in New York. The dressing rooms in that place were small and I remember seeing Joey Ramone changing his clothes. He had a huge scar down his back and I wondered what had happened to him, although I never asked. He had all sorts of health issues, and he used a lot of nose spray to breathe and eye drops to see. He had a beautiful girlfriend from LA. At the time I wondered how a guy like Joey could get such a hot chick, but when you saw him onstage, you figured it out. I started to love him too. I started to love all the Ramones. I loved the way they all wore matching clothes and moved together strumming their guitars in synchronicity. I knew every word to their set. They were very street, very rough, raunchy, and raw. The Ramones were like street rats with attitude on a rock-and-roll level.

I became friends with Joey's girlfriend. The only time I shot heroin was with her, when she injected it into one of my butt cheeks. It made me so sick! I threw up on the front lawn of her house. It was a disaster. Never again! I'm definitely not cut out for heroin. It never was my drug of choice.

After the long American tour with the Ramones, the Runaways headed for Europe again. One of my favorite shows in Europe was the Midsummer Festival in Stockholm, Sweden, that the country waited the whole year for. A fair combined with a rock festival, it was beautiful, crazy, wild, and full of all sorts of people: teenagers, families with young kids, and the Swedish Hells Angels. It seemed like the whole country came to this festival. When we stood on the stage, we could see the giant Ferris wheel lit up in the dark, turning in the distance, people screaming from the roller coasters, and thousands of people having fun, listening to music, eating, and drinking all weekend long.

During those two days, I met a journalist named Lars. He had longish, shoulder-length blond hair, blue eyes, and a chiseled face like a young Mick Jagger. He took a liking to me and I took a liking to him. I found him interesting, gorgeous, and sexy. We partied through the entire festival. I went back to his house with him after the show and stayed there overnight since we were off the next day. The following day, Lars took me around town. We went shopping and out on a boat to see these little offshore islands that you could only get to by boat. We cruised the waters and looked at all the houses on an island called Vaxholm.

Our next show was in Oslo, Norway. I told the girls and our British tour managers to take my luggage and go ahead without me—I would meet up with them in time for the Oslo gig. I wanted to stay with Lars and enjoy myself. His house was in an apartment-style building, and his neighbor was Britt Ekland. He cooked for me and told me stories—and as a journalist he had quite a few cool rock-and-roll stories to tell, especially about the Rolling Stones. I told him that my favorite song at the time was "Winter" by the Stones off the *Goats Head Soup* album. There's a line in the song that goes, "I wish I been out in California." When I was homesick, I would listen to "Winter" and it would make me feel better.

Lars was interesting and different. We enjoyed each other so much that I didn't sleep the entire weekend. I was so tired. But I had to catch the next flight to Oslo. I told him, "I'll be back soon," and took off for the Stockholm airport. Unfortunately, it wasn't a direct flight, so I had to switch planes somewhere. No one had forewarned me about the plane change, so, exhausted and feeling dreamy from the weekend, I passed out cold. When the plane landed in the city where I was supposed to get off and switch to a connecting flight, I didn't wake up. During that time a whole set of different people got on the plane. As we started for the runway ready to take off again, I opened my eyes and noticed the guy sitting next to me looked different. I sat up quickly and asked him, "Excuse me, sir, did you just get on this plane? Because you weren't here a few minutes ago, were you?"

"No, I just boarded."

"Where is this plane going?" I asked.

"Iceland."

"ICELAND!"

I screamed to the stewardess, "Stop the plane!"

She came running over. I said to her, "I have to get off this plane now! I was supposed to get off when we landed! I fell asleep! I need to go to Oslo!"

The stewardess asked the pilot to stop the plane. I couldn't believe it, but he actually stopped the plane. The back of the plane opened up and a staircase came down under the tail. I grabbed my stuff and ran for the staircase and onto the runway. I was standing on the fucking runway wondering how to get to the terminal. I was completely turned around. I didn't even know what country or city I was in. *Hold it together, Lita,* I thought to myself.

I saw a building in the distance and started walking toward it, hoping it was the terminal, which thankfully it was. I made my way into the terminal and found that I had missed my connecting flight. Shit. I was going to miss the show in Oslo for sure. I went to the desk at the Swedish airline and told them the story. They said, "We have one more flight that leaves for Oslo. It's the last one for the day." It put me in Oslo at the same time I was supposed to be onstage. My tour manager must have been freaking, pacing back and forth wondering what had happened to me. There were no cell phones back then. I dug through my purse and found a paper with his phone number on it. I called him and told him I had missed the connecting flight but would be on the next one. He started cursing at me, so I hung up on him. At least he knew I was on my way and not headed to Iceland.

When the plane landed in Oslo, I was already late for the show. My tour manager was at the airport to pick me up. I was so happy to see him, even if he was pissed at me. I think he got a kick out of my devious behavior, though. He gave me a little grin and said, "Did you have a good time, Lita?" We headed straight to the gig, where another sea of pissed-off and anxious, drunken Vikings were waiting to see the Runaways. We immediately jumped up onstage and did the show. We caused such a scene that night because of the delay. We gave them one of our best shows. After we got offstage I headed straight to the hotel for some shut-eye. As I entered the hotel room, the phone was ringing. It was Lars. He had called to play me "Winter" over the phone. And with that, all of my troubles calmed down. After that show, Lars would call me on a regular basis and play "Winter." We eventually lost touch, but I always think of him when I hear that song.

The European tour lasted two months. You would think from all the touring we would be getting some money by now. Nope. We were all broke, confused, and tired. With the exception of Vicki, who was on medication to manage her own medical issues, we were turning to drugs and alcohol to soothe our young, broken souls.

WHEN WE WERE finished with the 1978 European tour, Sandy, Joan, and I went to live on a ninety-foot navy-blue houseboat in London on the Thames River. We originally went to London thinking we were going to stay there and record our next album with a British producer named Phil Wainman, who had worked with the Sweet. But to be honest, again, no one really told us why we were there. Although I loved England and could have stayed there forever, I didn't realize we weren't confirmed to record with Wainman. Joan, Sandy, and I were not the right combo to pull in this guy to produce us. By that point we were all doing too many drugs and hanging out with British punk rockers who were doing too many drugs. We scared him away before we even got started.

The houseboat was next to the Battersea Bridge, off King's Road, which was full of shops, restaurants, pubs, and cool places. More important, we were right down the street from where the Sex Pistols lived. It was a prime spot for trouble.

We were deep into the punk era at the time, when "God Save the Queen" by the Sex Pistols came out. Sid Vicious, his girlfriend, Nancy, the drummer Paul Cook, and the guitarist Steve Jones would come to the houseboat all the time. Sometimes I loved having them there, but sometimes it made me uptight. It just depended on what drugs they were using, I guess. Sid was frightening and fucked up, although I could see a handsome little boy underneath all the razor-blade gashes and scars.

One time, I was just sitting on the sofa doing nothing and Sid walked in, very angry. He pointed his finger at me and yelled, "You!"

I said, "What?"

"You ripped me off!" he yelled again.

"Ripped you off of what? What are you talking about, Sid?"

Sid was in torn clothing with writing on his shirt. His hair was short and going in every direction possible. He was bleeding from where he had carved words and people's names in his arms and chest. What a mess. He just kept yelling that I'd ripped him off.

"I didn't rip you off," I told him. "Are you crazy?"

He pointed to my necklace. "That!" he said. "That's my necklace."

"No, it's not," I told him. "I've had this forever."

He did have a similar necklace, and he probably lost his. I was nervous as hell because he was not in his right mind. He was so fucked up! For some reason, Sid walked over to Nancy. They sat down, and then he dropped the necklace issue right away. A few minutes later, Sid got up and went into the kitchen to make himself a peanut-butter-and-jelly sandwich. We only had peanut-butter-and-jelly sandwiches that whole summer, and when we were finished with them, everyone would throw the plates out the window and into the river. We never had to do dishes that way.

While Sid was in the kitchen, Nancy was standing next to me. She was gorgeous, normal, and kindhearted. I couldn't understand what she was doing with Sid at first, but when Sid wasn't fucked up he was a really kind, gentle soul, so it started to make more sense. Nancy took a step closer to me, and that's when I realized she was coming on to me. I thought, *Oh shit! What if Sid finds out?* He'd either kill me or join in. I wasn't interested in either scenario. I told her, "You're very beautiful, Nancy. And I like you very much as a friend. But I'm not into girls."

She dropped the conversation when Sid came back into the room. I was really uncomfortable, so I went downstairs. I was changing my clothes when Paul Cook walked by my room. He must have been using the restroom. I didn't know he was down there or I would have closed my bedroom door completely. But I'm glad I didn't, because Paul, a very fair, handsome, blond-haired, blue-eyed drummer, saw me getting undressed through the opening in the door. I saw him and instead of covering myself, I locked eyes with him. He came into my room and I didn't stop him. No words were spoken, but we started to make out with each other and ended up having sex. Amazing sex. We stayed together a few nights here and there, but mostly we were just friends.

Steve Jones was the most businesslike of the group. He had dark hair and wore a black coat, clean looking, not all cut up like Sid or Johnny Rotten. Steve had written us a song called "Black Leather," and sometimes he and Paul Cook would get onstage and jam it with us.

Once day, Sid, Nancy, Sandy, and I went over to Johnny's house, which was within walking distance from the houseboat. When we arrived, I was shocked to see how fucked up his door was from fans who had spray-painted it and carved it up. I felt bad for Johnny. He was a recluse, and I couldn't blame him. We knocked and rang the doorbell over and over again, but Johnny never answered the door. He might have been asleep or he might not have felt like answering the door. So Sandy, Sid, Nancy, and I left. We walked around the corner to a pub for a few drinks and went back to the houseboat.

The houseboat was a lot of fun but basically a waste of time. The Runaways were beginning to fall apart. We couldn't get anyone to agree to produce us because there were so many drugs involved at that point. After a month, everyone left the boat and went home.

Kim wasn't around, so the hype around the Runaways had dropped. I stayed by myself a few extra days because I had relatives in London and wanted to see them. The boat felt really weird with no one on it but me. Like it was haunted. The doors would open and close by themselves sometimes because of the tide going in and out. I didn't like it, so I packed up and went back home to Los Angeles.

About a month later, in October 1978, I heard the news that Nancy had been found dead on the bathroom floor of the Hotel Chelsea in Manhattan. At first I thought she must have ODed, but then I learned Sid had been arrested. More details started to emerge. Her arms had been tied to a towel rack and she had been stabbed. I was heartbroken. The press began reporting on Sid and Nancy, but they got it all wrong. In reality, Nancy was a sweetheart. She was a beautiful, down-to-earth girl next door. She wasn't looking for anything other than a relationship, and she got sucked in by Sid's charm. He was out of his mind a lot of the time, but under there, too, was a nice person with a big heart.

I don't believe he meant to kill Nancy. I know he cared for her very much. Nancy was the love of his life. But Sid was so blown out of his mind on drugs that half the time he didn't know what he was doing anymore. It may have started as a kinky sex game that went horribly wrong. Who knows what the hell really happened. Ten days later he attempted suicide and was put in the mental ward at Bellevue Hospital. Sid was destroyed when Nancy died, and I knew it was only a matter of time before he'd die himself of a broken heart, which sadly happened a few months later when he overdosed while out on bail.

TOBY MAMIS BROUGHT in John Alcock, Thin Lizzy's producer, to produce the Runaways' fourth album. John thought that Sandy and I should be featured a bit more prominently on this record than we had been in the past. He was trying to put a different musical twist on the record by putting forth who he thought were the band's strongest musicians, me and Sandy. This was about drums and guitars, not vocals. Joan appeared to take it personally, as if Sandy, John, and I had some conspiracy against her. She was wrong. We didn't. Had she brought this to our attention, we would have eased her mind.

We all loved Joan. But I'm not sure she understood it that way. Although Joan didn't write everything, she often got credit for it during the Kim Fowley years. This time, because Kim wasn't around, Sandy and I were able to write and participate more in the creative process. In the end, we still didn't get enough credit for it. Sandy and I were a strong musical team. On *And Now . . . the Runaways,* I finally became the bass player everyone thought I was when I first joined the Runaways. To tell the truth, I really should have played bass all along on the studio albums. Sandy and I had the time of our lives working together as a rhythm section, and Joan must have felt left out, but that could not have been further from the truth.

WE WENT ON the road one last time in December 1978. On December 1, we did a show at the Palladium in New York City. Toby was driving us through Manhattan in his father's Mercedes. I was sitting shotgun. Toby often got on my nerves, and something came over me in that moment. I took my pair of handcuffs (we were the Runaways, we always had handcuffs around, in case you hadn't noticed), clicked them onto Toby's wrist, and locked the other side of the cuffs to the steering wheel of the Mercedes. I snatched the car keys out of the ignition and jumped out of the car, leaving Toby stuck in New York City rush-hour traffic. I saw Toby the next week. He never said anything to me about getting handcuffed, but he was irritated. He was usually annoyed at me about something anyway. That was just Toby. I got a kick out of it, though.

Soon after the release of *And Now . . . the Runaways,* Vicki was replaced by Laurie McAllister. Here we go again with another bass player. Laurie wasn't as good a player as Vicki, but we really had no choice at that point. When Laurie joined, the Runaways were hanging on by a thread. Jackie, Cherie, Vicki, Scott, and Kim were gone. Joan was fucked up and pissed off. Toby was a pain in the ass. John Alcock had turned into a nightmare. Sandy and I were going through the motions, and Sandy had started to lose her temper easily, which was unusual for her. She was tired and wanted a break. We all did. Laurie couldn't play as well as us, and we were too beat-up to take time out to help her learn like we did with Vicki. No one cared at this point. Not even me.

We had ten shows in California that December. The pressures of Cherie's departure and John Alcock putting more emphasis on Sandy and me seemed to be getting to Joan. At this point she was doing way too many drugs and was getting worse by the day. I saw her vomiting and in the middle of a conversation she would nod out. That was the end of the Runaways in a nutshell. One fucked-up person turning to another fucked-up person and wondering who was going to save whom. It was the blind leading the blind.

I could feel the band was done by the time we reached our last show, at the Cow Palace in San Francisco. We all just assumed the band was over. Nobody even said good-bye. The Runaways had fallen apart. It was as simple and as sad as that.

IN JANUARY 1979 I was only twenty. My life had just begun. I think no one really knew what was coming next. Was the band over? I knew Joan needed some stability in her life. It seemed as though all the girls had gone in different directions, and no one ever came back. So I moved on too. None of us ended with any bad feelings, except for Cherie and me.

I was a bona fide rocker by the time the Runaways broke up, which means not only had I grown into my own musical style, but also that I had become numb to the people in the music industry. I discovered they all really don't care about you. They want to use you. They want your money and they want your fame. And then they spit you out when they're done with you.

Being in the Runaways had prepared me for the rest of my career as a solo artist. There wasn't anything I hadn't gone through with that band. At least that's what I thought at the time. There was still a long road ahead of me, but I had graduated from rock-and-roll college, and I was ready for a new start.

PART II

GIRLS DON'T PLAY GUITAR

CHAPTER 7

GET A REAL JOB

I find you alone at night

Don't know what you're thinking

Don't know what you're dreaming of

Stay with me baby

—"STAY WITH ME BABY"
(WRITTEN BY LITA FORD)

AFTER THE RUNAWAYS BROKE UP, I WENT HOME TO MY PARENTS' HOUSE IN Long Beach. I was ready to take on the world, I just wasn't sure where to start.

My first step was to buy myself a new, reliable car to drive me from Long Beach to Hollywood. Recently, on my way to pick up Sandy one day, I had totaled the Monte Carlo in a four-car pileup caused by an old lady on a golf cart who shouldn't have been on the road in the first place. I took all the money I had made with the Runaways and bought a silver Pontiac Firebird. I paid for it in cash so I wouldn't have payments. The Firebird was a big, beefy sports car. It hauled ass and hugged a corner real well. After you turned the corner, you could just let go of the steering wheel and it would straighten itself out. Me and Edward Van Halen tested it out a few times going over Laurel Canyon's deep, winding, curvy roads, and on a steep turn, instead of hitting the brakes, we would just scream. Although it didn't help to slow the car down, it was a hell of a lot of fun.

I was still hanging out with Sandy and John Alcock at this time, because we shared the same musical tastes and we thought we would work on an album together in the near future. John was really sucked up by Sandy and had a crush on her. But how could you blame him? Sandy was a doll.

He had a house that looked down on Sunset Boulevard, and the house was usually filled with sex, drugs, and rock and roll. I had been around my fair share of drugs and wild behavior when I was in the Runaways, but John's house was on a whole different level. These people all seemed to have a death wish. Especially John.

John told us he had been diagnosed with cancer. The thought of John dying was not shocking, because of the way he abused himself. To tell you the truth, I wasn't sure how ill he really was. One day he told me, "There are a few things I want to do before I go. Would you do them with me?"

"Oh my God. I can't believe it, John. Anything you want to do," I said, "we'll do it. Where do you wanna go? What do you wanna do?"

"I want to ride the roller coasters at the new Six Flags in Valencia." A roller coaster!!! Oh fuck! Okay, John, let's go. Jesus! Why me.

I thought he was out of his fucking tree, but I agreed to go with him anyway. When we got to the first roller coaster, I read a sign that said: ANYONE PREGNANT OR WITH A HEART CONDITION SHOULD NOT BOARD THIS RIDE. It made me worry about John's health.

I said, "John, do you see that fucking sign?"

"Yes."

"And you're still going to get on this ride?" And that was a dumb question on my part. Of course he was going to get on!

"Yes, of course."

"Okay, let's do it."

John was a huge man. He was six foot six and weighed approximately three hundred pounds. When we boarded the roller coaster, all I could think about was how in the world I was going to scoop him up if anything did happen to him. I was starting to get sick of hanging around people who were so careless about life.

The final break came one night while I was hanging out at John's house with Sandy and a whole bunch of other people from the music industry. John had done so many drugs that he started firing shots at a target he had set up in the kitchen. From his balcony you could see the whole Sunset Strip, the place where it all started for the Runaways. As I was standing out on the balcony, I watched a reveler shoot into the sky over Sunset Boulevard, just for kicks. Then Sandy joined him. That was it for me. I couldn't handle being around the drugs and the stupidity anymore. I left, determined that I could make it some other way, without his involvement. That was one of the last times I saw Sandy. I believe John was the beginning of the end for Sandy, quite literally, as she got mixed up with the wrong people.

ANOTHER FRIEND OF mine—also named Patty (with a "y," not an "i")— and I decided to take a road trip, this time to Las Vegas, for some fun. It was my mother's favorite hangout. I'd always wanted to see what was so cool about Las Vegas. As a kid I wasn't allowed in the casinos, but in late 1979 I was twenty-one and I could get in to see what they were all about. We hopped into my Firebird and hit the road. On the way to Las Vegas we were hungry and stopped to eat at a truck stop. I ordered the fish and chips, a dumb thing to order at a truck stop in the middle of the desert. It was very greasy and I don't do too well with fried foods anyway, but I loved real English fish and chips. Obviously, we weren't in England, so I ended up with a stomachache. By the time we got to Vegas, I was sick. Patty checked us into our room because I felt like I was going to vomit any second. I went to sit down in the corner of the lobby on a red velvet sofa, and while I was waiting for Patty, a rock band walked into the hotel to check in. I was sitting in the corner so I didn't think the band noticed me staring at them.

Patty walked over and said, "Okay, let's go, I got the keys."

I said, "Patty, look at these guys. They're interesting, huh?"

Patty's eyes lit up. "Yeah! Maybe we can meet them later somewhere."

I said, "Yeah, that would be cool."

We were gathering our luggage when one of the band members walked over to us and said, "Hello girls," in a thick British accent. "I'm Glenn."

It was Glenn Tipton, Judas Priest's guitarist.

I said, "Hi, I'm Lita."

"What's wrong?" he said to me.

"I have a stomachache from road food."

He said, "Oh yeah." Glenn completely understood.

I had never met Glenn or the other Judas Priest band members before and had no idea why he would come over to me, unless he recognized me from the Runaways. I don't know. My God, he was cute, though!

Glenn said, "Well, come to my room and I'll make you feel better."

I thought, *Huh? Really? It's not like I've never heard that line before. How is he gonna make me feel better?* But he was so hot I couldn't resist, so I said, "Okay. Let me go to my room and clean up a little. I'll be right there. What room are you in?"

We exchanged room numbers since he had just been given his room keys by the tour manager. "East Tower, 1784."

"Let me go see what this Glenn guy is all about. I'll be right back," I said to Patty once we got settled. I also told her what room I was going to in case something happened.

I knocked on Glenn's door. He was waiting for me, and said, "Come in, my love, please sit down." He poured me a ginger ale from his minibar.

"How thoughtful. Thank you, Glenn," I said as I started to sit in the chair.

He stopped me: "No, no, no, darling, not there. Please sit here, my love, on my lap."

Ah! *Okay.* Glenn had such a wonderfully reassuring gentleman's voice. I loved his British accent. Of course I was more than okay with it. He put his hand on my stomach and said, "So, tell me about this tummyache of yours." I told him about the fish and chips at the truck stop, that we lived in Los Angeles, and that we'd driven four hours to Vegas for some fun.

"Fish and chips," he said.

"Yes, I'm British too. My father is a British gentleman," I told him. He was impressed.

His demeanor was so calming, and he started to tell me a story about a little girl with a dream as he held his hand on my stomach while I sat on his lap. I felt like I was twelve years old. The story sounded all too familiar. His voice was drawing me in and I felt in awe of him, almost instantly. After the story, he said, "How's your tummyache now?"

I had completely forgotten about it! "What stomachache?" I said. "You are magic, Glenn. I can't believe it disappeared just like that."

"Now do you feel better?"

"I do, yes!" I said.

We stayed in his room all night, talking and getting to know each other. Patty called the room about two hours later to see if I was all right. I told her not to wait for me, as she was excited telling me who this band Judas Priest was. I thought, *Go do your thing, girlfriend. I'm staying here with Glenn.* She gave her approval, and she went on her own expedition with someone else.

We had moved from the chair to the bed after a while to lie down with each other.

He was wonderful.

The next day I went back to see Patty. She sensed what was going on. Patty and I went to the pool to sunbathe, and she wanted to know every little detail. I told her Judas Priest was going to be playing that night in Las Vegas and that we should go see them, but that right now I needed to sleep. I passed out in the desert heat by the pool. Priest did their show that night, then had to pull out of town for their next show. Needless to say, I was a Judas Priest fan afterward—in more ways than one—and wondered if I'd ever see Glenn again.

EDWARD VAN HALEN was a good friend of mine and served as a great inspiration during this time in my life. Fans know him as Eddie, but he never really liked being called that. The Runaways and Van Halen grew up together musically on the Sunset Strip, along with a lot of other great bands. We'd go to Edward's mom's house after a night of partying and say hi to her. He'd make me breakfast by opening a packet of Carnation Instant Breakfast and adding milk. Edward had no time in his life for anything unless it was sex or rock and roll. He didn't even have an ignition switch in his car. He just said, "Fuck, I don't need a key," and he would put these wires together and off we went. It was a piece-of-trash vehicle with an amazing stereo system.

He had played me "Runnin' with the Devil" before it came out. I was blown away by how awesome and rockin' it sounded. Good old in-your-face rock and roll. It wasn't overly produced with tons of guitar and keyboard overdubs. This was during the Boston era. Boston was cool and had a badass album, but it was extremely produced. Van Halen's music was refreshing in a time when no one played the back-to-basics three-piece rock and roll. Everyone was too busy trying to figure out how to outdo each other, while Edward would just plug his guitar in and play the fucking thing. No questions asked.

Sometimes, for fun, Edward and I were lovers, depending on how many drinks we had in us. This was right before he met Valerie Bertinelli and soon after I had broken up with a forgettable guy named Mark, who I bonded with because we both drove Firebirds. Mine was silver and his was black and gold. I broke his heart—turns out a relationship needs to be grounded in more than a common taste in cars. One night soon after this latest breakup, Edward came to my apartment just above the Sunset Strip. We started fooling around and drinking Absolut vodka. He was trying on my clothes and I was wearing his. I happened to be wearing a T-shirt that said: BEAT ME. BITE ME. WHIP ME. FUCK ME. CUM ALL OVER MY TITS LIKE THE DIRTY PIG THAT I AM. TELL ME THAT YOU LOVE ME. AND THEN GET THE FUCK OUT. All that on one T-shirt. Ha! It was meant to be a silly T-shirt, not to be taken literally, but my mother hated that shirt. Months later, when she was doing the laundry, it magically disappeared.

After we got done goofing around with each other's clothes, we went into the kitchen to pour some vodka on the rocks. Then we lay down on the floor in the living room and started making out. All of a sudden I felt someone kicking the side of my ankle really hard. First I thought, *What the hell is Edward doing to me?* I looked down at my ankle and was shocked to see a third pair of feet. What the hell? It's not Edward. It was my ex-boyfriend Mark!

"How the hell did you get in here?" I demanded.

"I climbed up the balconies and came through the sliding glass door."

"What? You have to be kidding!" This is my house!

Edward and I were a little buzzed and Edward noticed that Mark was kind of a big guy, so he got freaked out. He backed his way toward the bathroom and said, "Well, if you're going to kill me, just bury me with my guitar." Then he slammed shut the bathroom door and locked it.

Not that that door would stay locked it was so flimsy.

Mark was really a sweetheart, but he should never have climbed up my balcony and into my apartment. I told Mark it was a crazy thing to do and that he had to leave. We weren't dating anymore, and it took me a few minutes, but eventually I got him to go.

After Mark left, I knocked on the bathroom door and said, "Edward, you can come out now. Mark is gone." But there was no answer. I kept banging and started to get a little concerned, so I kicked the bathroom door in. There was no sign of Edward anywhere. *What the fuck?* It was as if he had vanished. How the hell did he get out? There was a tiny, tiny window that was open over the shower. It looked as if there was no way a human could fit through it. I soon found out that he had some-how managed to squeeze his body through that window, scraping up his entire stomach. He dropped down four stories and went running down onto Sunset Boulevard. This was 1980. Nobody was bigger than Van Halen in 1980. And yet there he was, running down the Sunset Strip in *my* Levi's, *my* T-shirt that said CUM ALL OVER MY TITS, with no shoes and no money. He had to bum a dime off some kid so he could call 911 from the pay phone. The stranger said, "Hey, aren't you Eddie

Van Halen? Why do you need a dime?" They were my jeans, so of course there was no money in the pockets. The kid gave it to him and a few minutes later the police were at my door. I answered it wearing Edward's clothes. Mark had done the decent thing and had left when I asked him. But Edward was right to have called the police.

That was the last time we fooled around together, because not long after that, he fell head over heels for Valerie. I was happy for him. He is such a special person, and he influenced me in many ways.

You know how people sometimes say things to you that you carry with you for years and what they say can change your life forever? Edward Van Halen was one of those people for me. I was stuck in a world where not too many people listened to girls playing guitar. I didn't know what I was capable of doing, especially being fresh from the Runaways, which was an uphill battle. One day Edward said to me, "Lita, you can play guitar, what's your fuckin' problem? Just *do it*." Something so simple and true coming out of the mouth of Edward Van Halen made all the sense in the world to me. Suddenly my life became clear. I felt empowered. What was I waiting for? Approval? Fuck that! Just *do it*. Made perfect sense to me!

With Edward's advice in mind, I knew I needed to be the only guitar player in my band. I didn't want to give anyone the opportunity to say, "She's not playing that. He's playing that." So I decided I would get a guy to be the lead singer and that I would be the only one playing guitar. I started to audition lead singers, but I didn't know how hard that process would be. I had always just chimed in on the Runaways' backing vocals. First I found someone who had the right look but couldn't sing. Then I auditioned someone who could sing okay but looked all wrong. My patience quickly wore thin. I started to believe in the old saying *If you want something done right, you have to do it yourself.* So I decided to be the front person of the band.

I would put together a power trio à la Jimi Hendrix: bass, drums, and a guitarist who is also the lead vocalist (that would be me). I had been listening to a lot of Jimi Hendrix, and I liked how the power-trio structure automatically put him out front. There was no other guitar player to look at. I thought if I could pull that off, it would be something that would attract the record companies. After everything I had dealt with while being in the Runaways, I didn't want to face any more of the drama that comes along with being surrounded by teenage girls. At the same time, I wanted to prove something to the world: a female could really rock.

SINGING DIDN'T COME naturally to me, the way playing guitar did. Singing *and* playing the guitar at the same time is another skill altogether. Some people are born with it. I had to work my ass off to learn how to simultaneously play and work the microphone. I kept watching my fingers and never really focused on the vocals or the audience. But you can't just stare at your hands if you're going to entertain anyone. I went to Bernie Rico Sr. at B.C. Rich Guitars and had special guitars made without the markers on the fretboard, so even if I did look at the instrument, I wouldn't know where I was. I had to figure it out without looking. Next the frets came off. There was nothing on the guitar neck telling me where I was. I had to feel my way onto the right notes and chords. It was like Braille. I learned to look straight ahead. I hired vocal coaches to work with me. They showed me what to do, what not to do, and how to hit my notes.

I also went to concerts to watch musicians who could play electric guitar and sing at the same time—people like Johnny Winter, whom I loved and admired. He had bad eyesight and really couldn't see the neck of his guitar, which "allowed" him to sing and not have to be distracted by much. He played and walked around the stage effortlessly, with a white scarf flowing from the guitar as he moved.

I rented a warehouse in downtown Long Beach and set up a PA system, a guitar rig, and a mic. That's where I taught myself to sing. During this time I was also writing the album that would become *Out for Blood*. It was a shitload of work. But I knew it was only a matter of time before I'd have my own record deal and I'd be touring.

My parents supported my every move, but I didn't want to run to them for money every time I needed help. I was twenty-two and decided I would get a job to pay for my expenses. You would think after three years in a highly successful band I would have a few dollars in my pocket, but I didn't even have enough for gas, let alone to rent the warehouse I needed for rehearsals.

I got a job as a fitness instructor, which didn't last long because I told one of the clients to fuck off. Whoops! Then I got a gig at Broadway Stores (now Nordstrom) in Lakewood Mall. The mall was across the street from where my parents lived. I was selling men's cologne, and I disguised myself by putting my hair up, wearing glasses, and dressing very conservatively. I felt so out of place. I worked there almost six months. None of the customers ever knew who I was. Occasionally, someone would say, "You look familiar," and I would change the subject immediately. I was not happy about that job, but it was necessary for me to pay my way to something better.

One day when I was working at the department store, a guy named Ray Marzano came in with his girlfriend, Laura Johnson. He was shopping for men's cologne. He mentioned that he was looking to put together a band and needed a guitarist. At that point, I broke character and introduced myself and told him who I was. He invited me to his rehearsal facility.

Ray was a great stepping-stone. He had a rehearsal facility in North Hollywood on Lankershim. It was dark, like a cave. But I didn't have to pay for that warehouse anymore, which meant I could quit the department-store gig. That's the first reason I'm grateful to Ray. The second is because Ray helped connect me with a great drummer named Dusty Watson. Dusty was a young kid then and really green. When he came to the audition, he seemed a bit nervous. We went through three or four songs, and I then put my guitar down. I had never played with another drummer aside from Sandy West.

Dusty was a great player. I loved it! "God damn!" I said to him afterward. "No one has ever made my tits sweat like that before!" I was wearing a gray sweatshirt and a pair of jeans. I grabbed Dusty's hand and shoved it up my sweatshirt to show him I really was sweating. Needless to say, he got the gig.

WITH DUSTY ON board and Ray filling in temporarily on bass, my three-piece band was coming together. We started to play in nightclubs and word got around. During one of those gigs, I was approached by Neil Merryweather, an older guy who had written a few albums and had "been around." He told me he could help me. Maybe it was only because he looked like he could use some help himself, but I took him up on his offer. It turned out Neil had a lot of ideas. He handmade costumes for me—wild, Barbarella-type outfits, leather G-strings for crotch pieces, with bustiers and armbands. It was a heavy metal look, "out there," a little scary. But I decided to take the chance. I was living life on the edge anyway. Years later, Madonna, Cher, and Lady Gaga would make these sorts of fashion items the center of their entire look, but at the time no one else had ever dressed that way to play rock and roll.

Initially, Neil and I were just going to write some songs. However, as soon as we started to record, I discovered Neil was an outstanding bass player, and I asked him to play on the studio recordings, completing our stripped-down three-piece band. The trio fit with my vision of keeping the *Out for Blood* album free from overproduction. I wanted people to hear the individual instruments—the guitar most of all!

DURING THE TIME we were writing that album, I went with a bunch of girls to the Troubadour, a hokey—yet now legendary—little Hollywood nightclub. One of girls said to me, "If you could go out with anybody in this club, what guy would you go for?"

I sat there and looked around and as each dude passed by I would say, "Not him. Not him. Not him." And then this scruffy rocker-looking guy walked by with really dark hair and light eyes. He was wearing red thigh-high patent-leather "hustler" boots with a heel on them. "Him," I said.

"Go and say something to him," one of the girls said. They all chimed in and double-dared me to go talk to him. I didn't want to look embarrassed in front of my girlfriends, so I walked up to him and asked his name.

"Rick," he said. I immediately walked away. I knew his name wasn't Rick. "Wait, wait, wait," he called after me. "My name is Nikki. Nikki Sixx." It sounded like he wasn't sure what his name was. We talked for a while.

I asked him, "Would you like a quaalude?"

He said, "Of course!"

I stuck a quaalude on his tongue, which made him really happy. My drummer, Dusty, was having a party at his apartment in West Hollywood, and once the club started closing, we headed over. It was a dump with no furniture. Nikki took off his red patent-leather boots and his feet were all blistered.

"What's wrong with your feet?" I asked him.

"My shoes are two sizes too small."

"So why are you wearing them?"

"They're the only rock-and-roll shoes I own. Some girl gave them to me," he said.

They actually were women's shoes, and I'm sure they hurt like hell. He wore those boots for at least another year.

The quaaludes began really kicking in, and we were wondering how we were going to make it home from Dusty's apartment. Nikki didn't have a car, and I couldn't drive in my condition, so we spent the night. We slept together on the floor on a blanket and a couple of pillows. It was cozy, even if it wasn't most people's definition of "romantic." We had sex before passing out.

The next day, I dropped him off at his apartment. Nikki didn't have a car. Hell, he didn't even have the money to buy a pair of shoes his size. He lived in the "band apartment," because his band hadn't been signed yet. People had been talking about a unique-looking group that had three guys with blue-black hair and a lead singer with bleach-blond locks. I knew he was one of the guys from "that band"—Mötley Crüe, of course. As Nikki and I got closer, I started hanging out at their apartment a lot. It was a bona fide shithole. The front door had no hinges and was impressively banged up, owing to everyone's habit of kicking it, carving things into it, and slamming it. Needless to say, it didn't close properly. The only thing that held it in place was a deadbolt. Nikki slept on a mattress on the floor underneath the bedroom window. It was a ground-level apartment and they just threw the garbage on the back porch—it never made it to the Dumpster. There were stacks and stacks of trash bags out back; it became a thriving feeding-ground for rats.

I remember one night I was sitting in the living room drinking a glass of wine, and when I looked down in my drink, a German cockroach was floating in my glass. What a way to go: death by drowning—in wine. The oven was full of cockroaches too. When we turned on the oven, the heat would make them stand up on their hind legs, fall over upside down, and die. Nikki would do the Hitler march and salute them as they all perished. "Burn and die!" he would say. Then we would cook our meal.

Sometimes we would walk down to the corner restaurant and split an order of poached eggs. One egg for Nikki, one for me. That was all we could afford.

There was a map of the USA in the apartment, hanging on the wall next to the bathroom. Whenever Tommy Lee, the band's drummer, or Nikki had to take a shit, they would tear off one of the states to wipe their ass. That map got smaller and smaller. I always wondered who ended up with Rhode Island.

Eventually, because of the roaches, rats, and mounting property damage, the building was condemned, and the boys were forced to move out. Nikki and I decided to get a place of our own. We moved to a one-bedroom apartment on Coldwater Canyon. It wasn't big, but it was ours. We had a new mattress and even picked up a love seat, our only pieces of clean furniture. Above the love seat was a poster of a huge black pentagram, the sign of the devil. Throughout the apartment were half mannequins with fake blood all over them. Nikki was using them for his stage show. I had taught him how to make the fake blood because the Runaways used it in our shows. It was a mixture of red dye and pancake syrup, which of course would attract the ants. So we'd have these half bodies with blood and ants everywhere. It was lovely.

We celebrated Nikki's birthday soon after we moved into that apartment. December 11. He's a Sagittarius. I was excited to give him a special birthday cake that year. I had already bought him his first tattoo, which was a rose with a spiderweb on his upper arm. He was so happy with his ink. We didn't have much money for presents, so the birthday cake would be the gift. I found a custom cake place after doing a bit of research. This spot would make just about anything and everything you wanted in the form of a cake. I didn't want to do a guitar shape because the Runaways had ordered me one for my twentieth birthday, and also it was too big for just the two of us. I thought about what Nikki liked besides music. Girls! A sexy cake would be hysterical. I asked the bakery to make him a cake in the shape of a pair of boobs.

It was meant to be a joke, but when we stuck the candles in the nipples and lit them on fire, he got spooked. I have no idea why. He refused to eat the cake. I thought he was joking at first, but he wasn't.

I said, "What's wrong, Nikki?"

He said, "That cake is freaky."

"Really? With bloody mannequins lying all around the house, you are afraid of a cake?"

"Don't dig," he told me.

I was in shock. Mr. Rock Star, Mr. Woman Crazy, refusing to eat a cake shaped in the form of a woman's breasts. I never understood that one.

NIKKI GAVE ME my first '80s haircut. "Your hair is not rocked out enough," he told me.

"Okay, so rock it out," I said, handing him a pair of scissors. I trusted him as he confidently took the pair of scissors to my long, blond, '70s-style hair and cut it into an '80s shag.

I really liked Nikki because he had ambitions for what he was going to do with his life and knew what his future looked like. He was a leader. He had dreams, and he was going to make them happen. I felt this way about him because I shared the same dreams, and I saw he was willing to work as hard as I was to ensure they came true.

I watched Nikki put Mötley Crüe together from the ground up. Without him, there would have never been a Mötley Crüe. He was their creator and was constantly working to get them off and running. Nikki got ideas from a lot of different artists. W.A.S.P., Alice Cooper, Hanoi Rocks, you name it. He would get on the phone and work it himself. He would tell me, "I'm going to make an album called *Too Fast for Love*." "I'm going to make an album called *Theatre of Pain*." He told me he had written a song called "Looks That Kill" that was supposed to be about me. I told him, "Well, I'm going to make an album called *Out for Blood*." And then we both worked our asses off to make it happen.

Most nights, Nikki and I would walk into the Rainbow and grab a slice of pizza off a table. We didn't care whose pizza it was. The Rainbow was always so crowded at night, nobody could tell who stole your pizza anyway. One evening Tommy walked in, snatched a slice of pizza from someone's table, and while he was eating it, came over and pulled his dick out and flopped it onto the table. "Look," he said, "it still has cum on it from the girl around the corner." That was pretty typical everyday shit. Other than pizza, we basically drank our meals. Any alcohol would do. Whichever was cheapest.

We were leaving the Rainbow early one particular night when a redneck approached Nikki and started mouthing off because he didn't like the way Nikki looked. We were minding our own business and the asshole started calling Nikki names and getting in his face. Nikki gave me his drink because he knew he wasn't going to be able to get past this guy without a fight. I looked at him and gave him a nod of approval to go for it. Nikki didn't really have a choice. I took off the belt I was wearing. It had buckles and two ropes of chains that hung down. I handed it to Nikki and said, "Use this."

Nikki was skinny and didn't really know how to fight. The guy jumped on top of him and I knew right away that Nikki was fucked. So Nikki started to swing this belt around. The cops showed up and tried to break up the fight. Nikki didn't know the cops were there and he just kept swinging that belt. He accidentally hit one of the cops who got too close, smacking him upside the head with the chain belt. Needless to say, this cop was fucking pissed off! The police didn't like how Nikki looked any better than the redneck did. It gave them a reason to throw him in jail. Meanwhile the guy who started the fight talked his way out of any charges and just walked away.

As they threw Nikki into the cop car, I assured him I would get him out. I just didn't know how. I went to the sheriff's office and asked, "How much is it going to cost?" It was something crazy like $4,000. I obviously didn't have that money, but I had my beloved Firebird, which was paid off. It was painful, but I handed the sheriff the pink slip to the Firebird. I wasn't sure if I was really gonna get it back. They held on to the car for a few days until they finally let Nikki out. But that was the end of my chain belt, which I was pissed about. I wore that belt everywhere I went. It now belongs to the LAPD.

My parents loved Nikki from the moment they met him. When my mother started giving him gifts like socks, underwear, cookies, and money, it touched him deeply, but he never let it show, and when he was invited over for dinner, he would decline. I think he was afraid of being rejected by my parents because he had had enough of that in his own upbringing. He never talked about his own childhood. I think it was too painful for him. It was enough that my mother and father loved him, gave him gifts, and showed their affection.

UNFORTUNATELY NIKKI AND I didn't last too long once Mötley Crüe started to get big. He was becoming more famous by the second, which came with a lot of drugs and girls. I was focused on working on my album. It was a time when it was impossibly hard to remain stable and true to each other. He got sucked up by the music industry so quickly, and he started doing way too much heroin. It just consumed him. He wasn't the same guy I knew. I went to the Rainbow one night to meet him, and I saw him walking out with some girl, drunk and hanging on her. That was it for me. I was so hurt. I don't think Nikki even knew who the girl was because he was so high. It didn't matter to me. I was through. I went home and packed up all his shit and threw it out the front door.

Nikki moved directly across the fucking street on Coldwater Canyon into another apartment building. So close that if I lay in my bed quiet, I could hear his old Porsche start up. He'd bought a used Porsche after signing his first record deal. I hated hearing his car start up because I thought it meant he was going out to get drugs or was going to party. It was torture. I missed him terribly when we split.

When he tried to get back with me a few years later, I was shocked. I think it was a cry for help. He was looking for some stability in his life. He was so fucked up that I doubt he knew what he was saying to me. I think it would have been me against the world at that point—a losing battle. Although I cared about him, I knew there was nothing I could do to help him at that point, so I said no. He was a walking time bomb, and I had my own career to deal with.

CHAPTER 8

THE MAKEOVER

Get your ammunition,

I'm ready for war.

—"OUT FOR BLOOD"
(WRITTEN BY LITA FORD)

AFTER NIKKI "MOVED OUT," I STILL LIVED IN THE APARTMENT ON COLD-
water Canyon when the phone rang one day. "Hello, dah-ling." *Ah, there's
that voice,* I thought. I was so happy to hear that sound again.

It was Glenn Tipton.

"What are you up to, my love?"

"I'm cooking spaghetti sauce. Pasta sauce."

"Oh, sounds delicious. What do you put in it?"

I told him, as if he didn't know. "Garlic, olive oil, tomato paste,
tomato sauce. You know, Italian seasoning, onions. You'd love it, Glenn.
My mother taught me how to make it."

"Ah, your Italian mum," he said.

"Yes, you remember things well. Next time you come to town you'll
have to meet her."

"Come see me tonight. I'm at the Long Beach Arena." He was in my
hometown for Judas Priest's Screaming for Vengeance tour.

Oh, really! "Okay. I'll be there."

When I showed up later at the concert, he told me I smelled like garlic, which I may have because I was in such a rush to see him I hadn't showered before leaving for the show. He was only joking, but even so, it made me feel self-conscious. Still, the garlic didn't ward him off. Before the show, he said, "Stay with me tonight." I was thrilled. I left him alone for a little while so he could focus on the show. I went into the Judas Priest dressing room toward the end of the show and started to open a bottle of chilled white wine they had on ice. I was in there alone, fighting with a bottle opener trying to get the damn wine open, when Rob Halford walked into the dressing room and collapsed on a black leather sofa. I had watched him onstage and he looked so masculine with his black leather jacket covered in studs. The way he danced onstage was just awesome. He had worked so hard that when he came off the stage he was dripping with sweat! Looking for air. Now he slowly turned and looked at me. But Rob knew it was only me, the girl from the Runaways, the gal Glenn was with in Las Vegas, so he didn't say a thing, but he needed his space. I realized I was opening what was probably his wine, so without saying a word, I shoved it back into the ice with the corkscrew still sticking out of the top and left the dressing room. I waited for Glenn outside.

After Glenn cleaned up, he led me out to a limo back near where the buses were parked. He opened the limo door for me. Inside, a guy was waiting for us with a small white jar filled with blow. Glenn handed me a straw and said, "Ladies first." I'd never seen blow like this before—very refined stuff. I didn't realize that you were supposed to just take a bit with the tip of the straw; if you snorted it too hard into the container, you'd vacuum up the entire supply. Well, I messed up, and just stuck the straw in and snorted. *Oh shit.* I choked on the powder and had to go to the bathroom ASAP. Glenn looked at me and said, "Pig."

We both laughed. "Glenn, I don't know how to use this thing!"

He said, "We have to cut you off," and I said, "I know, I know!"

We went back inside, wandered around backstage for a while, and then went to a hotel around the corner where the band was staying. Glenn and I stayed up until about four A.M., then went to sleep. The next afternoon I snuck out, leaving Glenn a note on his pillow: "Good-bye, see you next time."

I was stuck and needed a ride home. So I called my father! Dad never asked me what I was up to, or why I was up so late, or why I smelled like cigarettes. He just drove me home. I was beat and hungry.

AROUND THIS TIME I decided to stop by to see how John Alcock was holding up. As I pulled up to his house in the Firebird he said to me, in his thick British accent, "What the bloody hell are you doing driving around town with the name of Joan Jett's hit single on the license plate of your car?" It read ILUVRNR, but I had no idea what John was talking about. I had been so focused on my own music and career that I hadn't listened to the radio or had a clue what Joan was up to. By this time, of course, her song "I Love Rock 'n' Roll" was climbing the charts. Once I got up to speed, I had to laugh. I was glad to see that John Alcock was still chipper and still alive.

I also caught up with my old friend Toni. I had not seen her in a while and was shocked by how strung out she was. Toni was the one who always had drugs because of an accident she was in, but she had never taken them before. It was clear circumstances had changed.

She had no job. She was in trouble.

"Lita," she said, crying. "I don't know what I'm going to do with myself."

"I do," I told her.

"You do?" she sniffled.

"Yes. You're going to go on tour with me."

"And do what?"

"Be my tech," I told her.

"But I don't know how to be a tech."

"That's okay," I told her. "I can teach you everything you need to know."

I knew she could do it. She was always a go-getter—a fearless, mighty person. The funny thing was, when I first met Toni, I had thrown her out of the Runaways' dressing room for giving drugs to the band members. Now here we were, five years later. She became my best friend. I cared about her very much. And just like that, we picked up where we left off, good friends and great partners in crime.

IN 1982, AFTER a year of working on the *Out for Blood* album—and with my new makeover now complete, featuring a leather G-string outfit and a handmade bustier that Neil Merryweather created for me—I was ready to show the world a female could shred on guitar. Denny Rosencrantz from Mercury Records, one of the same men who signed the Runaways, came to see us play and loved what he heard. He signed us almost immediately.

Awesome! My hard work and creativity had paid off.

Out for Blood, my first solo album, was released in May 1983. It was groundbreaking. A female had never fronted a three-piece hard-rock band before. Stores didn't want to carry the album because the cover featured blood coming out of a guitar. Not to mention a picture of me without pants. Mercury had to switch the cover so Walmart and other places would carry it. I wonder if it had been a guy on the front cover whether it would have been any different. But the formula worked: a girl on guitar, singing lead vocals, and dressed like Barbarella. It got a lot of people's attention. It was hard, fast rock and roll. The kind of music I always wanted to play in the Runaways.

Artie Ripp was our manager at the time. He sent us to stay in Oregon for a short while to keep us away from the evils of Hollywood—i.e., drinking and partying. Boy, he sure racked up the legal fees while negotiating a deal for us. At that time my total focus was on trying to get people to notice me as the only female guitarist in the band. I wanted credit where credit was due, damn it. In a three-piece band, the people had only one guitar player to look at: me, a female!

Management might have thought we'd write better songs in Oregon, but taking us out of our environment actually did more harm than good. It was sort of like being on Spring Break. We each chose our own bedrooms as soon as we arrived. "This one is mine," I said as I climbed up a ladder into a hole in the wall. The guys found some rooms downstairs. Then we located the nearest liquor store, and finally we hit the local grocery store to get meat to barbecue.

Neil didn't look the part or fit in with Dusty and me during live performances. He was too old, more like our father than a band member. So I ended up hiring Randy Rand to play bass. Randy was also older than us, but you never would have known it with his rock-and-roll attitude and long skinny body. Randy came to Oregon to rehearse and shoot the "Out for Blood" video. With Neil gone, we didn't want Randy to get hassled about the bass lines not being played correctly in the video. I looked around and saw an actual ax hanging on the wall. I grabbed it and shoved it up against Randy's chest and said, "Here, 'play' this." He was so tall and skinny, and he had a great sense of humor so I knew he could pull it off. Somehow it fit right in: the video was set in a twisted hospital, the kind of place where the doctors would give patients a transfusion of blood drawn from my purple guitar. My favorite part of the video is the ending, when Randy takes his ax and smashes my guitar, sending a bunch of blood squirting out. I still think about that every time I play the song. The video had some other innovative camera tricks too. Now everyone uses five-ounce GoPro cameras, but the first time I had ever used a camera on the body of the guitar was for the "Out for Blood" video—it weighed about fifteen pounds! It was hanging from the bottom of the guitar and captured me playing the solo. We got some great close-up footage of me shredding.

As soon as we were done shooting the video, we dove into rehearsals to get Randy up to speed, then set off on tour. Going out on the road as a three-piece band was a blast. A tour bus picked us up at the Oregon house, and we made our way back down the West Coast toward Los Angeles. Along the way we played a few warm-up shows before hitting the Hollywood spotlight. I remember us sitting on the side of the road, Dusty tripping on mushrooms, waiting for another bus because ours broke down. Thank God. Days later, we finally made it back home to

Los Angeles, and we were set to play the Whisky A Go Go. During sound check at the Whisky the night before the gig, a guy walked into the club holding two dozen roses. He was yelling out, "LITA! Who is LITA FORD?" As if he didn't know! There couldn't have been another person in the world who looked like I did standing there in studded leather and fishnet stockings. "LITA!" The bastard brought two dozen roses down to the stage area. I thought, *Oh, wow, that's so cool, who are these from!* I hoped it was a "congratulations" or something nice. But I was wrong, it was a summons from a scum-fuck attorney. Apparently I owed him $40,000 in legal fees that he said I hadn't paid. I had no idea I owed him, or any one else, that kind of money. I stood there with my mouth open. I tossed the flowers as the cowardly process server bolted for the door. This lawyer couldn't have called my accountant? My manager? Sent me a bill? We would have resolved the issue. So wrong! Looking back now, what's truly notable about the incident is how quickly I shook it off: by the time the man who had served me the papers had left the building, I had resumed my sound check. Mayhem was all in a day's work back then.

SOON EVERY VENUE in LA wanted our band. We landed showcase gigs at Artie's place. We'd do about three or four songs for each group that would come through. No one had much money, so anytime the labels stopped by they'd bring food. Dusty would run down to the pay phone to call the other guys and say, "Dude, you HAVE to get here NOW. There's free food." Dusty and I hung out a lot together, and this led to some great adventures. For example, Dusty had been in a disagreement with a dude over money he owed Dusty, but this guy didn't want to pay him. He knew Dusty didn't have a car back then, so he told him to come get the money in Riverside, just to fuck with him. Riverside was far: a good hour and a half toward the middle of nowhere. I felt bad for Dusty. This dick was holding his money, and he had no way to get there to pick it up. So I drove him. Dusty remembers us driving down the freeway with all the windows down, the heater on full blast, and the lights shut off—in the middle of the night. In my Firebird I always aimed for the triple digits on the speedometer. To this day Dusty says he's never been in a car going that fast. I just wanted to get to Riverside to collect Dusty's money. And we did.

Whenever we needed some good margaritas we'd go down to a place in Rosarita Beach, Mexico, just across the border. Lots of police and cameras and highway patrol officers were around because of drug trafficking and illegal immigration. Not a place to be fucking around. But did we care? "Fuck it! Let's go!" I'd say. It was only a two-hour drive there, but it could take us a couple of days to get back. Good margaritas. They have a way of warping time. Once I stayed so long south of the border that I returned to find my pet tarantula, Damien, had died. I figured that if his forefathers could evolve to live in the barren desert, Damien could survive a few days at my place in the Oakwood Apartments, a chain of temporary-stay, furnished apartments frequented by rock and rollers. Turns out rock-and-roll crash pads are a uniquely unforgiving environment. I came back to the Oakwoods to find full rigor mortis had set in. The poor thing. I put Damien in the microwave to try to defibrillate him, but Toni and I watched horrified as his limbs dropped off. So much for my pet.

Often on our way home from Mexico, we'd stop by my parents' place in Long Beach, where Mom would cook tons of food. I'd sleep if off, then eat until I got enough energy to go out for another week of gigs and rock out. Once, Dusty and Randy came over for a barbecue and Dusty wanted to impress my dad with his grilling skills. He didn't let the charcoal heat up properly so the fire went out. He kept putting lighter fluid on the briquettes and totally fucked up the steaks in the process. My dad just looked at him and said, "Yeah, the fire wasn't hot enough." He was so polite and respectful about Dusty's incompetence. My mom once prepared Dusty a huge roast to take back to his apartment. "I don't think you're cooking very much, so I made you this." Dusty ate off it for about a week. My parents fed everybody. Friends, relatives, neighbors, it didn't matter—they were always welcome.

ANYTIME THERE WAS no business going on, it got dangerous. Days off meant trouble! More specifically: a bunch of quaaludes, a bottle of Jack Daniel's, and usually some cocaine. We'd party and rock as hard and as long as we could. Our drug dealer was a fellow named Little John, who we'd claim was our "manager" when Artie Ripp wasn't around. All Little John ever did was try to get us to take the blow he was carrying on him. Someone had rented a floor's worth of rooms in Vegas for us to celebrate his birthday. I was in the car with Toni, while Dusty and his friend were in another vehicle. Dusty and his friend were wasted and in no condition to be behind the wheel. I took one look at them and said, "Oh Jesus. Let me go check us in." When I got back to the car, I could see some kind of fight was going on. Dusty and his friend must have exchanged words with a couple of working girls in the parking lot while they were waiting for me to get back. Evidently whatever they said to them really rubbed them the wrong way because the girls ended up kicking their asses. Yes, they literally got beat up. I walked over to Dusty and yelled, "You're always so fucked up, you fuck everything up!"

Later Dusty lost his friend somehow and was wandering the halls looking for him, knocking on every door. He happened to knock on my and Toni's door, and the next thing I knew Dusty was in my room and Toni was cleaning him up. They had ordered steak and Dom Perignon, the works. Great stuff. I had been crashed out on the bed, and when I woke up, I called Dusty an asshole so he got out of there. He must have found his friend again and headed home. It was a disaster. I have no idea how they got home in the condition they were in. We got blacklisted from that casino, needless to say.

AT THE RAINBOW ROOM you could buy cocaine from some of the waitresses. The restaurant had these tall menus that you'd put up—almost like a partition—and people would actually do blow right off the table. One time, we were eating there and a girl was trying to get into our booth. Dusty refused to let her in, and she started getting pissy. She threw her drink in his face and the entire table erupted in a fight. I grabbed her by the hair and tossed her onto the table; everyone was pushing and throwing people. We ended up getting booted from the establishment. There's a shocker. Dusty jumped into his car and drove off. That night, he ended up getting into a wreck, rolling his car over on Deadman's Curve about three times. His engine landed on the side of the road. A girl he didn't even know talked to the cops for him and managed to get them to leave the scene, and she drove him home. He was lucky to be alive. Dusty's days as a functional member of the band were numbered, however. One night he showed up late for a rehearsal that Edward Van Halen had dropped in on. I was pissed because I wanted to introduce the band to Edward, who was sitting in a chair with his back facing the door. Dusty didn't even realize who it was at first when he finally waltzed in. Then Edward turned around. Suddenly Dusty realized why I was so pissed he was late. At that moment I made the decision to fire him. It was a really difficult thing to do, considering he was one of my best friends. But his partying was compromising his ability to meet his responsibilities as a band member. As much as I loved Dusty, I couldn't let him derail my dreams.

I WAS OFF and running in the music world as the one-and-only guitar-playing rocker chick who could shred like I did. But people were still in denial about the female behind the guitar. Was there someone behind the curtain, maybe? I remember watching the looks on the audience's faces when I would rip into a guitar solo. They would be stunned. Pure shock! It was a powerful feeling to know that I could do that to people. Then there were the assholes who wanted to fuck with me.

Out of all of them, the worst offender by far was the band Dokken. Their lead guitarist, George Lynch, came up to me at the Country Club in Reseda, California. I thought he was going to say something complimentary.

Instead, he looked at me from head to toe, and said in a snooty voice, like a ten-year-old, "So. . . . I guess you're all . . . Joan Jetted out now."

"Excuse me?" I answered. *What?*

"Girls don't play guitar!" George declared.

To this day I still remember his ignorant words.

"You know, it's assholes like you who make me work that much harder."

George said nothing after that and scurried off and did his show. He seemed miserable the rest of the night.

At that same gig, my friend and tech Toni tore into him as well. She was rolling up our cables when someone said, "Hey, those are my cables!"

"No, these are mine. These are my cables," Toni said. She always kept an eye on everything because we had had our gear sabotaged several times before.

Toni had no idea who this guy was, until he announced that he was George Lynch from Dokken.

"You wanna know why I know they're ours?" She unscrewed the end of the guitar cable and showed them the writing in the cable that said "LF"—for Lita Ford. She had the cables specially made for me before we left for the tour and had written my initials with a black sharpie inside every cable. He walked away like some little boy who'd had his toy taken away. Toni said it was great to open that cord up and watch the look on his face.

It wasn't just Dokken. Sometimes guys from other bands or their crew would pull a tube out of my amp after sound check or mess with my monitor settings. We wrote the settings on duct tape so we could easily reset the amp without taking too much time. We were constantly dealing with this kind of bullshit. Some bands didn't want to be blown away by a girl, so they would try to screw me up any way they could. I guess they thought we didn't know what we were doing, but we knew how to fix nearly every problem, especially with a good tech like Toni.

I always had the lighting director turn the spotlights down so I wasn't blind. That way I could see if anything was coming at me and I could dodge it. At one show, a guy was standing directly in front of me, his chest pushed up against the stage. He didn't know I was watching him. He had a can of beer. He shook it up hard so that it would explode all over me. As he held the can up toward my guitar ready to open the beer, I kicked him in the wrist as hard as I could. I wouldn't be surprised if I broke his wrist; he was gone soon after that. Fucking prick. I don't think he saw that one coming. The beer went flying backward away from me and over the top of the crowded room.

The girlfriends of boys who were digging me frightened me the most. Experience taught me to always be en garde, watching out to avoid being hit in the face with something tossed by a jealous girlfriend. I was worried a woman might want to bring my looks down a notch by throwing an ashtray or a broken beer bottle at me. I may sound paranoid, but I had to be prepared for that kind of shit. Even when your back was turned, you had to be aware of what was behind you. This is all shit that you have in the back of your mind when you're onstage.

IN SEPTEMBER 1983, I went on a European tour with Ritchie Blackmore's post–Deep Purple group, Rainbow. I really wanted to make this tour a major statement since I was going to be touring with Ritchie, my all-time favorite guitar hero. My band, crew, and Toni all came with me, of course. It was hard to leave Dusty behind because we all loved him, but we were lucky to find an outstanding replacement in the late Randy Castillo. I've always had the greatest drummers, but there was something completely unique and different about Randy. I discovered him at a local Hollywood nightclub called Madame Wong's. Randy was a very handsome American Indian from Albuquerque, New Mexico. He seemingly had two or three girls in every town. I'd see him in the morning with a blonde, then at night he'd show up with a redhead. He talked a lot like Scooby-Doo, which Toni and I made fun of, even though we loved it. He was so funny and just a great spirit to have around.

During one of Randy's first shows with us, I fucked up really bad. Randy almost quit. Of course it had to do with a guy.

I had been hanging out at a house in the middle of North Holly-wood that was being leased by the Australian rock band Heaven. I had met the guitar player, Mick Cocks, and become one of the regulars at the Heaven House, which had become a major party spot. If I didn't stay at the house with Mick, Mick would crash with me at the Oak-woods. Heaven was a great band and wicked fun. One night, just prior to the European tour with Rainbow, we were to play the Wiltern The-ater in Beverly Hills. Mick had slept at my place the night before, which was a big mistake knowing that I had a very important show the next day. If you knew Mick, he was nothing but trouble, in a good way. He looked like a rock-and-roll Mel Gibson (the young version). As I started getting ready for the show, I hopped into the shower, and so did Mick. It was probably the longest shower I had ever taken in my life. He wouldn't let me out. Although at the time I wasn't complaining, it put me in a bad situation, because by the time I finally managed to get dressed I realized I was already late for one of our most important gigs. It was the Wiltern Theater, in our hometown with every record company executive sitting around waiting to see this novelty of an act. I knew I was fucked before we ever left the Oakwoods. I wasn't going to make it, and now I had to battle LA rush-hour traffic. The worst in the history of mankind. I was going to have to face the demons that were waiting for me.

At the Wiltern, it was already past my set time; my manager was dealing with the angry promoters, and Toni was being harassed by everyone and anyone—including the other band, Ratt—because she was not only my tech but my close friend, so people figured they'd get an answer out of her. "Where's Lita?" "Is she fucked up?" "Is she passed out somewhere? She must be." People were angry because I had already missed my entire show, and Ratt was just about done. As I entered the backstage entrance all hell broke loose. Everyone swarmed around me all at once.

"Where were you? What are you doing?"

"Do you realize what time it is?"

"We've been waiting for you!"

"Do you know who's here?"

No one asked me if I was all right. Except Toni.

In the distance, I could hear Stephen Pearcy saying "Good night" to the audience and then adding, "How come Lita's not here? Did she get her period?" Once he said that I couldn't hear anything else that anyone else was saying. His voice resonated through the building. All I could think of was putting my foot in his mouth.

How was I going to explain to everyone that between having sex in the shower and getting stuck in rush-hour traffic I had missed the entire concert? Not a very good way to start a tour. I didn't think about what I was going to say when I arrived until I heard someone in the crowd backstage mention a car accident when I walked through the door. I thought to myself, *I'll just go along with that,* since it's not an unusual event in Los Angeles, so I said "Yeah, that's what happened." That sounds like a good excuse.

After the show, I walked into Stephen Pearcy's dressing room and said, "You little motherfucker. I just got home from Mexico and you remind me of the stinkin' worm at the bottom of the tequila bottle." It didn't seem to faze him, and he just shook it off.

After the smoke cleared at the Wiltern Theater that night, it turned out Randy, happily, did not quit the band, I had my words with Stephen Pearcy, and the promoters decided to keep me on the Rainbow tour after all.

OPENING FOR ONE of my idols was a dream come true. Toni and I cheered on Ritchie and Rainbow each night from the side stage. We sang along to every word in their set. I became great friends with Joe Lynn Turner, the lead singer of Rainbow. He was an outgoing, fun, happy-go-lucky dude. He was a ball of energy: always ready to go. I would help Joe with his stage moves, his performance clothes, his raps, his stage makeup. Ritchie had a woman with him the entire time during that tour, so as much as I wanted to, I really couldn't get near him. Sometimes he would play a prank on me by taking over as my tech. I'd walk to the side of the stage to switch guitars, and there Ritchie was ready to hand me my guitar. I think it was his way of sharing a special moment with me, but I was onstage so all I could do was smile and laugh before I had to go back out and continue my show. I think it got on Ritchie's nerves that I paid so much attention to Joe during the tour.

After hours was always an adventure. One evening in Denmark some of us from the tour went to a transvestite bar that had a lazy Susan with cocaine, weed, and heroin on it. That night we lost Randy Castillo. We had to leave the next morning at eight A.M. so most of us went home at a relatively decent hour, but Randy stayed out until his attentions turned to a young "lady." Randy had to catch his own flight to the next city.

Randy Castillo used to wear parachute pants onstage because they were comfortable. He was playing a drum solo one night, and he had put his foot up on the floor tom to change the pitch. Those parachute pants don't give at all, and so when he lifted his leg, his entire crotch area ripped open. We were all side stage and noticed that Randy's manhood was exposed for the audience to see. The band is trying to tell him that his balls are hanging out all over the place, and meanwhile he's looking at us like *Yeah, look at me! Cool, huh?* No, not cool! If you ever saw him play, you know how vigorously Randy Castillo threw himself into his craft.

On that tour we got the opportunity to head over to Stuttgart, Germany, to open for Black Sabbath. Sabbath was the first rock concert I'd seen, and they had influenced me ever so severely since I was a child. Lead guitarist Tony Iommi was the Riff Master. To me, he was a god. At least I thought so.

During the first gig, Iommi took a liking to me and asked if I'd meet him at the bar after the show. Of course I would. *Awesome!* I headed to the bar with Toni. Iommi was there with Sabbath's lead singer, Ian Gillan, and bass player Geezer Butler. Toni and I sat down with these three guys, and I was drawn to Iommi right away. I thought he was nice, very funny, very drunk, with a thick Birmingham accent. He seemed so charming, confident, and handsome. I would later find out that looks are deceiving.

Toni chatted with Geezer Butler while I got to know Iommi. Geezer was a great guy, really fun and personable. Ian Gillan seemed to be in the wrong band, like he was an outsider and not happy with the way he was treated. At least this was the impression I got. As a Deep Purple fan, it was strange for me to see him in any other band, and I could imagine it was weird for him too.

Gillan didn't say much, but for a singer of his stature, he sure smoked a lot of cigarettes. As we were talking, the cooks came out from the restaurant kitchen and asked Toni and I if we wanted to go back and meet the chefs. We went back there, and I figured they might want a photograph or an autograph. Instead, they brought out a huge chopping block. Toni and I thought they were going to offer some German sausage or choice cuts of meat. But then the chef came out from behind the passageway and dumped a mountain of cocaine on the chopping block. Toni and I looked at each other, shocked. They cut the coke into massive lines. Crazy huge. At this point, Toni didn't do drugs, so I snorted a little bit of the coke for both us. We didn't want to be rude, after all.

We really had some fun that night. Iommi asked me if I would head back to his hotel room with him. Of course I said, "Let's go." When we walked into the room, I could smell the leather coming from his closet. He always had the best clothes. I dug through his jackets and boots, admiring it all. Everything was first class. We talked about music and guitars, and he told me the story of getting his fingertips cut off when he worked a construction job before he joined Sabbath. He was pushing some tile through the tile cutter and it clipped off his fingertips. How horrible for a guitar player! Tony had special tips made out of soft plastic and leather so he could continue to play.

I found out the guitar he was playing when I first saw him in 1972 was not a Gibson SG after all. It was made by John Diggins, who used to work for the famous English luthier John Birch, before going on to found Jaydee Guitars. That same guy also made instruments for AC/

DC's Angus Young. They were one of a kind. It was cool to hear Tony's stories. He asked me to stay the night with him, which I did. We fooled around a bit, but that's as far as he was able to get because he was so high. He was impotent from his constant drug use, and he was very embarrassed. I felt bad for him and didn't really know what to do. Eventually, I got him off. I left the next morning and went back to my hotel. We only did a few shows with Sabbath before I went back to the UK to finish the last few dates with Rainbow.

The record label would always fly me to the next city, but sometimes the rest of my crew wasn't so lucky. On one particular stretch of the tour with Black Sabbath, they put the crew on a ferry-type boat to get them from Stockholm to Helsinki. Toni hates small spaces, so she ended up sleeping on the top deck of the boat. If she wasn't in the bar drinking, she was on the top deck. It seemed to take them forever and when they finally made it to Helsinki, Toni knocked on my hotel room door and was in nasty shape.

"I need a bath, some food, and some sleep. Do you have a bathtub?"

"Uh, kinda."

"What do you mean kinda?" she asked.

I showed her the dirty little basin in the bathroom that was about four inches deep. You basically poured the water over yourself with a hose.

"I don't give a fuck!" she said.

She got in and used the body wash at the hotel, and in less than forty minutes she was covered in red bumps all over her skin. She was not happy, but I know she loved every minute of that tour—skin rash and all.

Before a gig at the Marquee Club in London, we had gone out for sushi and sake. Randy Rand had never had sushi or sake in his life, and by the time we got to the gig he and Randy Castillo were nicely buzzed. There were about three hundred shirtless guys in the audience and some of them were throwing darts at the Randys, who were terrified. I didn't notice because they weren't throwing them at me! But no matter where we were, we pulled it off. Our audience didn't want to like us, but by the time we walked off the stage, they loved us.

During the last part of the tour, I noticed another intriguing side of Ritchie that I hadn't seen when we spent time together during my Runaways days. For starters, he was really superstitious. He would never stay in a hotel room if the numbers added up to thirteen. He wouldn't have anything to do with the number thirteen, in fact. He had to have his back to the wall in an open room so nothing could come up behind him. He was also into occult rituals, but not evil stuff. He called it "white magic" instead of "black magic."

He liked to stay in Europe's old castles. One night we stayed in Dalhousie Castle in Scotland. Toni and I had rented a car and we were going to drive there to hang out with Ritchie and the rest of the band. I got in to drive but realized that since we were in the UK, everything was on the opposite side, and I didn't think I was going to be able to deal with the switch very well. I went to use the turn signal and turned on the windshield wipers. Toni said, "I'll drive." I was so impressed with the way she easily figured out where we were going. She didn't make one wrong turn!

Ritchie held a séance that night, attempting to talk to any spirits that were lingering in the five-hundred-year-old castle. He claimed to be talking to people who had been kings and queens from the 1800s. It was a pretty heavy-duty thing to see. It frightened me, but Ritchie also had me riveted.

After a show one night in London, four or five of us were in one of my favorite hotels in England, the Swiss Cottage Hotel. We were all sitting around a beautiful old stone fireplace having pints of beer. Ritchie gave me a pen and paper and said, "Write something down, but don't let me see it."

"Like what? A word? A sentence?"

"One or two sentences."

I thought for a moment about what I could write to make it really difficult. He turned his face away from me so he couldn't see me writing. I wrote a silly quote my father would always say: *Not knowing the situation of the consequences, I can't rightly say.*

I looked at his back and asked, "Now what?"

"Crumple up the paper and throw it in the fire."

I did as he instructed and watched the paper burn. Ritchie turned back around to face me. He looked at me for a few moments in silence, and then he said, word for word, "Not knowing the situation of the consequences, I can't rightly say."

How did he know? I wasn't even going to ask. I just went to my room, dumbfounded. He was really tuned in to much of the world around him, from the picture on the dashboard of my car the first time I visited him, to the spirits of kings and queens in castles. He was an amazing man. I loved him, and I knew he felt my heart. He was one of those rare people who actually deserve to be idolized.

The next day the entire band and all the crew had gone home after the tour except Toni and me. We were stuck in England because my passport had expired, so that meant a new passport photo. We were already so exhausted from being on tour, and you would think that after opening for Rainbow and Black Sabbath and spending one of those nights in my idol's hotel room I would have been glowing. Instead I had cum in my hair and makeup running down my face as they snapped a shot of me for my passport. It should be in a coffee-table book, *Classiest Passport Photos Ever Taken*. Page one.

WHEN TONI AND I got back from the tour, we had a day off in New York City. We hopped in a cab and headed straight to a Laundromat. There was no fabric softener at the Laundromat, so everything came out with maximum static cling. On our way back to the hotel, Toni said, "Let's go out for dinner."

I agreed. We returned to the hotel and got changed.

We went to a fine Indian restaurant and had a lovely time reminiscing about our European tour. It had been a hell of an adventure. As we were walking out I noticed something hanging from Toni's jeans.

"What's that?" I asked her.

She turned to look at what I was pointing to.

"Oh my God! Those are my underwear!"

The panties had been there throughout dinner! We laughed so hard we cried. Even rock and rollers need fabric softener, boys and girls.

That same fall, after we got back from the tour with Rainbow, my parents and I spent Thanksgiving with Toni's family at her mother's house. When Toni and I were leaving, Toni's mom gave us tons of leftovers because she was afraid we weren't eating right. And of course we weren't. Unless you call alcohol, cigarettes, and pills a square meal.

As we made our way back to Hollywood, we were driving down Santa Monica Boulevard when we stopped at a red light. A red Porsche Carrera pulled up next to us and the men inside rolled down their windows. We thought they were lost, and they thought we'd be impressed with their new Porsche. They were dressed in their best cheesy Hawaiian shirts. Toni and I were tired and grumpy that day, and we just wanted to get back to the hotel where we were staying—the Tropicana.

The guy in the passenger seat looked at us for way too long and then said, "Hel-looooo, baaaa-bbby!"

I got annoyed, and as I glared back at him, I reached into the backseat and felt around in the doggie bag Toni's mother had given us. I wanted to find something to throw at this arrogant bastard. I got my hands on some corn on the cob and yelled to him, "Hey, baby this!," as I threw the corn as hard as I could at his brand-new Porsche. It hit the side with such force it dented his door. I couldn't believe my eyes. There was a huge dent! But it shut him up.

I looked at Toni and said, "Oh shit! Floor it!"

Just then the light turned green and she hit the gas. Toni was driving a 1973 copper Pontiac Firebird with side pipes. She was a badass driver, and she knew what she was doing from all her days racing motorcycles. She was fearless. We were drag-racing down Santa Monica Boulevard with that yuppie. He chased us until we saw a hotel. I told Toni to pull over. I always felt safe at hotels. They were my home away from home. We turned into that hotel and the guys did too. They got out of their Porsche and started pouring beers on the roof of Toni's car and calling us bitches.

"Yeah, well, you shouldn't talk to a woman that way. Who do you think you are?" I shot back. I just wanted them to go away.

A security guard saw the commotion and asked Toni and me, "Are these guys bothering you?"

"Yes, they are," we said, with puppy-dog eyes.

The security guard told them to leave immediately or go to jail. The guys left, and Toni and I gave each other a high five. They turned around and yelled "Bitches!" as they drove off. We were both so sick of how we had been treated by men lately that the episode felt like some small victory that day.

CHAPTER 9

DANCIN' ON THE EDGE

You're always running for your life,

You can't escape.

You fall deeper in hell.

—"DANCIN' ON THE EDGE"
(WRITTEN BY LITA FORD)

I WAS IN CALIFORNIA AND STARTING TO WORK ON MY SECOND ALBUM
when I got a call from Tony Iommi. We had kept in touch since that first
night in Germany. He was still on tour with Black Sabbath, and we saw
each other more often. It was on one of those occasions that I first met
Ronnie James Dio. Ronnie stopped me one night in a hotel hallway. "Hey,
if you ever need a place to go, you are welcome in my room." He meant
it as a friendly gesture in case I was ever in trouble. It left me confused.
"Thank you," I told him. "That's so kind. I'm okay, but I will take you up
on that if I'm ever afraid." I felt like he was watching out for me the way
a big brother would. Ronnie James Dio was a very down-to-earth, caring
soul, as well as an incredible vocalist. I was very lucky for his invitation
and felt his warmth as a human being.

The first time my parents met Tony, they thought he was really odd.
My folks were the most understanding people I knew and had graciously
hosted my musician friends for years, so if they thought someone was
off, it meant something. He would come for dinners at my parents' and

sometimes we would sleep in the back house for the night. He would do weird things like jiggle the doorknob of the main house and then walk around to the rear entrance. My mother said to me in her thick accent, "Lita, I think he has a wheel loose." Boy, was she right. I was in love, though. What I didn't realize was that I was in love with the rock star, not the man.

As I would arrive at Tony's hotel in LA, I would always see another woman either coming or going. I assumed it was a second girlfriend or a drug dealer, and I didn't really care which it was. I always wondered who this "mystery woman" was, even though she never spoke to me. I didn't ask him about it, but she and I knew we were both there to see Tony.

When I read Tony's book, I found out he was still married but not yet divorced when we started dating. I felt sorry for his wife and daughter, even though I had never met them. He would spend hundreds of dollars a day on drugs but wouldn't pay child support. I thought it was horrible for a father not to want to support his child. He seemed like he couldn't be bothered with the little girl, and I hated that about him.

WHEN I WAS working on my second album, *Dancin' on the Edge,* I rented Shep Gordon's house in Hawaii to write songs and get away. Shep is Alice Cooper's manager, and I had met Alice when I was in the Runaways, so Shep was no stranger to me. I took my bass player Gordon Copley with me to write; his wife joined us shortly afterward. One afternoon, while Gordon and I were working on a song, I looked on the wall behind him and saw the biggest flying cockroach I'd ever seen in my entire life. I said, "Gordon, turn around. Look on the wall." Gordon was a little bit like Ron Wood—a good dude but a funny character. He didn't know how to handle this gigantic roach. It wasn't the kind of bug you would just step on. Gordon looked at the bug and then turned back around and looked at me and said nothing. I yelled at him, "Fuck, Gordon! Do something!"

"Like what?"

"I don't know! Hit him with your bass!"

He didn't like that idea.

I remembered seeing a bunch of magazines in the bathroom, so I led Gordon there. We went through the pile, contemplating: "Do we hit him with a *Better Homes and Gardens*? Or a *Popular Mechanics*?"

While we were trying to decide, the roach had crawled up Gordon and was on his chest.

"Gordon! Look!" I screamed, pointing to his chest.

Gordon flipped out and managed to knock the roach off his chest with the *Better Homes and Gardens*. It was like a roach rodeo. They were so big, you could saddle them up and ride them.

I'd never seen a bug like that before. Fucking prehistoric. Well, I soon learned the entire house was infested with flying Hawaiian cockroaches. We thought about going to a hotel, but I had paid so much money for this place, we ended up staying up all night, beating cockroaches and sleeping all day. When Gordon's wife, Lorraine, got there, she went to management and had the place sprayed. Why hadn't we thought of that? It wasn't exactly the most creative of environments.

WE RECORDED *Dancin' on the Edge* in New York and Philadelphia. Toni was still my tech at the time, and we stayed in Philly to record with the producer Lance Quinn and to be close to recording studios like the Power Station in New York City and the Warehouse and Studio 4 in Philly. We lived at a place called One Buttonwood Square. We always said it like we were Bugs Bunny: "One Buttonwood Squwah." We used to run up the Rocky steps and pretend that we were in shape. Then we'd go to the bar.

One Buttonwood Square was a cool little place. It just so happened Jon Bon Jovi and his bandmates lived close by and were also recording. Jon and Richie Sambora would come over to our place to hang out. We'd go to the corner bar, the Rose Tattoo Café, to have a drink. We'd have a lot of drinks sometimes, sit and talk music, and dream about how we were going to be big someday. We became good friends during those months.

One night, we were all in New York and staying at the Broadway Plaza Hotel. We went out to a club called Traxx, and Jon and Richie brought Aldo Nova. Aldo played keys on my *Dancin' on the Edge* album. Jon loved his red wine, but he had too much that night. As we were coming home from the club, he was clumsy, like a puppy when you first bring him home. I thought it was kind of cute. Soon enough Jon and I started making out. Richie caught on real quick and started making out with Toni. Aldo watched, sipping his red wine, as we tried to fit him in too. We all moved it to the bedroom, which had two beds. Jon and I took one bed, Richie and Toni took the other. Aldo stood in the doorway watching, still with wine in hand. Jon started feeling a little sick and began puking in the corner, right on the bedroom carpet. Toni hopped off of Richie as if to say, *Here, Lita. Try mine.* So I got in bed with Richie. Holy shit. Richie Sambora is the king of swing, I must say. Jon recovered from puking and Aldo finally made his way into the action, and it turned into girl-on-guy fun at the Broadway Plaza Hotel. We checked out the next morning, leaving the hotel room a complete disaster with red-wine puke in the corner.

DURING THIS TIME I was really falling into my own style. I was breaking away from the image I had created for *Out for Blood,* which was influenced by Neil Merryweather, and I was coming into my own as a vocalist. But I had made my bed and now I had to lie in it: I was the chick that played guitar. Not everyone believed in my vocal abilities, especially my producer. We had the time of our life making the record, but I would soon realize that it was also going to be one of the biggest challenges of my life, mainly because I was female.

Jon Bon Jovi had turned me on to the producer Lance Quinn. I couldn't stand him. Personally, I thought he was useless as a producer, but I was stuck with him for that album because of Jon's recommendation. He wanted his friend who thought he was Edward Van Halen to play guitar on "Gotta Let Go," my single on the album, but he didn't tell me. He was also pushing a guy named Geoff Leib on me to play keyboards. I couldn't understand it. I already had Aldo Nova playing keys, and he was great! Why the fuck would I need more keyboard players on an album like *Dancin' on the Edge?* It wasn't a keyboard-oriented album.

I had a great band for *Dancin' on the Edge.* It was one of my favorite groups that I've ever put together. Along with Randy on drums, I also had Bobby Donati and Gordon Copley. Bobby and I fit together real well. He was a singer and was very intelligent. Together we all looked hot.

On our final night of recording the album, I left the studio and the album was done. The record was supposed to have been turned in to the label the next day. Everyone went home except Lance. "I have a few last-minute things to clean up," he said. After we all said our good-byes, Lancey boy put in his friend's solo on "Gotta Let Go." I didn't know until after the album was mastered. Personally, I don't think Lance would have done that if I was a dude. In my opinion, he had his mind set on his buddy playing on my record, and because I was female, he took advantage of me. Even Lance Quinn couldn't wrap his head around the chick who played guitar. It blew my mind that after all I'd accomplished I still didn't have control over the production of my own album.

Dancin' on the Edge was the first album that actually crossed over to the other side. I became a chick on guitar with credibility, and I wasn't just a piece of ass. They actually managed to get me into clothes for the album cover. It didn't change anything in terms of how well I played guitar. The record label executives tried to change me and make me into this cutesie little pop star, but I just didn't have it in my blood to be that. I liked the raunch, and the shock value of being eccentric and playing guitar. They didn't know how to sell that side of me. But obviously it was working, because I was nominated for a Grammy. But still, the fight between me and my manager, Allen Kovac, and my label continued.

AFTER RECORDING THE album, I went to London for a few months with my band to shoot a video and do some gigs. The video was for the song "Gotta Let Go." While we were filming, my band and I were living in a house in Marble Arch on the West End of London. We went out to a bar called the Funny Farm quite often. It was a speakeasy open from midnight to seven A.M. that catered almost exclusively to musicians. A man named Frank Coe ran the bar. He was infamous in London and so was that bar. It was in the basement of a Greek hotel, and it only held eighty to a hundred people. You would have to knock at the door, and they would open the window to see your face. If they knew you, they would let you in; if not, they would tell you to fuck off. All the big British bands were in there: Thin Lizzy, Deep Purple, Whitesnake, et cetera. I met a musician named Phil Soussan in that bar. We hit it off right away, and from then on we hung out together almost every day. Phil was between bands at the time and would later join Randy Castillo in Ozzy Osbourne's post-Sabbath group. (Ozzy had split from Black Sabbath in 1979.) I would be working with my band, but at night we would meet at a Mexican restaurant to do shots and then go to a bar called Stringfellows or end up at the Funny Farm. This lasted for a few months, but then I had to hit the road again. At the time my main relationship was with rock and roll.

AS FOR TONY and me, we saw each other only on and off because we both traveled so much. He surprised me one day, however, when he said to me, "I want to take you to England to meet me mum." His father had passed away, and he rarely talked about him.

Tony had his keyboard player, Geoff Nicholls, whom he nicknamed Nick, with him at all times. Nick was never onstage with Black Sabbath—they kept him hidden off to the side of the stage during the shows. He came with us to England when we went to visit Tony's mom. Nick appeared to be Tony's safety blanket. He would laugh at Tony's jokes, do his drugs, and seemed to say yes to anything Tony asked. I didn't think much of Nick. I suspect Nick didn't like me, either. I think he was afraid that I would sweep Tony away.

Nick, Tony, and I were sitting on a jumbo jet, ready to take off for England. Boy, was I excited! And a little nervous. I was going to meet Tony's mother. I wanted to make a good impression, and that's all I was thinking about, when out of nowhere, as soon as the plane was in motion, Tony hauled off and punched me in the eye. For no reason! Something I said? Something I didn't say? Who knows! It was almost like he was trying to show off to Nick and show him what a "man" he was. A real man doesn't do that. It didn't look like Nick was as surprised as I was.

I got up and tried to find a place to hide. Fuck, I'm on an airplane, where do I go? I told the stewardess that my boyfriend had hit me and asked her to help me find someplace where he couldn't find me. She led me to a private area that they had curtained off for the stewardesses only. Tony came looking for me, but he gave up after a few minutes and went back to his seat. For the entire ten-hour flight from LAX to London Heathrow, I sat in the stewardesses' station. I was devastated. My hero, my idol, the man I thought I loved, had just punched me in the eye. And I had no idea why.

My eye began to swell up, and I knew it was going to turn black and blue. The stewardess gave me some ice. When the plane landed, I planned on turning around and taking the next flight back to LAX. Tony acted like nothing had happened. I wondered if Tony had taken some drug that had made him fly off the handle and I prayed that it had worn off and he wouldn't do it again. So I stayed, like a moron. But now I had to see his mother with a black eye.

We had to drive a couple of hours to Birmingham, where Tony had a place near his mother's. His home was a typical English house. Wooden and lined in river rocks, it was large but not extravagant. He showed me to the master bedroom upstairs, where I put my bags. Downstairs was the living room and kitchen area, which was really nice and clearly put together by a woman.

"Tomorrow me mum is coming over," he told me.

I figured the way to impress Tony's mom was to cook a full-blown

British meal. I was relieved that I had another day to figure out how to compose myself after what had happened. I went up the street to the butcher and bought a beautiful leg of lamb, bone in. You have to have the bone in. I also bought some sweet onions, brussels sprouts, and potatoes to roast with the leg of lamb, and a bit of mint sauce.

The next day I spent hours cooking, and I was happy because Tony left me alone. The whole time I was preparing the meal I wondered how I was going to get through the week. His mother came over that afternoon when I was just putting the final touches on the meal. She was really nice, and when we sat down to eat, she seemed impressed with what I had done. After she ate, she said, "Well, I give that dinner a ten!" I knew this meant that she didn't just like the food, but that she also liked me.

At one point in the night Tony went to get something upstairs and I was alone with his mother. I asked her, "Did you notice my black eye?"

"Yes," she said.

"Tony did it," I said.

"I figured."

"How? Why?" I wanted to know.

"His father used to do that to me."

Everything became clear to me. I had to assume it wasn't just drugs. It was aggression, passed down from his father. I was happy the father wasn't around—and I'm sure his mother was too—but I had finally realized what Ronnie James Dio meant about the possibility of me needing a safe place to stay while I was with Tony. Ronnie and I bonded as friends after that.

Tony and I stayed at his house in Birmingham for a week, and, thank God, he didn't hit me again. We returned to Los Angeles together, and I was lulled into a false sense of security. It was the first time a man had ever hit me. I stayed with him, hoping that was the end of the abuse.

TWO YEARS LATER I was still with him. While the abuse wasn't a frequent occurrence, it happened four and five times while we were together. Each time I was shocked by his sudden and extreme violence toward me.

We would travel and get fucked up a lot. He told me he had to leave England for six months at a time so the government wouldn't take massive amounts of income tax from him. So we would stay in California or sometimes we would crash at different places around the world. He would do cocaine to the point where he would think people were looking through the peepholes. Sometimes he would take a towel and cover the bottom of the door. I'd ask him, "Why are you doing that?"

"I don't want people to hear or see or smell what I'm doing." He always thought there were people in the vents, so he would close them all. He told me that sound and smells carried. He was a paranoid freak. Tony wasn't working much at this time—most of his energy was spent on consuming outrageous quantities of drugs. There were always large peanut-butter-size jars of downers around. He would take hundreds of dollars' worth of cocaine on a daily basis. He was so antisocial that the only people he talked to were me and his friend Nick.

All the while, the mystery woman whom I kept seeing sitting in the lobby of each hotel we were at was really starting to get to me. Was it a drug dealer? A hooker? Both? Even though I was curious, what bothered me about her wasn't the woman so much as Tony, from time to time, jokingly saying to me, "Hurry up and get out, I've got another one waiting downstairs." Did he think I didn't notice her? I felt like a fool, and it was really starting to piss me off.

WE GOT AN offer to play the Guitar Greats Show at New Jersey's Capitol Theatre in November 1984. It was a short jam session with all the top guitarists in the industry: Edward Van Halen, Johnny Winter, and Brian Setzer, just to name a few. It was a night to remember. As always, I was the only female surrounded by male musicians backstage. The pressure was on anyway because of the great guitarists who were on the bill. Johnny Winter was on before us. To follow Johnny Winter—

one of my greatest inspirations—was nerve-racking enough. I was supposed to go on separately, without Tony, but it all came to a head an hour prior to us hitting the stage.

"What am I going to play?" said Tony. "How will the drummer sound?"

"Tony, it's Kenny Aronoff!" I said.

"What? Who's that?"

Tony was nervous as hell because he wasn't really one to get onstage with other bands—he wasn't a jammer. Neither was I, really. By this stage in his life, he had forgotten nearly all his riffs because he was so fucked up all the time. I used to show him how to play his own guitar parts, which I hated doing because he had been my idol. But I knew them like the back of my hand, and he, sadly, did not. I would sit down and play them for him. He would say, "How did you do that?" I would slow it down and show him until he got it. It was the only thing he ever thanked me for during our entire relationship.

As we sat in a corner of the backstage area trying to figure out what Sabbath song he was going to play, I said, "Tony, why don't you just jam? Just don't worry. How about I just go onstage with you? I'll cover you for a song." He liked the idea, so we decided to go onstage together. It wasn't what was originally scheduled, but it was a cool idea. The idea of me being onstage with him made him feel better, but what he didn't know was that I had a plan to outshine him and leave his sorry ass in the dust. I dug deep into my soul and pulled out the times he hit me, the mystery woman in the lobby, and the nights he would stay up with Nick snorting line after line of cocaine until he would hallucinate. That, combined with the constant need to have to prove myself every time I picked up a guitar just because I was female, gave me more than enough motivation to do my best to outplay him onstage that night. I grabbed my pink B.C. Rich Bich, a powerful beast of a guitar, and walked out onstage with Tony. Kenny Aronoff said to me, "What do you want to play, Lita?" Tony was in the corner off to stage right plugging in. I said to Kenny, "How about a bluesy jam in E minor to start?" I had decided to give Tony a taste of his own medicine.

Gently adding in a little bit of "Heaven and Hell" to riff over, it was a ferocious jam. This was my chance. Tony needed a good ass-kicking. He managed to squeeze out a smile for the crowd about half-way through the performance. By the time our set was done, he was sweating bullets, and I knew by the crowd's reaction that I had more than held my own that night.

After the concert, we headed back to the hotel. Tony was relieved that the show was over. He didn't say much to me. I think he realized how much he'd fallen with all the drugs he was doing. I thought I'd get the shit beat out of me, but he didn't fly off the handle that night. Maybe it was done for good?

A few months after the Guitar Greats show, he gave me an engagement ring. It was a gorgeous, big solitaire diamond surrounded with more diamonds. There was no romantic proposal. It was more like *Hey, here, I got you a ring.* And that was it, we were engaged. But needless to say, I wasn't so sure about it. I went to visit my parents, and I made up a story about a girl who got hit by her boyfriend. I didn't tell my mother it was me. I wanted to see what she would say. She told me, "Lita, he do it once, he do it again." Those words would play over and over again in my mind.

SOON AFTER OUR engagement, I was at the Bellagio hotel in Los Angeles, where Tony and I were staying. He went off on the worst fit of rage I had ever seen. After snorting tons of blow, he got angry and choked me unconscious. When I woke up, I saw him holding a chair above my head. It was a big, heavy leather chair with studs around the arms, and he was about to smash it over my face. I rolled over, and luckily I moved fast enough that he missed me and the chair smashed into the ground.

I ran for the door because I knew he wouldn't go out into the hall-way in his underwear. I got into my car and drove to the closest place I felt safe, which was Nikki's house. I couldn't let my parents see me like this. My father would have murdered Tony Iommi. Literally.

I showed up at Nikki's with some hair ripped out and hand marks around my throat. Nikki said, "What happened to you?" I explained what Tony had done.

"He could have killed me," I told Nikki. "He hit me in the head and gave me a concussion."

Nikki said to me, "I'll be right back; I have something that will help make you feel better." He got in his Porsche and drove over to his friend Robbin Crosby's house. He came back with heroin.

"Are you crazy?" I said to him. "I don't do heroin, Nikki."

"It will take the pain away."

And I *was* in so much pain. My heart ached more than anything. I was willing to try anything. I snorted a little bit of it, because I refused to shoot it after that horrible experience when I shot it with Joey Ramone's girlfriend.

I curled up on Nikki's water bed and fell asleep. My head was pounding from the concussion. I could barely move. Nikki let me have his bed that night while he slept on the sofa.

THE NEXT DAY Tony was in rehearsals with his new band, which included members of my own band that he had recruited for himself. Stealing my band was the icing on the cake. He had beaten me, choked me, and now he had taken my rhythm section too: Eric Singer, my drummer, and Gordon Copley, my bass player. What a gentleman. That's when I was finally done. Of all the drummers I've ever played with, and helped in terms of their careers, Eric Singer was my least favorite. If Tony had asked me, I would have gladly handed him over. But to ask him behind my back, that's a pretty dirty, low-life thing to do when you're a musician of his stature. He's Tony Iommi, for fuck's sake. He could have had any band he wanted. Why steal mine, his fiancée's? Because it was convenient for him and he only thought of himself. I decided to leave for good. I waited until he was in the studio, then I made my move to leave. I packed up all my stuff and left.

I wrote him a note that read: "You're not a man. You're a mouse. Squeak squeak."

I ended up selling the engagement ring he gave me at a pawn shop for a piddly amount. It had to have cost him thousands, but I got only a couple hundred. I didn't care. That was what he was worth to me. I guess I held on so long because I had an idea of what he would be like as a person, and I kept hoping that man would come through, but he never did.

After I left Tony, I was heartbroken despite it all. My all-time idol turned out to be an abusive, backstabbing drug addict. He didn't deserve to be idolized. He was a dirtbag as far as I was concerned. I was so hurt and disappointed that someone I had looked up to could be so horrible. I became angry and self-destructive by doing all the things Tony didn't want me to do. Tony hated tattoos. They just weren't proper to him. I rebelled by getting a tattoo on my right shoulder of a dragon wrapped around a guitar. It represented strength in guitar playing. After our breakup, I went on crazy drinking binges because Tony never let me touch a drop, not even on long flights, which was something I always did—a glass of wine relaxed me and helped me sleep. Besides, back then the drinks were free.

To this day I still idolize the original Black Sabbath lead guitarist I saw onstage at the Long Beach Arena when I was thirteen. The one I never met. The Tony Iommi I knew and became engaged to is now gone from my heart. He wasn't worth the torture. Only the guitar riffs will linger in my memory.

AFTER THE TERRIBLE ending with Tony, seeing Glenn Tipton again was the breath of fresh air I needed. Judas Priest came through Long Beach again in 1984 with their Defenders of the Faith tour and, as usual, I went to the show. This time Glenn invited me to go with them to their next show in San Diego. He had the following day off and then a show the night after that. I said, "Well, how will I get back home?"

"No worries, my love. We can drop you back at your car when we come back up the coast."

Awesome!

After the show in Long Beach that night, Glenn cleaned up, took me by the hand, and walked me onto their tour bus. Glenn was such a lovely gentleman and a kind person. We crawled into his bunk and waited for the bus driver and the other band members, then started to make our way down the coast to San Diego. We stayed in his bunk the entire night. It's one of my favorite places to have sex.

The next day in San Diego we fooled around all day, went to the mall, had some food at a nice restaurant, and then later that night Glenn, Rob, his friend John, and I all went to go see the movie *This Is Spinal Tap*. Man, we laughed our asses off, especially at the miniature Stonehenge set that Rob Reiner had ripped off from the Black Sabbath shows. Glenn and Rob were waiting nervously to see what "inspiration" Reiner had drawn from Judas Priest. Still today I find myself doing Spinal Tap things backstage. Not being able to find your way around backstage or not knowing where the dressing rooms are is the most common, but then there are other classic moments like the time I was playing a show in LA and drove my 1969 Corvette to the gig. It was a great-looking car, but it didn't always run great. I had my mother with me, and as we approached the Reseda Country Club, I noticed the line of fans that went around the block. I was trying to look as cool as I could, and some fans noticed me: "Hey, look, it's Lita Ford!" All of a sudden, my car stalled out. It wouldn't start. "Lita, what are we going to do?" my mother asked. We were at a standstill in the middle of the street.

"Get out and push, Mom."

"Lita, I'm not going to push. I'll go inside and get a roadie."

My mother came back out with two roadies, and once the fans saw what was going on, a couple of them came over to help as the roadies pushed my car into a parking spot. I don't think there's one rock band that doesn't find themselves having a Spinal Tap moment at some point.

After their San Diego show, the guys from Judas Priest headed back up the coast and drove me to my car in Long Beach. I said my good-byes and couldn't wait till the next time they came through town.

ALLEN KOVAC MANAGED me for a time during my *Dancin' on the Edge* tour. At the time I hired him, Allen was a wannabe rock-star manager trying to "reinvent" me. I think he didn't believe in me and would have preferred me to be a sweet little pop singer. Everything I tried to do he tried to changed, just like Lance Quinn had done during the recording of the album. He drove me nuts. He kept a suffocatingly close eye on me. I was still in my rebellious phase, and he would slip notes under my hotel room door telling me to "Be a good girl," "Don't drink so much," "Don't put on so much makeup," "Get some sleep." Fuck off!

On one occasion, we were in Lowell, Massachusetts, for a show near where I used to live as a kid and where my aunt Livia still was. She was my mother's youngest sister and one of my favorite relatives. We had a day off and I wanted to go visit my aunt, who had just been through a difficult divorce. She was going to cook a feast for my entire band and crew; my cousins were going to come by. But Kovac had a hair up his ass because he thought I was going out to score drugs. He was wrong. Way wrong. Kovac had told my tour manager, who then ordered the bus driver not to take us anywhere that day. I ended up taking a cab by myself. I fired Kovac soon after that. He pissed me off one too many times, but this time he fucked with my family. My aunt went out to get steak and chicken and all the fixings, and all the work she had done went to waste because I was the only one who showed up for the wonderful meal she had prepared. Soon after that she was diagnosed with and forced to battle lung cancer. She was very special to me. I'll never forgive Kovac for killing that visit.

GLENN AND JUDAS PRIEST came to town again about a year after I had seen him last, and we picked up right where we left off. I invited him over to my parents' house after the show. He had one of Priest's truck drivers bring him over in a black semitruck. That's the kind of down-to-earth guy Glenn is, to visit me at my mother and father's house after a show.

We sat up all night in the back house exchanging guitar licks, talking about instruments, and doing what little blow we had. My mother had to be at work by four A.M., so she came into the back house at around 3:30 A.M. to say hello to Glenn. Glenn had heard so much about her and had been looking forward to meeting her. My mother loved Glenn too.

We got talking about guitar picks, and he asked me what kind of pick I used. I handed him my odd home-plate-shaped pick, and he showed me his medium, regular-shaped pick. I told him he shouldn't be using those picks because they weren't thick enough, and that he should use something thicker for more attack on the strings. He looked at me as if to say, *Really? You* are telling me what kind of pick to use? We both laughed.

Glenn's driver slept in the truck while we stayed up all night. Until next year, Glenn. Ta-ta.

CHAPTER 10

LITA

> If I close my eyes forever,
>
> Will it all remain the same?
>
> —"CLOSE MY EYES FOREVER"
> (WRITTEN BY LITA FORD AND OZZY OSBOURNE)

BY THE TIME I HAD TOURED THE HELL OUT OF *DANCIN' ON THE EDGE,* IT WAS 1986. My manager at the time was Don Arden, who was Sharon Osbourne's father. Don Arden was considered the Al Capone of managers. His aggressive tactics were well known throughout the industry, and he was both respected and feared. I was happy Arden liked me, and I never saw the scary side of him that some promoters had experienced—like dangling them out a hotel window asking them where his money was. Don respected me and the feeling was mutual, although he didn't do that much for my career in terms of getting me on great tours or the covers of rock magazines. He, unfortunately, was another one who didn't know what to do with me. Was it really that hard? You'd think that with a Grammy nomination for Best Female Rock Vocal Performance for *Dancin' on the Edge,* someone would get a clue. I really loved Don, and his team members were all wonderful gentlemen to me. They just weren't the right fit.

I already had a new album written. I had a song called "Under the Gun" that Mike Chapman liked, which soon led to us working together.

What unfolded was the *Lita* album. He brought me "Kiss Me Deadly," a song he had in his publishing catalog. "Broken Dreams" was an idea inspired by a poster I saw of the James Dean movie *Boulevard of Broken Dreams*. He looked sad in the poster, and the lyrics of the song are me singing to him. For "Back to the Cave," Mike already had the chorus, so I wrote the lyrics and the guitar line. It was about the pressures and bullshit of day-to-day life and how you sometimes just want to go "back to the cave" to escape them all. It could be interpreted sexually too, which is why it works so well lyrically.

Mike had seen the David Lynch movie *Blue Velvet* and wanted to write a song about it. Instead of having the female character as the "sex toy" who does whatever the male character wants, Mike reversed the roles and had the female—me—singing the song as the sexual aggressor.

Motörhead's Lemmy and I had met at the Rainbow one night while I was working on the album. He had an apartment down the hill, within walking distance from the Rainbow. Since the Rainbow closes at two A.M., and we were still hanging out, he asked me if I wanted to go to his place for more drinks. I ended up staying at Lemmy's house for three days! We had shots of Wild Turkey, did lines of meth, and ended up writing "Can't Catch Me." I eventually called my friend Patty and asked her to help get me out of Lemmy's house. I was so fucked up there was no way I could drive home. I remember walking in the front door of my new apartment: there was no furniture, only a bed, and I collapsed on the living room floor for probably another three days because I was so fucked up. Once I came to I stumbled over to my bed, where I slept for what seemed a few more days. It was a week before I realized we had written a song.

I already had Mike Chapman in place as record producer. I had a record deal with Dreamland Records, which was Mike's label. Now I just needed a manager who could take me to the next level.

I WAS SITTING at the bar on the *Queen Mary* in Long Beach with a gorgeous guy from Anchorage, Alaska. We were downing oyster shooters and drinking Bloody Marys. I said to him, "I want a manager who I can relate to as a human being and who doesn't just see me as a piece of meat or a dollar sign." The old record label and Kovak had given me a hard time about wearing too much makeup, my clothes, and my look. "I need someone who can understand what it is like to be a woman in the music industry," I said. I thought a female manager would be appropriate. Who would be able to take me to the next level I was after? I thought about it for a minute and realized it was Sharon Osbourne. Right then I picked up the phone and called her from the *Queen Mary*. I told her I was managed by Don Arden and that I needed someone who understood where I was coming from and could help me get to where I wanted to be. At the time I did not know Don Arden was her father and her rival because of a falling-out the family had had. Maybe she saw an opportunity to outdo her dad and believed she could make me a success. She said yes right away.

I was thrilled, and my Alaskan friend and I left the ship and headed toward the freeway. I was driving a Jeep and had taken the top and the doors off. I was talking a mile a minute, imagining the possibilities of my career moving forward with Sharon. I was so happy to have her on my team. Well, as I got onto the freeway, I turned to look at my friend. He was gone! I looked in the rearview mirror and saw him rolling on the freeway. Shit! Thank God there isn't much traffic in that part of town. I pulled over and ran back to get him. "Are you okay?"

"Yeah, I just ripped my knee open," he replied.

I'm not quite sure how or why, but he was wearing the new green suede-leather pants I had bought in Germany. I'm convinced those leather pants saved his leg that day. The pants were torn, and the gravel from the road was stuck in his knee. I helped him into the Jeep and we drove to the first bar I could find. I ordered him a cognac and handed it to him. He started drinking it.

"No! It's not for you to drink! It's for your knee! To disinfect it."

I grabbed the cognac and poured it over his wound. He screamed in pain—the normal reaction when someone pours alcohol on an open wound. This was definitely rock-and-roll first aid.

I ABSOLUTELY LOVED Sharon and respected her. She was a teetotaler and helped me sober up. Sharon and I would go shopping together. We could be real girly girls together, which was nice to have in a manager. She showed me all the best stores and hairdressers in Hollywood and helped me create my new look for the *Lita* album. Most important, she put me on better tours and shows.

But before I could tour, I needed musicians. I remember hiring Charlie Dalba after he came into the audition and we played "Into the Arena" by Michael Schenker. We immediately had chemistry, and it stayed that way the entire time he was in my band. Shortly afterward, I hired Tommy Caradonna to play bass. He walked in, played one song with us, and he killed it. He was tall, dark, and sexy and could play that bass like a motherfucker.

"That kicked ass!" I said.

Tommy left the room and I turned to Charlie and said, "What do you think?"

"I like him."

I sent Dave-O out to get Tommy and when he came back in, I said, "If you want the gig, you got it."

We had our bass player.

We went through a lot of guitarists before we landed on Steve Fister. Everyone would come in to the audition trying to do their own thing, but Steve came in and played what we needed him to play and got the gig. The four of us—Tommy Caradonna (bass), Charlie Dalba (drums), Steve Fister (guitar), and me—did some warm-up shows in small venues before "Kiss Me Deadly" made it onto the Billboard charts.

We were getting ready to go out on tour and I wanted to try dyeing my own hair. I had never done it before because I was always horrible with hair, but I thought to myself, *How hard can it be?* I went to a local pharmacy and bought some hair color. Bleach, to be exact. Unfortunately, I didn't know there were different strengths of bleach for hair, so I bought the strongest bleach I could find and went home to "color" my hair.

I read the directions. "Leave color in hair for twenty minutes, no longer." *Okay, I can do this. It's easy. What's the worst thing that could happen?* I mixed up the ingredients and blobbed it onto my hair. Just then, the phone rang. It was an old friend from London. We talked and talked. I was standing in my bathrobe with bleach in my hair and realized that the twenty minutes had quickly turned into forty-five minutes. "Oh shit! I gotta go!" I hung up the phone. I washed out the bleach in a hurry, got dressed, and hopped in my car to drive to a meeting in Hollywood. I didn't have time to dry my hair, so when I got in the car I rolled down the windows to let the wind dry it from the movement of the car on the freeway. My hair was so wet that I decided to run my fingers through it, thinking that would help it dry. It felt good: soft hair, warm California day, driving to a meeting on the freeway, and no traffic. As I ran my fingers through my hair, I noticed a little clump in my hand. I did it again just to see where the hair was coming from. Was it *my* hair? More strands of hair came out in my hand. What the fuck? It was coming out by the handful! Oh my God! I was freaking out. Strands and strands of hair were coming out in my fingers. There was so much of it that I was throwing it out the window of my car as I pulled it out of my head. I realized I had burned my hair with the bleach by leaving it on too long. All the hair behind the back of my neck was burned off. I didn't know what to do. Do I cut it all off? Do I shave my head? Shit!

Sharon took me to a professional hairstylist, who suggested hair extensions. Hair extensions? What the heck are those? I had never heard of them before, but I had to do something: I didn't have a choice. So Sharon and I decided to give me a new look. Like it or not, I bought the finest hair extensions and had the salon put in blue-black hair underneath the back of my neck, and the blond extensions on top. I had a full head of hair again, and my real hair had a chance to grow back. The extensions looked cool and were definitely different. The funny thing was, a lot of Lita fans started dyeing their hair blue-black and blond too. It became a look, but no one really knew the truth behind it.

Sharon was great at creating my new images, but she also had a list of changes that she wanted me to make. "One thing is you must get rid of Toni, your tech."

I said, "Why?" Besides being my close friend, Toni was a great tech, and I saw no reason to get rid of her.

Sharon said, "Because everyone will think you are gay." But I didn't believe it was the real reason. I think it was a control issue. Sharon had to have things her way, and Toni was always looking out for me and looking over everybody's shoulder. I don't think Sharon liked that. I didn't want to do it, but Sharon let Toni go, which made me resentful. However, Sharon also booked me on Jon Bon Jovi's New Jersey Syndicate tour, which was huge for me. I had to put business before personal.

Around this time, I was with my friend Patty, driving along a side street in Hollywood when I spotted an electrical worker working on a telephone pole. He was wearing a pair of jeans that were shredded all the way up the front, and I thought that they might look good as a part of my new look. I said to Patty, "I want those jeans." I just didn't know how I was going to get them. I asked Patty if she could get them for me. I handed her $100 and she got out and asked the worker for his jeans. He told Patty he had another pair just like them at home, so Patty arranged to meet him at the same telephone pole the next day, with another $100 for his torn work jeans. I gave them to my clothing designer at the time, and they became the jeans that I wore in the "Kiss Me Deadly" and "Close My Eyes Forever" videos.

I was walking my dog in the front yard one day at my parents' house, and my mother was motioning with her hand, pointing toward the ground, as if to say, *Come here!* I looked at her and said, "What?"

"Get in the house!" she said through gritted teeth. She was angry. "I don't want the neighbors to see you in those jeans."

Little did she know that they would be on heavy rotation on MTV. They became quite the fashion statement in the late 1980s and remained a part of the rock-and-roll dress code for years to come. I like to think I had a part in making that happen. Sorry, Mom!

WHEN IT CAME time for me to do a video for "Kiss Me Deadly," I enlisted the help of a great choreographer named Anne Marie Hunter. She had booked time for us—just her and me—to work on the various parts of the video in Jane Fonda's studio. When I arrived, Anne Marie handed me a bottle of Jack Daniel's and a small rinse-and-spit cup: "This is to help you loosen up." I liked this woman already!

I had a few shots of the Jack Daniel's and we got to work. Anne Marie had some of the girls from a Roller Derby league come in and show me how to fall and slide without putting pressure on the wrong parts of my body. As crazy as it sounds, she had to teach me how to fall in order to get that slide on knee pads just right for the video.

The video for "Kiss Me Deadly" became a hot, sexy anthem on MTV, but it sure didn't start out that way. I guess I must have been a little too loose after the Jack Daniel's, because as I was working on the choreographed moves Anne Marie had shown me, I stumbled and slammed into the wall behind me. The problem was that the wall was made of mirrors, and before I knew it, there was glass all over the place. By the time I was done bumping into mirrored walls and sliding across the floor on knee pads, I owed Jane Fonda's studio $750 worth of mirrors. It was money well spent. Anne Marie really helped me prepare for what would become my signature music video.

During the filming, they put Charlie's drum kit up on a forklift, and he was convinced that the whole fucking thing was going to come crashing down. The video was directed by Marty Callner, who used the same warehouse we were shooting in for later Aerosmith, Poison, and Cher videos. I remember the taping session lasted twenty-four hours and that years later on MTV's show *Pop Up Video,* they mentioned that the band and I had nothing to eat that day because we had no money. I found out just recently that Charlie had seen the show on TV and had his attorney call MTV to tell them to remove that "bubble" from the video because "it was a fucking lie." It was misleading. We ate and were treated well for that video shoot, and once it hit MTV, it changed everything. We went from playing smaller clubs to playing in front of twenty thousand people in arenas around the world. My bassist Tommy Caradonna said to me that he'd never forget the loud screams and "little girl" squeals that filled the stadium when they announced my name at the first gig we did. It was such an incredible feeling.

OZZY AND SHARON used to come over to my mother and father's house for dinner or a drink. There was nothing Ozzy could do to freak my parents out. They had already seen it all in the Runaways days. In fact, they were amused by Ozzy, and they liked him and Sharon very much. How could they not? The Osbournes are wonderful people. When they would pull up to my parents' house in a big black limo, the entire neighborhood would poke their heads out to see what was going on and then realize, "Oh, it's only Lita with her rock stars."

Being with Sharon and Ozzy was always an adventure. He passed out once in the aisle of a jumbo jet on the way to London. Sharon was poking him with a fork and putting holes in his favorite suit. She wanted him to get up, but he was out cold. He woke up as we were landing and found a bunch of holes in his coat. He was screaming, "Why do I have these fucking holes in me bloody coat? Sharon?!"

She calmly told him, "You were blocking the aisle. Nobody could pass by you."

Nikki and I were still friends around this time, and one day Mötley Crüe had the studio booked for the day to do some drum overdubs. I was in the next studio. There are a lot of little rooms in Record One, and Nikki had a few minutes to hang out with me in a little side room that had a piano in it. While we were in there we wrote "Falling In and Out of Love." I was writing and recording the *Lita* album in the studio, and David Ezrin—Bob Ezrin's son—was there with me working on the keyboard overdubs together with Mike Chapman. I was kind of running loose.

One day, Sharon and Ozzy came to the studio to bring me a gift, a life-size replica of Koko the gorilla. We started playing pool and drinking wine. Hours went by and Sharon got bored and left. That night, in another little room with a keyboard and a small guitar amplifier, Ozzy and I ended up writing "Close My Eyes Forever" into the wee hours of the morning. It was totally unplanned.

As the sun rose I said, "Ozzy, the fucking sun is coming up."

"Oh shit," he said. "I've got to get home. You have to drive me."

"I can't drive," I said to him. "We've been drinking all night. Take a fucking cab." I couldn't make that Laurel Canyon drive drunk! Ozzy took a cab, and later that day, I drove home with the gorilla strapped into the passenger's seat. Of course I put her seat belt on: we have to be safe after all.

Right before I fell asleep, the phone rang. It was Sharon. "Well, I've got one sniffer, now I've got two," she said. She was pissed. I wonder if she thought Ozzy and I were fucking each other, but all we did was play guitar and sing.

She asked me one day, "Lita, I was gone for three days, out of town on business, and when I came back, I found a tampon underneath Ozzy's bed in his hotel room. You don't know anything about it, do you?" I didn't hang out with Ozzy during those three days, and I didn't know anything about it.

Sharon also got pissed at me because I wouldn't get into bed with some guy for the "Back to the Cave" video. I wanted to do a live performance-based video, which I hadn't done before. During the actual shoot, I was trying to decide who would say the part of the song that Mike Chapman speaks in the studio version, where he says "I don't want to waste your time." Mike wasn't there, so I said "Let's have Tommy speak those parts." When I look at the video, I can see Tommy Caradonna laughing because he had a hard time keeping a straight face.

I had been voted Best Female Rock Vocalist by *Metal Edge* magazine, and Ozzy was voted Best Male Rock Vocalist at the same time. Together, both being managed by Sharon, we were a hit. I didn't know it at the time, but Sharon had tried to stop "Close My Eyes Forever" from being released. She didn't want Ozzy and me together on screen for the video, but I never understood this until much later. I went to the record company and asked them, "Is this true? Does she not want to release this as a single?" They said, "Yes, but we're going to release it anyway." For once, Sharon didn't get her way. It was released on my label under Lita Ford and became a Top 10 hit single, which is something none of us predicted. It is still one of the greatest rock ballads of all time, in my opinion. It was No. 8 on the Billboard Hot 100 list. Ozzy's first—and only—Top 10 hit single ever!

DURING THE RECORDING of the *Lita* album, I had a rare night off and needed to unwind. The Scorpions, the German heavy metal group, were playing a concert in Irvine, California. The Scorpions are one of my all-time favorite bands, with two great guitar players and one kick-ass vocalist, Klaus Meine. I headed down to Irvine by myself.

Irvine Meadows is an open-air amphitheater that holds approximately twenty thousand people. The only trouble with the place is the horrific traffic. It just doesn't move, especially when twenty thousand people are trying to get into or out of the same venue. As I was sitting on the freeway in traffic stopped dead, I was starting to get anxious. I said to myself, *Hell, I don't have to play tonight.* I was almost there and didn't need to worry about driving much farther, so I took out a joint I had with me. It was huge, but it was also organically grown pot that had purple hair on it. I lit it up and smoked it while I sat in that traffic. Oh my God, did I get stoned. My eyes were like slits I was so baked.

When I finally arrived at the show, I went backstage to say hello to the band and then planned on sitting in the audience. They were just about to go onstage when Doc McGhee, the Scorpions' manager at the time, saw me and called me over to talk. Doc is a great man. He said, "How would you like to jam with Klaus tonight?"

"Oh, Doc, thank you so much," I said, "but it's my day off, and I'm just going to go out in the audience to watch the show." Normally I would have loved to jam with the Scorpions, but not when I was stoned out of my mind. I headed to my seat, and on the way I spotted a white-chocolate cheesecake inside the Scorpions' dressing room. It was two tiers high with chunks of shaved white chocolate stacked up on the cake. The munchies had started to kick in, and I considered taking a slice, but then I heard the show starting so I quickly headed into the audience. But I thought about that cheesecake until the show was almost over. During one of the last songs I said to myself, *Fuck it. I need that cheesecake.*

I walked back to the empty stage area, and the only two people backstage were Sebastian Bach and Christina Applegate, who were making out. They didn't look like they were going to get between me and that cheesecake. I grabbed a great big piece and dove in. As I was chowing down, I could still hear the Scorpions playing in the distance, and then I heard Klaus say, "We have Lita Ford in the audience tonight! Lita, come up here and sing with me!"

Oh no! I started choking on my cheesecake. There was no way I could go out there! I was too baked, and the cake was more important to me in that moment. I had no idea how I was going to stay out of sight, and I was looking around for what I thought would be a safe place to hide for just a few minutes in case someone came looking for me. I looked at the table, which had a long, floor-length tablecloth on it, and decided to hide under there until it was "safe" to come out. So there I was, in the Scorpions' dressing room, stoned, hiding under a table with a slice of white-chocolate cheesecake in my hand. Thank God nobody found me.

After the show, Klaus said to me, "Lita, I called for you to sing with me, but you didn't come out." I felt like an asshole for leaving him hanging, but I didn't have the heart to tell him that I was too busy stealing his cheesecake—which was really fucking good, by the way. Now every time I see a piece of cheesecake, I think of the Scorpions.

AEROSMITH IS ANOTHER of my favorite bands, but whenever I try to go see them, something always seems to happen. The very first time I went to see them was at the California Jam II, held in Ontario, California, the site of the original Cal Jam. I got there and from the parking lot I heard Steven Tyler say, "Thank you, good night!" I wasn't even in the venue yet. There goes Aerosmith.

My second experience with Aerosmith was in 1989, and I remember wearing low-cut pants and a tiny shirt that came just under my boobs. We got to the venue and I went to my seat, which was about ten to fifteen rows from the stage, looking down from stage right. I noticed that there was someone in our seats.

"Excuse me, you're in my seat," I said to the girl who was sitting there.

She turned and spit in my face.

"You fucking cunt!" I hawked the biggest loogie I could and spat right back in her face. I had learned how to spit in the punk era, so I could launch a mean loogie.

Her boyfriend pulled his fist back and was going to hit me. The guy I was with hit him, and they both went tumbling down the stairs. My friend left his high school ring imprinted on the guy's forehead.

Security came running over.

"You're Lita Ford. Why are you watching the show from here?"

The girl who spit at me and her boyfriend got thrown out, and I got taken backstage. I got to sit next to the amp that Joe Perry's tech uses to hear what's going on, which was cool, but I wanted to see the show from the audience.

When we got backstage, Steven Tyler walked over to me, pushed me up against the wall, and planted a kiss on me. He looked me up and down, checking me out, and said, "Is it really you? You're really here?" Turns out he had always wanted to meet me, just like I had always wanted to meet him. I explained to him that I had been in the audience but that some chick had spit in my face and we had gotten into a fight in the stands.

"Holy fuck, that was you up there?" He had seen the whole thing from the stage. He had this huge bodyguard stay with us for the rest of the night.

As we were leaving through the loading dock, the girl who had spit on me and her boyfriend were waiting for us. The bodyguard walked me and my friend to my car, and we got out of there without further incident. To this day I still haven't seen an Aerosmith concert from start to finish. What is it about that band?

ON ANOTHER NIGHT off, in 1987, I went to see W.A.S.P. perform at the Long Beach Arena. I remember watching the guitar player, Chris Holmes. He was six foot six with long flowing hair and a handsome face. He looked hot and menacing when he was onstage. He resembled a Viking, but covered in tattoos. Back then nobody had that many tattoos, so it was different and interesting. I met him backstage after the show, and he turned out to be a really sweet guy. We exchanged phone numbers so we could meet up another night for some drinks. We decided to rendezvous at a club called the Cat House. Afterward we ended up at my apartment, and we started seeing each other from that night on. I would go with Chris on tour, and he would come with me.

I soon moved out of my parents' home and into a house with Chris in the Tujunga/Angeles Crest Mountains, which were twenty miles outside of Los Angeles with huge properties nestled in the mountain range. While living together, I found out that Chris is an awesome cook. He could make the best chicken chili I'd ever had, and he would often create delicious barbecue feasts. Who would have known that W.A.S.P.'s guitarist knew his way around the kitchen as well as he did a guitar?

As much as I loved Chris's house, I really wanted to be able to purchase a home of my own. Sharon and my producer Mike Chapman were kicking ass for me. Sharon brought me up to another level of success, just as I had hoped she would when I first asked her to manage me. I was making more money, in larger chunks, and I ended up buying my own dream home in Angeles Crest. It was a country-style house: one level, high beamed ceilings, a huge fireplace, and a backyard that overlooked a massive mountain range. My next-door neighbor had five horses and he used to open up the stables and the gate and they'd eat the long grass in my yard. He'd let us use the horses whenever we wanted, and we'd go horseback riding for hours into the mountains in the twenty-five miles of riding area of that range. We'd party all night, people would sleep over, and then the next morning we'd all go horseback riding. Even if they didn't know how to ride horses, I would put them on the horses anyway. It kept their mind off their hangovers, that's for sure. The trails were narrow and steep, and there wasn't much room for a mistake. Kim, my neighbor, would grind his own wheat and make awesome hotcakes for all of us when we'd get back from the ride. We'd see coyotes, snakes, and poison ivy. My dogs had full run of the yard. I had two rottweilers at the time; Chris had named them Chopper and Crusher. They were friendly dogs, but when Ozzy came over for a visit one day, they took one look at him, walking in his usual hunched-over stance with his hands sticking slightly out in front of him, and they started to growl. Ozzy backed off right away. Settling into that house was a wonderful moment in my life. I had plenty of time for partying, writing, and enjoying my own home. I had a guest room for my parents. But best of all, it was all mine.

BEFORE WE LEFT to go on tour with Bon Jovi in 1988, my father and I met up for our annual fishing trip to Oregon on the Deschutes River. We fished for steelhead salmon and trout, which is my favorite thing to do next to playing guitar. My dad drove there, and I flew in a couple of days later because I had to work.

When I arrived, I noticed him limping, which wasn't uncommon for him because he had tripped in the rocks a year before and twisted his ankle. I said, "Dad, did you twist your ankle again?" He said yes.

It wasn't bruised. I had a feeling he was lying, but I left it alone and decided to deal with it after the trip.

As we were driving home, I saw a huge tree trunk on the side of the road. I screamed to my dad, "Stop!"

My father said, "Why do you want me to stop?"

"Did you see that tree?" We pulled over and together we picked up the trunk and strapped it to the roof of the car. When we got back to

LA, I took it to B.C. Rich and asked Bernie Rico Sr. to make a guitar out of it. Bernie had the best luthiers in the country, and I knew he would make a beautiful guitar from that trunk. Neal Moser ended up being the luthier who built the guitar. Everyone at B.C. Rich wanted to know where I got the wood. It had three different types of maple in it: curly maple, burled maple, and fire maple. We didn't want to hide the beauty of that wood, so the guitar was coated with a resin finish instead of painted. I named the guitar Fishing Wood. Every time I play that guitar, it takes me back to the beautiful memory of fishing for steelhead and trout with my father.

I am so glad I asked my dad to stop for that tree trunk, because it gave me a memento of the last trip I ever took with him. Soon after we got back from Oregon, an entire side of my father's body became paralyzed. We took him to the hospital and he was admitted immediately. They told us he'd had a stroke, and that they'd found a giant brain tumor. They did a biopsy on it to see if it was malignant. The results came back: inoperable stage IV cancer. There was nothing they could do. I remember my mother screaming from the other room when she got the phone call. It was a sound I had never heard before.

Unfortunately, Chris wasn't very sympathetic during my father's illness. I had just moved in with him, and I really wanted to spend time together, but my father was sick and I needed to be there for him. Chris would get upset at me for visiting my father so often instead of spending the nights with him, and it frustrated me. He just didn't get it. Driving from Long Beach back up to Angeles Crest was exhausting, but I went to see my father as often as I could, regardless of what Chris said. Sometimes he would stay at my parents' house so I wouldn't have to make the drive back to Angeles Crest. I was dealing with Chris and coping with my father's illness. I was full of mixed emotions at the time.

ONE DAY WHILE leaving the hospital after visiting my father, Toni, my mother, and I were in the elevator when I noticed a lump on the side of my mother's neck. Toni and I looked at each other and knew exactly what it meant: my mother's cancer had come back.

My mother had originally been diagnosed with cancer in 1980, but she didn't tell me at first. I had invited her to come to Hawaii with me, but she said, "No, thank you, I'm going gambling in Vegas." I should have known something was up because she loved the beach and the sun. She ended up admitting herself to St. Mary Medical Center and had a mastectomy of her left breast. When I came home, she pulled open her shirt and showed me the scars left from the surgery. I knew I had let her down for not going with her. "Why didn't you tell me?" I said. I was crying, devastated.

"I didn't want to ruin your vacation," she said.

God bless her.

IN THE WEEKS that followed my father's stroke, he lost his speech, then his hearing, and then slipped into a coma. He passed in January 1988, soon after that fishing trip. My mother and I buried him with his favorite things: photographs and pieces of our jewelry. My mother and I were devastated. My father had always been my hero and my best friend. I was his only child: his daughter *and* his son. He taught me things most fathers did not teach their girls, like how to fish, hunt, shoot, hook a worm, and skin a fish. There was no fluff and pink lace in my childhood, but there was a lot of love and laughter. My father was the funniest man I'd ever met, and he loved me and my mother with all his soul. He was such a good man—the kind of man that as a woman, you wonder if you'll ever find for yourself. I never once heard my father raise his voice or argue with my mother. I could always call him to come bail me out of any situation and there would be no questions asked. Who was I going to call now?

Looking back, I'm saddened that my father never got to meet his two grandsons, James and Rocco. He grew up with nine female siblings. He was always surrounded by girls. Imagine if he knew he had two grandsons! There are no words to express how happy he would have been.

My parents had been happily married for forty-four years, and my father's death destroyed Mom. I had to go straight from the funeral to the airport to catch a flight to New York. What hurt the most was having to leave her behind, knowing she was sick and now had to deal with the void left in her heart by my father's death.

My father never got to see the success of the *Lita* album. I only wish that he had been there to enjoy those moments with me, as my father was always proud of me, but he was too ill at that point. I felt like something awful had happened in exchange for something really great. The album went platinum, and I was nominated in 1988 for an MTV award in the Best Female Rock Video category for "Kiss Me Deadly." I took Tommy Caradonna to the awards show with me, and he sat between me and Robert Downey Jr. He was nervous as hell on the red carpet, but he totally pulled it off. He looked so disappointed when "Kiss Me Deadly" didn't win. David Coverdale from Whitesnake and his wife, Tawny Kitaen—the hot chick who danced and did acrobatics on the hood of a car in the Whitesnake videos—sent me a huge basket of the most beautiful flowers with a note that read "You should have won, Lita."

Other bands like Warrant and Poison followed with similar videos after the MTV nomination. "Kiss Me Deadly" helped open the door for other rock bands to have a "hot rocker chick" star in their videos, and I can't help but wonder if David and Tawny's gift was a way of showing their appreciation for the look I had helped make so popular at the time.

SOON AFTER MY father died, Chris and I were talking and decided we would get married. It wasn't like we couldn't live the rest of our lives without each other. It was just something to do. We weren't a couple who walked around calling each other honey or baby. Marriage just came up in conversation; there was no real proposal. I think I agreed hoping Chris would fill the void left by my father's passing. If he had been alive, there is no way my father would have agreed to the marriage.

The wedding was in Lake Tahoe, Nevada, in 1988. I only invited my mother, Sharon Osbourne, and a few of my very close friends. Right before the wedding, my best friend's boyfriend asked me, "Lita, are you in love with Chris?"

I said, "No."

"Then why are you marrying him?"

I was trying to fill a hole in my heart.

Of course, marrying Chris did not do that. The night we were married, Chris met some stranger at the bar and spent the entire night talking to this drunk. I left him at the bar drinking. It was like our marriage was a kind of game. I went to my girlfriend's hotel room and stayed with her. The next morning I ran into my mother in the hallway. She said, "Lita, where are you coming from?"

"I was just getting coffee," I told her.

But she knew I didn't sleep with Chris that night. And we both knew I had just made a mistake.

BEFORE THE EVENTS of my father's death and then my marriage to Chris in 1988, though, I took my mother and my aunt Livia with me for the Italian dates of Jon Bon Jovi's New Jersey Syndicate tour, which was a thrill. Jon and I had been friends since my *Out for Blood* days, and I thought I'd be in good hands on the road with him. In late 1988, the tour lasted eight weeks throughout Europe. My goal was to get all three sisters together, and since my aunt Rosetta lived in Rome, I could make that happen. They weren't getting any younger, and I knew it was only a matter of time before they wouldn't be able to be together again. My aunt Livia was the youngest of the three sisters, and she would be the first to pass two years later. Every night before the show she'd say to me and the band, "Go kick ass!"

The New Jersey Syndicate tour was one of the biggest tours out there at the time. Our bands were a perfect fit. Jon was really nice and accommodating and was always asking if I needed any help with the monitors or anything. Of course, I'd had enough of taking his advice after the Lance Quinn incident.

Jon's band had learned a couple of Beatles songs for the tour, so if any celebs would show up, they'd be asked to get up and jam with Jon's band. One show at Wembley Arena he invited Elton John, Brian May from Queen, and Rick Allen from Def Leppard to come up and play "Come Together." I went running backstage to my bandmate Steve Fister and asked him to show me the guitar parts to that song. Then I went running back onstage. Jon scooped me up and swung me in his arms in front of a packed Wembley Arena. I was wearing a miniskirt. I whispered in Jon's ear, "I don't have any underwear on." Jon quickly put me down like a gentleman would, and I laughed and walked off to grab my guitar.

We got to our places onstage: Sir Elton John was on keyboards, Rick Allen on drums, Brian May and me on guitars, and Jon on the mic. What a surreal moment it was when we all started to jam. It was a blast and truly one of the best nights of my life and career.

At another stop on the tour, my drummer Charlie Dalba got to jam with me, Bon Jovi, and the Scorpions. That same night we went to an after party where I met the legendary blind guitarist Jeff Healey for the first time. He was sitting in a corner drinking some chicken soup. He got up and walked over to where the food was and was eating out of everyone else's discarded food trays. I took his chicken soup and handed him a bottle of champagne. "Here, drink this instead."

Jeff and I got drunk together off this bottle of champagne and he said, "Let's get out of here."

"What do you want to do?"

"We'll go back to my room and order some room service."

We tried to order food and they told us that we'd have to go down to the front desk and get a menu. Jeff led me to the elevators, and knew where everything was, which amazed me at the time. We got to the front desk and the guy working there said, "Would you like to see a menu?"

Jeff was completely drunk by this point and yelled, "I'm fucking blind! Are you kidding me?" We laughed hysterically. We went back up to his room and I ordered food for us. I will never forget how Jeff poured the wine for me—he didn't spill a drop. It was amazing to watch him. We ate and then went back to the party. I had my arm wrapped around his and was leading Jeff toward the party, but then I realized the party was downstairs, not upstairs. "Hey, Jeff, the party is down here." Before I knew it, we tripped on each other's feet, fell down the stairs, and flopped right into the Scorpions party. At that same party, Charlie Dalba hooked up with a gorgeous blonde. She later told him that she had come to the party with Richie Sambora. Turns out Charlie ended up taking the girl away from him without even knowing it! The next day Richie was pissed at Charlie. Oops!

I always traveled with my band on the tour bus, and I stayed in the same hotels as they did. They were family to me. I had also hired a keyboard player for the tour, Martin Gershwitz, who was a wonderful human being. He was very European, with long hair and a German accent. He was a joy to be around, but we always made fun of him because he wasn't really into personal hygiene. God bless him and I love him dearly, but he was a stinky guy. Every once in a while, one of us would buy him a can of Lysol, mouthwash, or deodorant as a gift. Once, there was a bee on the tour bus and I used the Aqua Net hairspray we had bought Martin as a blowtorch to kill it. The bus driver wasn't too impressed with me.

Our drummer Charlie had a video camera with him and would film everything we did—on the bus, at sound check, anywhere—and caught a lot of beautiful memories on tape. At one gig, one of Bon Jovi's security guards came into our dressing room while we played our set and took Charlie's camera. During the sound check that day, Charlie had been filming while they were testing the harness that Jon used to get strung across the stage and swung over the audience. The security guards thought he was going to sell the footage, and so they took his camera and erased it. They were also going to keep the camera. Jon came over and said, "You weren't gonna sell that, were you?"

"No, man. I just want to keep it to show my kids some day!" Charlie answered.

Jon Bon Jovi turned to the security guard and said, "Man, give him his camera back. He's not gonna sell anything." Charlie thought it was a really down-to-earth thing for a megastar like Jon to do.

Tommy, our bassist, used to like to run around all over the stage. Bon Jovi and their crew never gave Tommy any orders about what not to touch or where not to go onstage, unlike when we had opened for Ted Nugent. The Motor City Madman's crew wanted to know where you were going to stand and didn't want us putting our feet up on the monitors. I never told my band what to do onstage or where to stand. Sometimes that meant we'd run into each other, like the time Tommy was going nuts onstage and didn't notice me standing next to him until he swung around and hit me in the leg with the headstock of his Fender P-bass. I had apparently yelled out when he hit me, but the part Tommy remembered was that the next day, I had four bruises on my leg—from the four machineheads on his P-bass.

When we got to Paris, Jon and I had a chance to hang out. Jon said, "Lita, tonight I will take you anywhere you want to go." One of my favorite places in Paris was the Crazy Horse strip club. It is a high-class burlesque club that you needed to make reservations to get into months in advance, but because it was Jon Bon Jovi and Lita Ford, we got in right away.

I put on my favorite black lace dress with black high-heeled shoes and curled my hair, and Jon was dressed in a silver-gray suit, which complemented his light eyes. He looked very handsome, and he smelled so good. Jon rented a limo so we could drink and not worry about driving. First stop: the Crazy Horse. We drank champagne, more champagne, and *more* champagne. We stayed for hours at the Crazy Horse, watching the girls dance. They were hot! It was a turn-on, I have to say.

Then Jon said, "Let's go get something to eat." We were already drunk, and the dress I was wearing was skintight. There was no room for a big meal. We had some nibbles of food and drank the rest of our dinner by doing shots of tequila.

After we tore up Paris, we went back to Jon's hotel. I pulled off my dress and asked Jon for some sweats. By this time it was five A.M. and I had to get back to my hotel. Chris usually called me at around six A.M., so I wanted to be there for him when the phone rang in my room. I said my thank-yous to Jon in more ways than one, then I took off for a cab dressed in his sweats. He was so thoughtful and kind. As soon as I walked in the door of my hotel room, the phone was ringing. I ran to answer it. It was Chris. Phew. Good timing.

The next day, Sharon kept asking me, "What did he smell like?" I couldn't describe it, so we went to a mall and searched the men's cologne section, trying to find the one that smelled like Jon. We never did.

WE WERE DOING gigs, press, radio, photo sessions, and traveling from country to country. I was wiped out half the time. I asked Sharon if I could have one day of rest. She said to me, "If you can't take the pressure, then get the fuck out of the music business!" It was kind of a shitty thing for my manager to say to me. I'm not a complainer at all—she knew that. I was simply asking for one day of rest, but she refused.

That night we arrived in Munich, Germany, which was the headquarters for my record company, BMG (Bertelsmann Music Group). I crawled into my hotel room after arriving from the airport exhausted. We had just wrapped up the German leg of the tour and needed to be near the airport for an early departure the next morning. All I could think about was sleep. Almost instantly after arriving at the hotel, there was a knock at the door. A man with a huge arrangement of beautiful white flowers was standing there. I tipped the guy and he left the flowers in the room. I read the note that went with the flowers: "Lita, Welcome to Munich. Tonight we take you out to your favorite restaurant." It was signed by all the BMG executives.

To tell the truth, I was way beyond sleep, and if I didn't rest, I knew I would be sick. My immune system was running on empty, but how do you refuse your record company? I called them to try to explain to them that this was my only night off and I would love to go, but I needed the sleep so badly.

"No, no, no, Lita. You are in Germany. We must take you out tonight. I'll send a car for you at eight P.M." *Click*. The guy hung up. Oh, man. I could barely walk, I was so beat-up and tired. How was I going to pull this off?

Eight o'clock rolled around. I chose the same restaurant I had been to in the past so I was familiar with it. I walked in and was greeted by the entire artist-relations department. They were so kind and friendly. I ordered a soda, but they were not happy with me drinking soda, so I caved and ordered a shot of tequila, hoping to kill the pain of being exhausted. They brought me white tequila, which I had never had before. It tasted like nitroglycerin! Oh boy. This was going to get interesting.

After I had a few shots of this stuff, I was toast. I said to the artist rep from BMG, "Please get me out of here. Now!" He could see in my eyes that I wasn't doing well at all. He grabbed me under one arm while another rep grabbed me under my other arm, and we headed for the front door.

I remember that my feet were dragging behind me.

The BMG reps drove me back to the hotel. Being in the moving car made my head spin. I never even got a chance to order my food at the restaurant. I was so embarrassed.

When I got back to my hotel, I ran straight for the toilet bowl and puked my guts out again and again. Clearly I had alcohol poisoning combined with being exhausted, but I had a flight to Italy the next morning at six A.M. and there was no time to do much about my situation. The phone rang the next morning. It was my mother. She was so excited for me because I was going to Italy: her country. I told her how beat I was and how sick I was from last night. She said, "But, Lita, you are going to Italy. I'm going to order you an orange juice and some breakfast." Before I could tell her no, she hung up. I called her back and said, "Mom, I can't eat. I'll just puke it up." And then I threw up some more.

Six A.M. came around fast. I still had on my leather pants from the night before. The rest of my clothes were spread out all over my hotel room. Makeup everywhere. I wasn't packed at all! Sharon sent over her assistant Lynne to help me. Every time I moved an inch I had to vomit. Lynne placed my stuff on the bellman's trolley. I was still clutching the toilet bowl. "Lynne," I said, "if I move, I'm going to puke."

"So puke, then," Lynne told me.

I asked her for something to puke in while I tried to get through the lobby. I knew I wouldn't make it all the way to the car. She handed me a plastic bag. I made good use of it while I made my way to the car from the hotel room while they took care of the bill. I got in the cab and headed for the airport.

When we arrived at the airport in Germany, we had to check our bags, then get in a shuttle to take us to the gate. I was puking at every bathroom I could find. By now I was getting dehydrated and had the dry heaves, but I managed not to puke on the shuttle bus.

Of course when we got to the airplane, it was a small prop plane. Oh, fuck! Great. This wasn't going to help. I sat at the very back, in the last seat so no one could see me, and grabbed a sick bag out of the seat-back pocket. I still had the dry heaves, and everyone was looking at me for the entire flight.

When we arrived in Florence, Italy, I got off the plane and went straight to the shuttle, which took us to the terminal. Sharon and Lynne went to baggage claim while I went to the bathroom. Again. When we got in the vehicle, I closed my eyes, held my guts, and managed not to puke all the way to the hotel. An accomplishment.

After arriving at the hotel, I was relieved but exhausted. Sharon knocked on the hotel door and said, "How are you now? Any better?"

"Fucking horrible."

"Good. You're shooting the cover of an Italian magazine. You've got an hour and a half, then a car is picking us up."

What? Oh, dear God. Another car? Really?

"Okay, Sharon. I'll be ready," I promised. It's not like I had a choice.

When we arrived at the photography studio, everyone was excited to see us. They directed me to the makeup artist as I sat there sipping a soda, trying to munch on a Quarter Pounder. The makeup artist made me look beautiful. Wow, I sure didn't feel as good as I looked. They cranked some Aerosmith and I felt a whole lot better. I rocked out to the music while we shot the cover of this Italian magazine. The session was a success. It was a miracle.

After the photo shoot, I made my way to sound check for a show that night. No rest for the wicked. Unfortunately, I didn't get to see much of Florence outside of souvenir postcards. However, my mother had taught me to say "Good evening, Florence!" to the audience in Italian: *"Buona sera, Firenze!"* They went wild and we rocked them so hard. I was so beat-up but still kicked ass. Ah! The magical powers of a Quarter Pounder with cheese. Some things never change.

AT THE END of the European tour dates, there was a huge party. Jon had sixty-three people on his crew. I didn't go, because I am not good at good-byes. I sent him a note that said: "There will always be a place for you in my heart. Lita xo." Soon after that tour, Jon eventually married his girlfriend. I was really happy for them, and I wished them both well.

I flew home on Pan Am from London's Heathrow airport. For some reason, there was a last-minute change and we switched gates. I didn't think anything of it at the time. A limo picked me up at LAX. As soon as I walked in the door of my house I turned on the television and saw that a jumbo jet flying out of Heathrow headed to New York had gone down over Lockerbie, Scotland. Everyone was killed. The airplane had left from the very gate I was originally supposed to fly out of before the switch. *Oh my God. That could have been my plane.* I wondered if Jon or any of his crew were on that flight. (Thankfully they weren't.) I dropped to my knees and began crying in horror.

COMING HOME FROM Europe after the Bon Jovi tour, I was so jet-lagged and my system was so out of whack that I decided to go to my mother's house for a few days to get a home-cooked meal and some rest.

After a day of being home, I told my mother I had some stomach issues, probably due to jet lag.

"Mom, I can't go to the bathroom."

"Lita, what's wrong with you?"

"I haven't gone to the bathroom in three days and my stomach hurts."

"Oh, Lita, I'm going to get you the castor oil," she said in her Italian accent. "You'll go tomorrow morning."

I took the castor oil. Nothing. The entire day passed.

"Mom, the castor oil didn't work."

"Oh, Lita, we'll get you the Ex-Lax." I was on day five by this point.

I took the Ex-Lax, and nothing happened.

"Mom, nothing is happening. I have all of England, Ireland, and Germany in me and I feel awful."

"Oh, Christ, Lita, we're gonna have to get you a dynamite."

So I went to the health-food store and got Smooth Move tea. I made it using four tea bags instead of one. It was really strong. The next day, still nothing.

"Mom, I need to go to the bathroom. I feel like I'm going to die. What am I going to do?"

I was in Long Beach and had a lunch-hour meeting in Hollywood. I was stuck in the midday rush-hour traffic on the 101, going two miles an hour in the fast lane, when I felt all of England drop into my lower intestines.

"Holy fuck! I've gotta shit and I've gotta shit now!"

I managed to pull off the freeway, and the only place I could find was a tiny little hotel. I went flying past the front desk yelling, "Where's the bathroom?"

I get into the bathroom, and I'm shitting out all of Europe while holding my tampon string. All of a sudden, I notice there's someone's eye looking through the crack of the bathroom stall.

"Excuse me?"

"Excuse me, but are you the girl who sings 'Kiss Me Deadly'?"

"Yes, I am. And if you wait for me in the lobby, I'll give you whatever you want," I said in a panic, my voice cracking.

"My daughter would love an autograph. She loves you."

"Oh, how nice. I'll be right out and give you an autograph."

I sat in there for about ten to fifteen minutes and then walked out and gave her an autograph, but I felt like I carried the smell with me. God, the luxuries of touring.

Sharon threw us a beautiful party after we got back from the Bon Jovi tour. She had a gorgeous old house that was built in the 1800s with something like twenty-four rooms. She had a tent and hosted Bon Jovi, me, and our crews. They had drums and amps set up and we all jammed; Jon's drummer, Tico Torres, got so drunk that he fell backward over the monitors and into the drum set. We all had such a great time.

PRIOR TO THE Bon Jovi tour, we were opening for Poison on their US tour in support of their album *Open Up and Say . . . Ahh!* I kept to myself on that tour and didn't get too friendly with the guys in Poison because of the way they treated women back then. It scared me away, although the tour was awesome.

During the show, they would have one of the road crew pick women out of the audience, then after the gig they would herd them into a room backstage. The band would go into the room and take their pick of which woman they wanted to be with that night. The rest were offered to the road crew, for second pickings, or sent home. I hated this and didn't want anything to do with these guys because of it. It was disgusting. The women probably thought they were going to a party, but they were just pieces of meat for the band and crew that one night. It was a game to them. It was degrading to women in general, and it was upsetting to me to see other women being treated like fucking cattle.

I never partied with them or went on their bus. Chris came with me to a few shows, so I mostly stuck with him and my band. The final stop of the tour was Dallas. On the last day of the tour, the headlining band often plays a prank on the other band. That night, right in the middle of my set, I saw something coming down from the rafters. I looked closer and saw it was my roadie and one of my best friends,

Roger. He had been duct-taped to a chair and was hanging from the rafters. The crowd starting cheering. I began laughing even though I was really pissed. I kept right on playing. Then another roadie came down from the rafters. Poison's crew started throwing pies at the band. Steve and Martin got hit, but Tommy managed to dodge every pie they threw at him. During "Kiss Me Deadly" they poured a huge bag of flour all over Charlie and his drum kit. He kicked his kit right over and dumped the whole rack forward. The crowd cheered louder. Poison was ruining our show. Then a male dancer comes out of nowhere and starts humping me; all of a sudden a bucket of whipped cream came down all over me. That was it. I was pissed off. These guys didn't know me. They weren't my friends. We didn't hang out together. Who the fuck did they think they were?

I was using Bret Michaels's wireless mic that night because mine wasn't working. I held it in my hand, ready to throw it at something. I didn't want to toss it into the audience in case it hit someone, so I sent it flying as hard as I could back over the drums. It struck the top of the backdrop curtain and came down onto the ground. The sound man couldn't find it, because he wasn't sure where I had thrown it, and all he could hear were people walking back and forth, because the mic was still on. Then I jumped forward off the stage and into the orchestra pit. I ran around to the side of the stage because the audience was gated. On the side stage I saw all of Poison's keyboards lined up, polished and clean and ready to go onstage. This was thousands of dollars' worth of equipment with all their backing tracks in them. I kicked them over one by one, sending them flying, destroying bits and pieces of their keys, and wiping out their backing tracks. Next I saw C.C. DeVille's guitars all lined up, cleaned, and polished. "Tie up my road crew," I mumbled under my breath. "Who do you think you are?" The Italian in me was coming out. I was fuming, my blood was boiling, and I was already pumped up from the show.

I made my way for C.C.'s guitars. I thought that if I kicked the first one, maybe it would trigger a domino effect and they would all fall over. I lifted my boot, ready to kick over the first guitar, when I felt two large arms being wrapped around me from behind. They were holding my arms down and picked me up so my feet weren't touching the ground. It was Poison's tour manager, a six-four dude. He carried me from stage left to stage right, where the buses were. On the way I managed to work one of my arms free. Just as we passed Bret I punched him in the jaw. "Fuck with me and my crew, Bret," I yelled out. "Fuck you!"

The tour manager took me back to the bus where Chris was just waking up and didn't have a clue as to what was going on. He saw that I was in a bad mood and he said, "What's the matter with you? Did you get a little bit of whipped cream on you?" I slept on the bus that night, having nowhere to shower and no hotel where I could clean up. I did get some joy from the fact that Poison's show was delayed by an hour and a half because of faulty backing tracks. The next morning Chris said, "Eww, you smell like sour cream." *No shit!* Thanks.

TWO YEARS LATER I was leaving a recording studio in West Hollywood. In the dark, coming from the parking lot, I could see a familiar shadow walking toward me. As he got a little closer I realized it was Bret. I hadn't seen him since that night in Texas. How was I going to handle this? I wasn't about to turn around. Shit. We had to pass each other. As we got closer, I took a step sideways and stood in front of him. He looked down at the ground. I stuck out my hand and said, "No hard feelings?" He looked up at me, smiled, shook my hand, and said, "No hard feelings." We both laughed and then went about our business. Years later, in 2012, we would tour together again, this time with Def Leppard.

CHAPTER 11

LISA

Lisa, Lisa, say you're gonna live forever,

Only you know who I am,

Only you really understand.

—"LISA"
(WRITTEN BY LITA FORD AND MICHAEL DAN EHMIG)

IN THE LATE 1980S, PUTTING A WOMAN ALONE ON THE COVER OF A ROCK
magazine still was unheard of. To her credit, Gerri Miller, who ran
Metal Edge magazine, used me on the cover all the time—but always
crammed alongside lots of other guys, sometimes twenty or thirty
dudes. Then along came my dear Lonn Friend. We met while he was
a senior editor at *Hustler* magazine; Lonn had interviewed me for a
feature for the music section of that magazine. (Yes, it was more than
nudie pics.) After seven years at *Hustler,* he left to become the editor
of *RIP* magazine, one of the top hard-rock/heavy metal publications
in the United States. Lonn had a pedigree in porn and sexuality. Larry
Flynt, the owner of *Hustler*'s porn empire, had told him, "Rock and roll
will come and go, but sex will always sell." Coming fresh from *Hustler*,
Lonn knew the impact that a cutting-edge cover photo would have on
the rock world. And so in October 1988, for Lonn's first issue as editor
of the magazine, *RIP* plastered me on the cover in skintight leather and
high heels, holding a gorgeous black guitar, under the headline OUR

EXCLUSIVE COVER STORY: LITA FORD GROWS UP (WOAH!). That definitely broke the ice. Way to go, Lonn!

At that time, the men were looking more like women than the women were anyway. It was all becoming androgynous, so Lonn said "it made sense to put women with chops and credibility on the cover. They deserve just as much pulp as the men." It was groundbreaking news and a few months later he mixed things up again when he put Doro Pesch and me together on the same cover. Doro is a hard-rock singer from Germany with a huge heart; she's a wonderful person. She bought me a gift of perfume when she came to the session. I was so flattered. It was a magical photo session and that issue was the number-one-selling issue of 1989. It made a statement about the importance of allowing women to compete on equal footing in rock and roll. The testosterone was so heavy at the time that you had to have balls or a background to even get on the bill. Lonn Friend seemed to be one of the few who got it. Lonn said, "What's better than a hot blonde with a guitar? Two hot blondes on the cover of *RIP*!"

Lonn made *RIP* a special magazine. Rock fans would look forward to it coming out each month. Then, in early 1989, Lonn said to me, "Do you think your mother would want to write an advice column?"

I said, "You mean like 'Dear Abby'?"

Lonn replied, "Yes, exactly!"

Of course, with me having grown up in the Runaways, my mother was the right person for the job. She knew everyone in the industry by the time the Runaways were through. And so we made the column happen—it was called Dear Mama Ford. Fans would write in and Lonn would forward the letters on to my mother in the mail. They'd send her questions about relationships, drugs, music, homosexuality, tattoos, music, and all kinds of other topics. Sometimes my mother would get stuck and call me. She'd say, "Lita, what do I say to this one? Do they really do that, Lita?"

Ha ha! "Yes, Mom, they do that!"

"Oh, okay then." She was paid on a weekly basis and it helped take

I love this wedding photo of my parents, Harry Lenard "Len" Ford (wearing his British Army uniform) and Isabella Benvenuto. They were married on January 19, 1945, in Trieste, Italy.

My dad with his beloved Norton motorcycle. He had the soul of a rocker.

My mom and I hit a high note at our flat in South London.

Me with my first guitar, my favorite possession, in our Long Beach, California, home. Little did I know where it would take me . . . *Len Ford*

A Runaway flanked by her parents. *Brad Elterman*

A publicity photo for our 1976 tour. *Left to right, back:* me (lead guitar), Sandy West (drums), and Jackie Fox (bass); *front:* Cherie Currie (vocals) and Joan Jett (rhythm guitar). *Chris Walker*

Left to right: Laurie McAllister, Sandy West, Joan Jett, and me during the filming of a video for "Mama Weer All Crazee Now."
Donna Santisi

"Punk lives": Thrashing at the El Mocambo in Toronto, 1978. *Doug Cawker*

Maestro Kim Fowley with the band at the Whisky A Go-Go. *Henry Diltz/Corbis*

At Rusk Studios: Joan and I powwow with John Alcock *(third from left)*. *Donna Santisi*

Joan and I share a rare moment together during the filming of a video for "Mama Weer All Crazee Now." We never connected personally, but what we accomplished together has stood the test of time. *Donna Santisi*

Left to right: Laurie McAllister *(rolling a joint)*, me, Sandy, and Joan in a hotel room on tour, 1978. *Toni Francavilla*

Have blackberry brandy, will travel. *Donna Santisi*

With the Hamer Explorer–shaped cake that the Runaways got me for my twenty-first birthday. *Donna Santisi*

Hanging with Johnny Ramone. *Jenny Lens*

Stepping out on my own:
A filmstrip from the
Out for Blood era — circa 1983.
Donna Santisi

Me and Jon Bon Jovi, 1990. Jon, we'll always have Paris, baby.
Ron Galella/Getty Images

Young love: Me and Nikki Sixx. I bought Nikki his first tattoo—seen here in the reflection in the mirror. *Jack Lue*

The poster for Jon Bon Jovi's New Jersey Syndicate Tour dates in Italy. Look who got top billing.

Me and Ozzy Osbourne in 1989, while we were both managed by Sharon. Our duet "Close My Eyes Forever" was a Top 10 hit.
Gene Kirkland

Cover girl: *Rip*, October 1988.

Metal's revenge: Tony Iommi, me, and Geezer Butler take on the guys from Spinal Tap. I actually loved the movie! *Toni Francavilla*

Jamming with my onetime hero, Black Sabbath's Tony Iommi. After we got engaged, I saw a very different side of the man. *David Plastik/Getty Images*

With my band, my true soulmates, in 1984. *Ray Palmer*

Out with my first husband, Chris Holmes. Marital bliss eluded us whenever the party ended. *Lisa Darbon*

Mama Ford, shortly before her passing. Her loss cast me adrift. *Gene Kirkland*

Pregnant with James, my first child, 1997.
Motherhood was a precious gift in my
otherwise tragic second marriage.
Cynthia McCarthy

Me and my "Sweet Baby James,"
1998. *Cynthia McCarthy*

Rocco (*left*) and James (*right*) in
the Turks and Caicos Islands.
The boys were my lifeline
during the most difficult period
of my life.

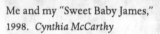

Welcome to the
family business:
Rocco (*left*) and James
(*right*) pose with
me and "Grandpa
Alice"—Alice
Cooper, that is.

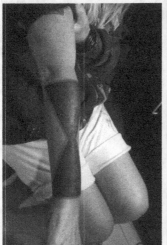

One of the first things I did after filing for divorce in 2010 was to cover up the tattoo of my husband's name on my arm.

In the studio with Gary Hoey (and my dog Churro) while recording *Living Like a Runaway*, 2012. Gary and his wife, Nicole, gave me sanctuary while I was finalizing my divorce. *Matt Scurfield*

Missing my kids, Malmo, Sweden, 2013. *Henrik/In the Rearview Mirror*

It broke my heart to write "Mother," but it was essential to the grieving process. It's been inspiring to see the fans' response too. Here's a pic I took of a fan who had the lyrics tattooed on her back.

The Black Widow returns. *Erin Williams*

I took it as a sign when this real black widow visited my apartment. *Left:* Here she is trapped in Tupperware. *Below:* My bandmate Marty O'Brien shows off the paperweight he made out of the bitch. *Marty O'Brien*

I have the greatest fans in the world. They give me so much love, and my mission is to give it back. Here I'm playing in Three Forks, Montana. *Marty O'Brien*

My band of brothers: Patrick Kennison, me, Marty O'Brien, and Bobby Rock. *Dustin Jack*

LAX, zero-dark-hundred: Life on the road isn't for everyone, but I love it.

One of my favorite honors: *Guitar Player's* Certified Legend Award. *Marty O'Brien*

You never know who you're going to run into; this time it was Nikki. It's been a blast to reconnect with my buddies from the old days. *Marty O'Brien*

Facing the light: I still cry for my boys every night, but after years in the darkness, I feel blessed that my fans let me wear the crown of "the Queen of Metal." Don't count on my giving up the title any time soon!
Peter Fagerbacka

her mind off the fact that my father was gone. My father had died in January of the year prior, so Dear Mama Ford was a really cool thing for her and the magazine.

MY ALBUM *STILETTO* was released in May 1990, and it was produced again by Mike Chapman. The cover was shot by Herb Ritts, who had photographed icons such as Madonna, Michael Jackson, David Bowie, Nicole Kidman, Tom Cruise, Michael Jordan, Cindy Crawford, Elizabeth Taylor, Richard Gere, and many more. However, if you look, you won't find his name in the credits. At the time, he didn't want to be associated with heavy rock. I never liked him after that. We paid him WAY too much money for what he did. He thought his talents were more special than they really were, in my opinion.

Holly Knight, who was known for writing some of Tina Turner's, Aerosmith's, Pat Benatar's, Heart's, and John Waite's biggest songs, cowrote the title track with me. Working with Holly Knight was an absolute honor. She's a great writer and a better person. I went on to become Holly's maid of honor at her wedding. I asked her if I could bring my husband, Chris, with me, and Holly said, "He has to remain on his best behavior or he can't come."

I told Chris, "Holly said, 'Put on a suit, and don't get drunk!'"

Chris listened to every word Holly said. He was a complete gentleman that night, and I was proud of him. My expectations were pretty low!

"Dedication" is a song that was written by Mike Chapman. It was basically written with two chords. It forced us to give the song dynamics without changing the chord structure, and that gave the song a lot of attitude.

"The Ripper" was the song I wanted to write with venom. It's fast and aggressive—a real guitar-driven song. In my mind were all the times I had been told that someone didn't "know what to do with me." I thought, *Who says girls can't play guitar?* It gave me that fire I needed to play its solo. I downed a pint of Jack Daniel's and played that solo with such aggression. The whiskey definitely helped with the attitude. I think it's one of my favorite solos of all time: it takes you to a different place.

FILMMAKER PENELOPE SPHEERIS contacted Chris to be one of the rock stars she interviewed for her 1988 documentary *The Decline of Western Civilization Part II: The Metal Years*. She used Chris for an infamous scene shot by a pool where he pours out a half-gallon vodka bottle on his face, while his mom looks on, and proudly declares, "I'm a full-blown alcoholic." I was standing there watching her record it, thinking, *What is she filming?* He was performing for the camera, giving Spheeris what he thought she wanted. It was a horrible thing to do to Chris. It made Chris look pathetic. I'm sure she didn't think for a second it would help destroy his career, but in my opinion it did.

Chris and I used to have some intense but silly arguments. He had come home drunk and cocky one day and our argument became heated. I was so angry. I took one of his favorite guitars out into the middle of the road and smashed it to pieces. Chris took the incident in stride.

"Where is my guitar?" he said.

Ah, yeah! It was in the road, it was on the trash, it was in the driveway . . . it was everywhere.

"Do the pickups still work?" he said in a really monotone voice.

"I don't know. Probably."

I had a Stratocaster that Yngwie Malmsteen had given me on tour. It was a vintage white/faded yellow guitar with a scalloped-out ebony fretboard. Shortly after the guitar-smashing incident, my gorgeous Strat magically disappeared. I wonder where it went? Chris said he didn't do it.

MY MOTHER WAS one of the finest women in the world as far as I'm concerned. Such a lady. She spoke fluent Italian; she never used bad language, smoked or drank too much liquor, and never dressed in risqué clothes. She was always kind to people no matter if she liked them or not. If they were black or white, stoned or straight, my parents didn't care. My mother was a diamond. She was so beautiful inside and out. Wherever she went, people fell in love with her. After the death of my father, she went everywhere with me. During the next few months, I would call my mother and say, "Mom, meet me at LAX. Bring a friend. Tomorrow we fly to Rome." Or New York. Or Texas. Always somewhere. She didn't want to go home. I took her to the New York City Music Awards in New York City, where I was asked to be a presenter. All the biggest stars were going to be there, including Tina Turner, Keith Richards, Little Richard, et cetera. I knew my mother would like seeing them.

I was having my hair and makeup done, getting ready to go onstage to present the award. My mother was tired of waiting for me. She said, "Lita, I'm going to wander around and talk to some of the guests while you finish getting ready."

I said, "Okay, Mom. I'll be done soon, and I'll come find you."

Well, I wasn't done soon. My hair was a production, my makeup had to be perfect, and my clothes were tight as tight could be, so it was a process to get into them. The whole thing took me a couple of hours.

When I was finally finished getting ready, I went looking for my mother. The show was starting and I needed to know if she was okay, where she was going to sit, and so on.

I walked around the entire backstage and couldn't find her. I looked everywhere. Finally, I found her sitting on a sofa backstage with a guy. I walked up to them and my voice cracked from nerves as I called out, "Mom!"

She looked up and saw me standing there and said, "Oh, Lita! I was just talking to Dave. He wanted an orange juice." She was hanging with David Bowie! Holy Christ. *Good choice, Mom,* I thought to myself.

I knew David Bowie reminded her of my father. He was handsome and charming and had that British accent. His blue eyes were similar to my father's too. I shook his hand and he looked at me from head to toe. He turned back to my mother and said, "Is this your daughter?"

"Yeah, Dave. Dat's Lita," my mother answered in her Italian accent. She was a proud mama.

"Do you always let her dress like that?"

"Yeah, Dave," she told him. "Dat's rock and roll."

I said, "Hi, David, nice to meet you." And then, "Come on, Mom. I have to present the award soon." My mother shook David Bowie's hand and said, "Wonderful to meet you, Dave."

As we walked away I told my mother, "You have amazing taste in men!"

"Why, Lita?" she asked, not knowing anything about David Bowie.

The show was starting, and I didn't have time to explain. "Just trust me on this one, Mom."

She grinned.

ONE DAY IN 1988, I got a call from my mother's best friend, Jaylee. She told me, "You need to come and see your mother right now." When I walked in, I asked my mother what had happened. She told me she had been driving home from work and all of a sudden she couldn't see well and pulled over to the side of the road. She knocked on a stranger's door and asked to use their phone to call Jaylee to come get her. My mother had had an anxiety attack that had been brought on by the death of my father. After that, my mother never drove again, and she never went back to work. This was the beginning of the end for her, sadly.

Her cancer had spread. I thought I was going to lose my mind. I went outside and did something I'd never done before: I said a prayer and asked God to help her, to let her live for three more months. *Don't take her from me yet.* I didn't think that was too much to ask. Three months! *Thank you, God, for listening to my prayers.* I moved in with my mother into the house in Long Beach where I took care of her. Chris came down on occasion.

My mother hated Chris's drinking. I hired a registered nurse to care for her when I couldn't be there.

When I first heard my mother was diagnosed with breast cancer, I wanted to give her a gift. A lot of people write their loved ones a song after they die, but I wanted to finish it while she was still alive. I wanted to give her something she could watch being made and recorded, that she could take with her to show her best friends: something to take her mind off the horrible things that were happening to her, not to mention the recent loss of my father.

I decided to write a song called "Lisa" for her. When my mother first moved to the USA, no one could say her real name, Isabella. So they called her Isa for short. Jaylee, who was from Texas, nicknamed my mother Lisa Jean, which was hysterical because of her thick Italian accent.

It was a very difficult song to write. How do you put pen to paper to create a song for your dying mother? I wrote the guitar part first. It's an intricate acoustic progression that seemed like a gift from God. Some of the parts were written backstage on one of Chris's guitars while W.A.S.P. played the Hammersmith Odeon in late 1989.

I was in a writing session with a songwriter named Mark Spiro, who cowrote "Bad Boy" on the *Stiletto* album. Mark Spiro is represented on more than one hundred million records worldwide, but the song I wrote with him wasn't the track that rose from this album. Instead, it was another song I wrote with Michael Dan Ehmig, whom I had met in Mark Spiro's driveway. When I crossed paths with Michael Dan, I felt as if I had known him my whole life, like he was a brother, even though we had just met. Turns out he had watched a VHS tape of mine after that first meeting, and he had told his publishing people about this "phenomenal person who has this great song. Do you think I could write with her?" They said yes, and he called me soon after.

I answered the phone, "Michael Daaaaaaan! I haven't been able to stop thinking about you!"

I bonded with Michael instantly, and I told him, "I want to write a

song about my mother." I already had written a beautiful guitar piece
for the song.

"Well, Lita, my mom and I have always been close, so I'm the guy
for that."

That reassured me, because my mom and I were as close as a mother
and daughter could be. We weren't a cliché. My mother and father had
always been my biggest fans all my life. Most moms would have been
afraid to have a daughter in a rock band, but not mine. I just couldn't
come up with the words for a song about how much she meant to me,
but I knew deep in my heart that Michael was the guy who could con-
jure the right language. I could feel it. He asked me about my mother,
and I told him all the wonderful things I could think of. I started to play
him the guitar piece, and the words just flew out. It wasn't tedious or
a struggle. It was like magic. After writing a song like that, you don't
just say good-bye and walk away. You become family. At least we did.
"Lisa" became my most powerful ballad next to "Close My Eyes Forever." Together, Michael and I would go on to write some of the era's
greatest hits. "Lisa" was both the beginning of a lifelong friendship and
the song that my mother would take to her grave.

"HUNGRY" WAS ANOTHER collaboration with Michael Dan, and one of
my favorite songs on that album. After the magic of creating "Lisa"
together, I told Michael Dan that I wanted to write something really
in your face and sexual, like George Michaels's "I Want Your Sex"
but from a girl's perspective. I couldn't wait to see what Michael Dan
would come up with. He sent me the first verse to the song, and he
told me later that he thought I'd find it awful, but I absolutely loved
it! I thought it was brilliant. He said he had been watching the *Dating Game* on TV and this woman described her date as someone who
"melted the nylons right down my leg." Michael said to me, "How
about you call it 'I'm Hungry for Your Sex'?" The name "Hungry"
stuck, though the song presented some challenges for Michael, who is
a devout Mormon. He told me that one guy at his church went up to

him, put his arm around him, and said, "You know some of the young people in the church really look up to you. What's this 'Hungry' song about?"

"There's another one too, called 'Cherry Red,' that a Chippendales dancer in Las Vegas is dancing to, so you might as well go buy the album and listen to it all and decide if you still want me in your church," Michael answered. They didn't throw him out, but I'm sure the songs turned some heads among the members of his church, to say the very least!

At the time, a song like "Hungry"—sung by a female—wasn't something that would get played on the radio. As a result, it was banned from radio, and the video turned out to be a disaster. Jesse Dylan, the director, thought it would be a good idea to have a child in a video for a song with sexually charged lyrics. It was supposed to have been an Alice in Wonderland–type concept, but it would have looked more at home in a video for Jefferson Airplane's "White Rabbit." I think Jesse Dylan did a fucking horrible job and cost me a fortune. With a large lump sum, he produced a video that looked cheap to my eyes. I had chosen Jesse Dylan because he was a familiar name, and Sharon wasn't around to offer advice. But it was a disaster. It was banned in the UK, and MTV chose not to air it because of the strong sexual lyrics, although they had no problem playing 2 Live Crew's "Me So Horny." Another fucking battle for me as a female in the industry. With a $300,000 budget for a video you'd think that your manager would have been involved, but Sharon was back in England fighting her own battles.

WHILE RECORDING *STILETTO,* my bandmates—Myron Grombacher on drums, Donnie Nossov on bass, and David Ezrin on keys—and I would hibernate in the recording studio, then come up for air and food. It was like the movie *Goodfellas:* work and lots of food. One of the first times Michael Dan came to the studio while we recorded some demos of the songs we had written, I was craving English chocolate, so I gave him about $100 and asked him if he'd run over to the specialty shop.

"There's a little shop on Sunset and they have all kinds of English chocolate."

It was more like a chocolate warehouse. He was gone for about an hour. When he got back, he had made his way from the elevator in the back into the recording studio with a huge brown paper grocery bagful of chocolates. Michael told me years later that I was leaning up against the mixing console, with my head back and my eyes closed, playing my guitar. When I opened my eyes, I noticed Michael standing in the doorway, shocked and mesmerized. I smiled and closed my eyes again and kept playing. When I get into that zone, it takes me to a special place—I can't stop playing. I played for another two minutes or so, then turned to Michael and said, "Did ya bring any chocolate?"

"Lita, I had no idea! I knew you could sing, you're beautiful, and you're a performer, but I didn't know you could play like *that*! It sounded like Eric Clapton or Leslie West was playing in here!" He handed me the big brown paper bagful of English chocolates, still astonished.

"Oh wow, did you get any change?" I asked.

He thought I had meant to spend the entire wad of cash on chocolates. Oh well. It definitely didn't go to waste! And I certainly didn't mind.

AS A FOLLOW-UP to *Lita*, *Stiletto* should have gone quadruple platinum. We all expected it to skyrocket. But that didn't happen. Bob Buziak was gone, and the BMG/RCA record label was in turmoil. There was no leadership. A lot of the top folks at the company left when Bob was let go. They were trying to figure out who to bring in and what to do, and as a result, the album didn't get the promotion it should have.

That was the beginning of a downward spiral for me.

Meanwhile Sharon Osbourne was letting me slip through the cracks. I had done a cover of Alice Cooper's "Only Women Bleed," and I thought that with "Hungry" having had the issues it did, it would make a great comeback single. At four A.M. one night, I was sitting quietly with a friend listening to the radio, and Cooper's "Only Women Bleed" came on the radio. I heard it and thought to myself, *That's it! I have to cover this song. It would be perfect*. I asked Mike Chapman what he thought, and Mike was up for the challenge. "Yes ! Let's do it." I had called Dick Wagner, who was once Alice's guitar player; he taught me the guitar parts over the phone. It turned out great.

But Sharon said, "You can't release it as a single."

I said, "Really, Sharon? Why not?"

She answered, "Because there is another artist out there who just released 'Only Women Bleed.'" What the fuck was she talking about? "There's another band who has recorded and released it. It's out and doing well," she said.

"I haven't heard anything like that, Sharon."

She said, "I have. It's really great. Radio is playing their version." To this day, I have no idea what band Sharon was talking about. I was really pissed because the amount of effort it took to rerecord that song was enormous. Mike had two guys come in to provide backing vocals. They sang like angels but looked like plumbers with their butt cracks showing. They were characters. The guitars were a challenge because I had to duplicate two of my favorite players, Steve Hunter and Dick Wagner. I learned pedal-steel guitar, lap steel, and improved my slide-guitar playing. The song even had an orchestra on it. I couldn't fuck it up. I didn't want to give anyone any more reason to bag on me, or to say that Alice Cooper's version was better. It had to kick ass, and I had to own it. When we recorded it, I felt it was a masterpiece. Nobody could have done a better version. Sharon was full of bullshit.

Sharon also helped ruin my relationship with Mike Chapman. She was against putting a song that he had written on the album, and it created a rift between Mike and me. I said, "Sharon, Mike has artistic control over the album. If he wants to put the song on the album, he can."

"Not if you fire him," she said. It was terrible advice.

Fire Mike? Oh my God, no! But at the same time, I had my doubts about the song. I let Mike know Sharon and I didn't love it, but he was pushy and insisted it was a hit. I didn't agree and neither did Sharon, but at this point I wasn't sure who to listen to. I ended up firing Mike Chapman, and we didn't do the song. No one has recorded it since.

As much as I truly loved Sharon, I couldn't help but feel she was undermining my hard work. I continued to wonder if she thought I had fucked Ozzy. Maybe that was why she was doing this. Let me tell you, he was fucking everything that moved, so to speak—*except* me.

Sharon managed me during the worst time of Ozzy's drug use. A few weeks after the release of "Close My Eyes Forever," I went to a party full of celebrities, and I ran into Ozzy. He looked at me, pointed his finger in my face, and said, "Do I know you? I know you, right?"

"Holy fuck, Ozzy. We have a top-ten hit single together." The one and only top-ten hit single *you've* ever had in your life, and you don't know my name? Wow!

He stared at me blankly. I walked off. The lights were on, but nobody was home.

Ozzy and Sharon's marriage was in trouble, and it was affecting the working relationship I had with Sharon. She said she was going to put Vixen on tour with Ozzy, not me. *What?!* Nothing against Vixen, but what kind of manager puts another female band of Lita Ford wannabes on the tour with her husband, Ozzy Osbourne, when *we* were top ten on the US charts? Not only was I fighting the music industry, now I felt I was battling my manager too. Sharon evidently didn't want me anywhere around her Ozzy.

The last straw was when I had a show at the Long Beach Arena, and I couldn't get her on the phone. It was a huge gig for me because I was in my hometown, at the arena where I had first seen so many of the biggest bands. I had tried to speak with Sharon for days prior to that gig. I got no response. Nothing! I was starting to get annoyed, and I needed my manager. She never returned my calls. The night of the Long Beach show, I called her hotel and told her I was coming over. When I arrived at her hotel door, it was ajar and she said, "Come in." Sharon and Ozzy were lying in bed with the covers up to their necks, trying to convince me they were all ready to go to sleep. I threw my hands up in the air and walked out. That was it. I was done with the bullshit.

I was truly heartbroken when I had to fire her, but I felt she was no longer helping me. She seemed to be doing the opposite: sinking me. Ozzy was incredibly fucked up on drugs all the time; it felt like I was going down with both of them. It was a horrible feeling, but I knew I had to jump off the ship or go under.

I took her out to lunch to fire her. We had a very civil discussion. In the middle of it, I excused myself to use the restroom, and when I came back, I saw Sharon walking out of the restaurant. I backed up toward the restroom and didn't go after her. I was relieved she was leaving. It was over.

THE 1990 VIDEO for the song "Lisa," directed by Wayne Isham, was magic. He used the original 8 mm film and photographs that my father had shot of me and my mother when I was four years old living in England. I could see that I looked just like my beautiful son, Rocco. I was the spitting image of him at that age.

My mother was there when we filmed the video. She was so proud. Although it was incredibly hard for us, writing and filming "Lisa" was a really great way of helping her to take her mind off her cancer and the hell she was going through. It was my way of letting her know just how incredible I thought she was.

She even came on the next Mötley Crüe tour with me. We put "Lisa" in my set, and each night I dedicated it to my mother. She sat backstage with her nurse, watching me from a wheelchair, an oxygen tank attached in case she needed it. As I played the song live I would look back over my shoulder at my mother, so proud of her song. I would get a lump in my throat, which made it hard to sing. I had to fight back the tears, watching this beautiful woman in her last days sitting in her wheelchair. This was not the woman who had raised me. My mother was always so full of life and a force of nature. It was so hard to watch her like that. I felt completely helpless.

By this point, my mom was going through chemotherapy every two weeks. She took the "Lisa" video with her every time she went to the hospital. She played it for the doctors over and over again. The doctors and nurses must have been sick of that song.

My mother's illness progressed. Finally, I took her to the doctor, who informed us she had three days left to live. When I told the home nurse, she cried and cried. She had no idea my mother was so close to dying. I told her I was sorry for not telling her, but that those were my mother's wishes. For the last three days I sat beside the woman who had stood by me and my dreams for my entire life.

I took care of her the best I could at home. I tried getting her to drink or go to the bathroom. I cleaned her fingernails and talked to her constantly. I told her over and over again how much I loved her. "It's okay if you go, Mom," I told her for three days. "If you need to go, I will be okay." I saw how badly she was suffering, and I wanted her pain to end.

The second day I was on the sofa, sitting next to my mother. She was sitting in the reclining chair, which seemed to be the most comfortable for her. Her lungs were filled with fluid, and her breathing was labored. She was slipping into and out of a coma. I asked her, "Mom, where are you right now?"

Much to my surprise, she answered, "I'm doing the laundry."

"Mom, who's there? Who are you with?"

"Livia." When she told me this, I knew in my heart she would be okay and that she soon would be with my father and with my aunt Livia, her sister who had died only three months prior. She made me swear not to let her die in St. Mary Medical Center: she had worked there for twenty-five years. I tried to follow her wishes, but eventually I had no choice. By the third day, I was forced to dial 911. The paramedics arrived within minutes and rushed in through the front door. They barged into her bedroom before I could say a word, then looked me in disgust and said, "She is dying!"

"I know," I told them. "I need to get her to St. Mary Medical Center. That's why I called you."

"No, we are taking her to Doctors Hospital. It is much closer." By law they had to go to the closest hospital.

"No!" I begged them. "She doesn't know anyone at Doctors Hospital. Do not take her there. I don't care what it costs. Please take her to St. Mary. Her doctors are waiting for her there."

They finally agreed. I rode in the ambulance with her, but they wouldn't let me sit in the back; I had to ride up front with the driver. I stared through the glass window into the back of the ambulance and watched my mother during the drive. It seemed like the longest journey of my life.

When we arrived at St. Mary, Father Mike, our family friend who worked at the medical center, came to see her. My uncle Gordon and I stayed up all night watching her and praying for God to let her suffering end. Neither of us slept a wink. The home nurse was by my side while Chris slept in the corner on a cot.

At ten o'clock the next morning, August 16, 1990, her heart stopped beating.

I looked up because I knew my mother's spirit was above me and she could see me leaning over her body. I waved and said, "Good-bye, Mom. I love you. I love you."

Father Mike came in and gave her her final prayers, and we all said one last good-bye. It was the most empty I have ever felt in my entire life.

Hundreds of people showed up to my mother's funeral. There were magazine editors from *RIP* magazine, journalists, guitar reps, rock stars, record-company executives, and many close friends. The crowd was so large that we needed a police escort to get to the funeral site. Nikki Sixx sent her twelve dozen white roses in one big bucket. Ozzy and Sharon sent flowers, even though we had split and gone our separate ways. Sharon knew how special my mother was to a lot of people.

Finally, we played her song, "Lisa." At that point, I completely broke down.

TWO WEEKS LATER, I went to a meeting at a movie producer's house. A friend had set it up. The producer wanted to do a film on my mother and her death. I took my dog with me, as always. When I arrived at her house, she said, "You can let your dog out of the car. My dogs are in the house and locked up." I looked into the house and saw her two rottweilers inside through the living room window, so I let Porky, my little wiener dog, out of my car. Porky was the last living member of my immediate family other than my cousins, who I unfortunately don't get to see that often. The next second, her dogs pushed open the door with their paws and came flying over to Porky. A 135-pound rottweiler sank his teeth into my fifteen-pound wiener dog before we even knew what was happening. I grabbed one dog by the back and kicked him in between the legs, but it was as if he didn't feel it at all. The producer tried to pull her dog's mouth open, but there was nothing either of us girls could do. The rottweiler had crushed my dog in seconds. I picked Porky up and placed him on the hood of my mother's Cadillac. There was so much blood. We got into my car and I held Porky in my arms as we raced down the street to the nearest vet, but it was no use. He was dead on arrival.

The producer said to me, "If you want, I can buy you another dog." I looked at her and didn't say a word. Instead I called my girlfriend Robyn to come get me. I was too upset to drive. Robyn picked me up and took me for a stiff drink. Everyone in the bar stared at me; I must have looked like I had committed a murder. I was covered in dried blood, but I didn't care at that point. I ordered enough drinks until I couldn't feel the pain as much, then went home alone and distraught. I climbed into my bed and didn't want to ever come out.

For days after, I barely slept or ate anything. I turned to drugs and alcohol to help numb the pain. One morning, after staying up all night, I looked in the mirror and saw my mother's image. She said, "Lita, drugs are for sick people. You are not sick. We didn't raise you to be like this."

I thought, *Lita, you can do drugs and die, or you can stop and be healthy and strong, and live.* I chose to live. It was a matter of making up my mind: I didn't want to do drugs anymore.

I went to one AA meeting and decided it wasn't for me. Instead

I traded in one habit for another and started exercising obsessively. I began running and lifting weights. I hired the choreographer Anne Marie Hunter again, this time as my trainer. She was a beautiful soul and came over every morning; we'd run the fire roads in the hills behind my house. It was twenty-three miles of steep roads in the San Bernardino mountain range. It was such a therapeutic place for me. This was a time of recovery in my life, and Anne Marie was a huge inspiration. She got me healthy, off drugs, and she was there when I needed someone to talk to.

My next plan was to divorce Chris. He had been less sympathetic than I had hoped during the illnesses and deaths of both my father and my mother. It was an amicable split. Chris was a great guy with a huge heart, but we really weren't right for each other. We both knew it.

My career was hanging by a thread. Sharon was out, Mike Chapman was gone, my father and mother had passed, my dog was dead, and now Chris and I had split. What could possibly be worse than losing all that?

CHAPTER 12

BLACK

Black, is it your medicine?

Your soul, your hole, or the shape you're in?

Black, is it your wedding gown?

Your eyes, your lies, or the truth you've found?

—"BLACK"
(WRITTEN BY LITA FORD AND MICHAEL DAN EHMIG)

SIX MONTHS AFTER MY DOG WAS KILLED, I WAS WALKING THROUGH THE Beverly Center Mall and I saw a little dachshund puppy in the window of a pet store. She seemed to call to me as I walked by. She looked exactly like Porky, but only a puppy version. I picked this dog up and she immediately started to gently chew on my diamond earrings. Porky used to do the same thing. Something so little made me so happy. I held this little puppy in my arms and asked the guy who worked there how much.

I negotiated with the guy at the store, and I began to cry as I handed him my American Express card. This dog was the beginning of a new life for me. I took the puppy home and named her Chili Dog because that is what Chris used to call Porky.

I'd had dachshunds since I was a child. My first wiener dog, Maxy, was bought for me by my parents as a birthday gift when I was four years old. From that point on, I always loved those little sausage dogs. Chili Dog was my constant companion. She went wave running with me, she went horseback riding with me, she went into the studio with me. She was my little buddy. I had guitar picks made with her on them. I had a beautiful Alvarez guitar that had an airbrushed photograph of her on it. It looked exactly like her. Chili later had four puppies and I kept one as a companion for her. I named him Pork Chop. All my dogs from that point on were named after food. The two pups went everywhere with me.

At this time I was working on writing songs for a new album and I was running every day to help me cope with the pain of losing my parents. After a year, I had a really toned body and a full album written. I was ready to go into the studio. When we started to record, my producer on the album, Tom Werman, would ask me each morning, "How far did you run today?" I was a totally different person from the girl who'd stepped into the music scene seventeen years before.

MY ALBUM *DANGEROUS CURVES* was released in November 1991. *Dangerous Curves* was a title that came from Sammy Hagar, who is one of my favorite people on this planet. Sammy had started to write a song called "Dangerous Curves," which we were going to finish writing together. Sammy and I couldn't coordinate a good time to complete the song, but he let me use the title for my album. I wrote "Shot of Poison" and "Playing with Fire" with Michael Dan Ehmig and Jim Vallance during a songwriting session that lasted a few days in Vancouver, British Columbia. Jim Vallance had picked me up at the airport dressed as a limo driver, holding up a sign that said RITA WARD. I saw the sign, but I was expecting Jim, not a limo. Since I didn't know what he looked like, it definitely threw me for a loop. I loved Jim already. With a sense of humor like that, I thought, *YEAH!* I knew we were in for some great songs.

"Holy Man" was born when Michael Dan drove to my house one day and rang the doorbell. When I answered it, he stood there and sang, "Lead me / Into temptation / Save me with your healing hands . . ." The words had come to him while he was driving so he sang the line over and over until he got to my house. When I write with Michael, we always go on the "feel" of a song. If it's working, great. If it's not getting me to where I want to be, then we scrap it. I don't like to have any "filler" on an album. Each song has to stand on its own, and if I'm not feeling it, I won't bother finishing that song. "Holy Man" definitely worked. Just like all the other songs I've written with Michael, it was effortless once one of us had the initial idea for a lyric. As we worked on the album, we wrote all our ideas on masking tape and stuck them up on the door in the recording studio. When the album was finished, the door was covered with tape.

By this time, I weighed 111 pounds of pure muscle. I was ripped to shreds, which I proudly showed off in my "Shot of Poison" video. On a trip to Vegas, I heard that one of the Chippendales dancers was using my song "Cherry Red" in his routine. Naturally, I wanted to go see for myself, and I figured since he was using my song, I'd be able to get backstage. So off I went. I met Bernie Tavis, the guy who was using my song, and introduced myself. He was hot! All the guys backstage were hot! I quickly learned that Bernie was married, but he introduced me to his brother Jimmy. Jimmy was hot too! "Gee, you guys look alike!" I said. I ended up dating Jimmy, but I cast Bernie in my "Shot of Poison" video.

I thought "Playing with Fire" was one of my best videos and one of my finest songs. We had to climb up the Burbank Dam to film it. If you looked behind you, it was a thirty-foot drop to the bottom. The crew threw down this thin rubber mat and told us, "This is just in case you fall." Right. Like a thin little mat was going to help you if you fell thirty feet! Some airplanes were trying to land at the nearby airport and radioed into the air traffic control tower in a panic because the "dam is on fire!" They managed to send someone out to the dam to see what was going on. "It's just Lita Ford making a music video. That's why the dam is on fire." With that, they cleared the planes to land.

I was really happy with *Dangerous Curves:* both the album and the videos were great. But that happiness was short-lived. Bob Buziak, the former president of my label, BMG/RCA Records, had been replaced with Joe Galante, who was a big country music fan, but my impression was that he had no idea what to do with a female, platinum-selling, rock-and-roll artist. Bob Buziak had given me nothing but encouragement and everything I needed to succeed. He was a gem. A real rock dude. To this day I will never understand why they pushed him out of the company.

I knew I was in trouble, but I didn't know how bad it was until I went out to get my mail one morning and found a letter from BMG/ RCA records. I opened it expecting to find something nice, but instead I got a handwritten letter from the new president of the label. It read: "Lita, you are one kick-ass lady. I'm sorry to let you go." What? I was dropped off the fucking label? I had the rug pulled out from under me once again. I had cleaned up, and physically I was in great shape. I was singing better than ever and playing guitar like a champ. I didn't understand. What the fuck was wrong with this country music guy? It was a sign of the times—by 1991 rock was in a tough place, and country was the hot ticket, with artists like Garth Brooks selling millions of records and crossing over to dominate the pop charts. This was not good news for me.

I was sick to my stomach. The "Playing with Fire" video was supposed to have been sent to MTV, but it never made it off the label's desk. The record company completely stopped moving forward with anything and everything. Basically, I had been shelved. Once that country-western jackass took over BMG/RCA, I no longer had the backing I needed to stay on top. When I physically showed up at BMG to find out what was going on, I learned that the staff who had worked on my records and supported me were all gone. The ones who were left wanted nothing to do with me. They were literally slamming the door in my face. Much to my surprise, I received an anonymous phone call from someone at the record label who tipped me off that "Shot of Poison" had been nominated for a Grammy for best female rock vocal performance. I attended the Grammys alone that year, which was such a horrible feeling. Unbelievable. Thanks, Joe Galante!

JUST AFTER "Shot of Poison" made some waves, I got the opportunity to guest star on the TV show *Herman's Head*. They gave me a script for one episode, which was about one week of work. Shooting started early in the morning, and for a rocker, that was unheard of. Full hair and makeup and then you had to be ready to deliver your lines. After the show's taping was done, I went out with the girls from the cast and crew for some wine. At that point in my life, I wasn't a drinker anymore, so the two glasses of wine I had went straight to my head. I stopped at Jack in the Box and ordered a coffee. I downed the coffee and started driving home in my 1990 black on black Corvette. I was speeding and swerving, listening to Van Halen in the CD player, when I looked in my rearview mirror and saw a cop behind me. I pulled over thinking, *Oh my God, I'm going to get a DUI!* The officer walked over to my car and I rolled down my window, batting my eyelashes. He flashed his light at my coffee cup and said, "Have you been drinking?"

"No, I don't drink."

"What's in the cup?"

"Coffee." I showed him the cup.

"Do you realize you were speeding and swerving?"

Oh. "I had Van Halen's 'Poundcake' in the CD player. I'm so sorry."

"Okay. I totally understand."

And he let me go. Just like that.

I WAS DOING some press in Detroit in April 1992 when the officers who beat Rodney King after a high-speed chase in 1991 were acquitted in their trial; we all had seen the infamous video of King's beating by then. The acquittals set off a wave of riots in LA. All of Los Angeles County was being looted, stores were being burglarized, and people were beating each other to death. It was a full-on war zone. I was watching the TV, and I was almost in denial about what I was seeing. The violence and mayhem seemed to be getting worse by the minute. And I was about to fly into the heart of that hell the very next morning.

The plane got closer to LA and the pilot came on the loudspeaker and warned us all to get in our cars and go straight home once we landed. As we descended into LAX, I looked out the window and saw that many buildings across different areas of the city were on fire. The plane almost landed at Ontario airport, more than fifty miles outside of LA, but LAX gave the okay for our flight to land. We were the last ones allowed to land there that night. Then they closed the airport. They closed the city!

I had a driver pick me up from LAX, and as we started to drive toward Hollywood, I noticed that all the streets were completely empty. The driver explained to me that the streets were closed, and if anyone was out past six P.M., they would go to jail for breaking the curfew. It was like we were driving through a ghost town. It was a spooky feeling. I had never seen Los Angeles like this. It's always crowded, but that day it was completely desolate. We drove up the foothills to where I lived. I was really freaking out because I lived alone, but I was starving and had no food in the house. There was a grocery store two blocks down the hill. Much to my surprise, it was open—but also completely empty of people. I grabbed some food and quickly went back home up in the hill. From there I could see the entire city, and it was still burning in places and completely deserted in others. A few days later city officials lifted the curfew and people slowly trickled out of their houses. It was a weird, edgy time to be living in LA. Everything seemed to be falling apart.

DURING A SHOW for Dick Clark, I met Clarence Clemons, Bruce Springsteen's legendary sax player. He was putting together a house band for Howie Mandel's new talk show, and he asked me if I wanted to be in it. I was hired to play in the band for every taping of the show, which was done over the course of six weeks starting in July 1992. I wore high heels and tight leather clothes every day and ran up and down through the audience. The contrast and chemistry between me and Clarence was hot! It was sexy and electrifying. I had the time of my life filming Howie Mandel's show with the late, great Clarence Clemons.

We stayed in Anaheim during the filming of the show. One morning, we were awakened by a huge earthquake. It shook the Anaheim

Hilton like a fucking tree. It flipped me out of bed and knocked out the electricity. *Man,* I thought, *I'm dead for sure!* My life flashed before my eyes. I crawled to the front door as it swung back and forth. I stood up, holding the edges of the doorway. I watched families running down the fire-escape stairs. An automated lighting system came on and gave a little light, enough for me to be able to walk down the hall to Clarence's room.

Clarence stood way taller than me, so next to me he was kinda like Darth Vader. I was running down the hallway, yelling, "Clarence, we're gonna die! We're gonna die!" I was hysterical. Clarence was holding a cognac in his hand looking completely calm. He asked me if I would like one. "Fuck yeah, pour me one of those," I said in a panic. I was speaking ninety miles an hour because I was freaked out. We were on the unlucky thirteenth floor; the damn hotel was rocking and rolling, literally. Apparently the Disney Hotel, which was next to us, cracked in half.

Clarence came back and said, "Come inside and stop worrying. This is nothing. I've been in way bigger earthquakes than this; I lived in the Bay Area for a long time. Here's your drink." I downed it. Keep in mind it's still only five A.M. We had to perform to a huge studio audience later. "Clarence," I said, "all these tremors, we have to blow off the show! What if the building caves in and kills all the people?" I was worried because the Celebrity Theatre was in the shape of a dome.

Clarence put his hand on my shoulder and said, in a thick southern-style accent: "Lita, when it's yo' time, it's yo' time. If it ain't yo' time, it ain't yo' time!" Huh? Oh! Yeah, that makes total sense, Clarence. It ain't our time?

Later that day we had to go get ready and leave for the venue to tape the TV show. In the elevator on the way down, I was standing there with Clarence and Howie Mandel. There were still aftershocks from the quake. I was still screaming "We're gonna die!," trying to convince Howie not to do the show. I explained about the building caving in on all the people in the audience. Howie said, "Lita, do you want me to slap you?" I stopped and thought to myself, *Shit, I must be overreacting!*

We did do the show that night. The aftershocks stopped as soon as we started to play.

WHEN JENNIFER BATTEN quit Michael Jackson's band during the Dangerous tour in 1993, I got a phone call from Michael's people right away. Who else would they have called? Ha! I went to get the songs they wanted me to learn. I needed to learn the solo to "Beat It," so I called Edward Van Halen, who originally played it for the recorded version, and asked him to show me exactly how he played it. When I went over to Edward's studio, he gave me a red signature Music Man guitar that played like a dream. I decided to drop-tune the guitar two whole steps—down to C—and it made the song sound so ferocious. It was fun to play it like that. When I played it for Michael's band, they were floored. They loved the hard, heavy vibe I had given the riff. Even though I knew Michael wouldn't have gone for it, the band loved it and we had a blast.

I needed to learn the rest of the show too, and I had to get the tapes from Michael's musical director to do so. The musical director lived on Lookout Mountain, filled with tight, winding roads. On the way to his house, a car coming in the opposite direction slammed into my Corvette. It was a head-on collision, similar to the one I had years ago coming from Blackmore's house. My car was a mess and barely drivable. After calling the police, my tech and I drove over to pick up the tapes from the musical director. When we got there and knocked on the door, no one answered. I knocked and rang the doorbell over and over, but no one came. Finally, my tech walked over to the back of the property and basically opened the door and found the musical director asleep in his bedroom. I don't know what he said to him, but we got the tapes pretty quickly after that. There wasn't much time to learn the show, and I wanted to get it perfect before we left to go on tour. In the weeks that followed, I had stage clothes made and received the tour itinerary from Michael's people.

About six weeks into rehearsals, I went to a nightclub and mentioned to someone that I was playing for Michael Jackson, and they said, "No, some girl named Becky is playing for Michael Jackson." I laughed it off and said, "Yeah, right."

The next day, I showed up at SIR rehearsal studios, and they told me I wasn't allowed in. They blocked the door like security guards and wouldn't let me or my tech in. I was pissed. I put my ear up against the door and I could hear the other guitar player. I asked one of the guys, "What kind of guitar is she playing?" "A Strat." A Strat? Wouldn't it have been easier to just call me and tell me, instead of making me find out about being replaced on the street? My manager called the musical director and reamed him out. "Why did you do that to her? Couldn't you have just picked up the phone and let her know?"

About four days later, I got a call from Michael's longtime guitar player, Dave Williams. He told me that Michael didn't want me in the band because I had too much credibility and had my own name in the industry. I told Dave I respected him for his honesty and thanked him. "Please, Lita, don't say anything," he said. "I'll lose my job." I gave him my word that I wouldn't say anything. *Bam* magazine, an LA industry paper, later wrote an article that claimed I had auditioned for Michael Jackson and "failed miserably." The bullshit never ends.

BY NOW I was getting pretty tired of the games of the music industry and almost wanted to quit. I thought about getting a lead singer and kicking back and just playing guitar like I had originally tried to do when I went solo. Playing in someone else's band appealed to me because it meant I could focus on my guitar playing without having to deal with the pressures that come with being the lead singer. I pondered my options for a while, trying different ideas, talking to labels and different management companies. I even called John Kalodner, who had his success with Aerosmith. He gave me $13,000 to put on a showcase for him. I had found a lead singer and put together a band. We wrote songs and we were great, I thought, but John said to me that the lead singer was not the star I was. "So sign me," I said to him. But

he said, "No. I don't know what to do with you." I thought he didn't
know what to do with a *woman*. The great John Kalodner didn't know
what the fuck to do with me, either. At least he was honest and didn't
give me the runaround.

I was offered a deal with Atlantic Records. But I turned it down
because the only one who really believed in me at Atlantic was their
A&R guy, but he was at the bottom of the food chain over there, so the
president could overrule him in a hot second. I felt like it was a "Let's
throw her against the wall and see if she sticks" kinda thing. Fuck that.
I walked. I wasn't going to be shelved again.

Instead I decided to go with a little label called ZYX that believed
in me wholeheartedly. There were definite drawbacks to going with
a smaller label. I knew I was in trouble commercially either way we
sliced it. Rock had completely changed to make way for the grunge
era, which I didn't fit into at all. Everyone had started to look like
they crawled out from under a fucking boulder. Either that or they
had no look at all—bland, slickly produced "adult contemporary"
schlock with zero edge dominated the charts. Rock stars were dropping off the face of the planet like dinosaurs. In 1993, for instance, not
one rock act would be represented in the top twenty of Billboard's
year-end Hot 100 Singles. I made a decision to give the music scene
one last chance. I decided that if I was going to go down, I would go
down swinging.

After I left Sharon, I had signed with the agency Gold Mountain.
They also managed Nirvana, and most of their attention went to Kurt
Cobain and his wife, Courtney Love. According to news reports at the
time, Courtney, who was then pregnant, was alleged to be shooting
heroin, and child welfare services in California launched an investiga-
tion. Kurt was also doing so much heroin; between the two of them,
they were a handful and dominated almost all of Gold Mountain's
bandwidth. There was no place for me; meanwhile I was running
out of money. I was in a dark, depressed place. But I was determined I
would write one more album before I hung it all up. It would be called
Black, because that was my state of mind.

A FEW MONTHS before I decided to walk away from the music scene, the Northridge earthquake hit the San Fernando Valley in January 1994. It was one of the most devastating and costly natural disasters in US history, racking up more than $65 billion in damage. It was about four thirty in the morning when it struck, and I did what I always did when an earthquake hit: grabbed my .357 revolver, my bottle of Absolut vodka out of the freezer, and my dogs. The revolver was for the looters, the vodka for my nerves. I remember sitting at the breakfast nook in the kitchen. I had the front door open and all of a sudden I saw a giant flashlight coming down the walkway. It was my friend Gavin. He had driven from North Hollywood up into the area where I lived. I couldn't believe he had driven that far because some of the freeways had collapsed. He brought in a little radio that ran off batteries, and I was so glad to see him. I was just sitting there with my dogs, Gavin's dog—who I was babysitting—my revolver, and my Absolut. My house was one of the few that wasn't damaged because it wasn't in the Valley, where the earthquake had hit the hardest. Many of my friends ended up staying at my house and brought their dogs, their kids, everybody. I was handing out sleeping bags and pillows.

> **AUTHOR'S NOTE ON WHAT FOLLOWS:** Out of respect for my children, I have chosen not write in detail about their father, my husband of almost eighteen years. It was a very difficult decision. There is much the world needs to hear. But now is not the time. Thank you for your understanding as you read forward.

The period that followed was one of the worst times of my life, both emotionally and careerwise. To make matters infinitely worse, I met a man whose name I refuse to mention because of the awful memories I will always associate with the seventeen years he was a part of my life. I sometimes get asked, "How did you meet someone and marry them after knowing them for only two weeks?" The answer is not a simple one, but the consequences were life-changing.

I went to Texas to do a few gigs before heading into the studio to record what would be my last album before taking a fifteen-year hiatus from the music industry. I was with a friend, and we went to catch a local band. They weren't bad. The place was packed. I was standing on the side of the stage, all dressed up, when I felt somebody poke me on my shoulder. I turned around, thinking it might be a friend or someone who needed to get past me. I saw a cute stranger standing there. I turned back to watch the band. He poked me again. I turned around again. This time he introduced himself.

"Hi, I'm Lita," I replied.

"I know," he said.

Two weeks later, I was married to this guy. After a horrible few years—with my parents' deaths, then changes in staff at BMG destroying the success it took me decades to build, then the disruption of the hard-rock market—I was left without music and without family. I was all alone. I was extremely vulnerable.

My dream wedding was to be married in Rome surrounded by my Italian relatives, the warmest, most wonderful people I had ever met in my life. Instead, I got hitched by a Texas justice of the peace. I was wearing an old, torn-up pair of jeans and no makeup and hadn't even had a shower. Nobody else was there, just my new husband, me, a little old judicial officer, and his wife.

We were married in May, on Friday the thirteenth.

We went to Denny's for breakfast right after we were married, and we drove back to our hotel room in a truck littered with beer bottles and soda cans that we had borrowed from one of the workers at the Chicken Ranch, a local tittie bar. I had just gotten married in bum-fuck Texas to a man I hardly knew.

I was thinking, *What the hell did I just do? Why did I marry this guy? I don't even love him!*

I called some people with the news. None of my friends even knew I was seeing anyone. I rang my manager and told him. "What? *Who* did you marry?" he asked, puzzled. It was a great question. I quickly came to realize I had no idea who this guy was.

What had I done?

BACK IN CALIFORNIA, I looked into having the marriage annulled; I called the justice of the peace. It would have meant flying back to Texas to take care of the paperwork, though, and I was already in the studio recording *Black*. The musicians I had hired were there, on the clock. Michael Dan Ehmig was staying at my house, and I had booked and paid for studio time. Not to mention that I knew this might be the last album I would ever record, and I wanted to make it great. I couldn't leave. The annulment idea slipped away.

Still, something inside me was not happy.

I sought Michael Dan out to get his feedback and opinion. I needed some reassurance from someone whom I truly trusted. Michael has a way of finding the beauty in anything and everything. He would always tell me he loved me like a sister. I said to Michael, "I don't know, something doesn't seem quite right, but I can't put my finger on it." He replied with "Yeah . . ." in a slow, southern drawl. Michael later told me he felt the same thing I did but didn't want to say it.

AFTER DEALING WITH so much bullshit while trying to make the album, the grunge scene pushing heavy metal out the door, and dealing with the pressures of being married, ZYX released *Black* in early 1995. Their slogan was: "Lita Ford is back, and she's black." REALLY?!? What the fuck is that? That's when I knew it was time to hang it up. I was not happy with the album that was released. The demos I had recorded were fucking awesome, but the record company insisted on using the Robb Brothers as the producers, because they owned Cherokee Studios. They mutilated my songs by rerecording all the demos. Even Michael Dan was devastated when he heard what they had done to my songs. "You should just produce yourself, Lita. You know exactly what it should sound like and you're so good at it," said Michael. That was it. I quit. *Black* was the end of the road for me. I didn't even recognize the music industry anymore, and I thought no matter what I did at that point, it would have been a losing battle. I was so beaten down and so exhausted. I didn't have it in me to fight for my career and try to get a divorce, so I decided to be a loyal and faithful wife. It would be the most disastrous decision of my life.

Looking back, it's eerie to reread the lyrics to the title track of the album I was recording: *Black / Is it what you hate / the hangman's hood or the offering plate / Black / is it nightmare or dream is it midnight sky or silent scream / Black / is it all you see when you close your eyes and you think of me / Black / Black / Black.*

The next decade and a half of my life would be a nightmare, a silent scream. I withdrew from the music industry and faded to black.

CHAPTER 13

MOTHER

When you look in the sky at a shining star,

Listen to your heart and know who you are,

And I'll always be your mother.

—"MOTHER"
(WRITTEN BY LITA FORD)

AFTER THE NORTHRIDGE QUAKE I WAS REALLY DONE WITH LIVING IN CALI-
fornia. I agreed when my husband decided to search for a new place
to call home. We just didn't know where. He wanted to get out of the
United States. We traded in my black Corvette for a pickup truck. We had
a shell put on the back of the truck so we could actually sleep in it if we
needed to. The next day we got in the pickup truck as soon as the *Black*
album was finished and we started driving north. My beloved LA faded
into the rearview mirror.

The plan was to drive north, then hang a left and come back down
south. We went up through Nevada, Utah, Idaho, Wyoming, and Montana. We ate junk food and camped in RV parks; chipmunks nested under
the hood for a few hundred miles. One night I ran out of the tent and into
the woods to evacuate the latest terrible meal; when I got back to the
tent, I realized I had stepped in my own shit. I was not in my element.

We made our way almost up to the Canadian border, and then turned
around and headed toward Washington and Oregon. The chipmunks

stayed with us until we got into Redwood, California. Unbelievable. We drove back down the West Coast and digested all these places we had seen. Did we want to live in any of them? We went through all the free *Homes & Land* magazines we had collected, and my husband decided upon a house in Lincoln City, Oregon, that was unfinished but worth good money if we fixed it up. He thought we could make a profit, so we decided to fly back to Lincoln City. It was beautiful: so green and peaceful. We got a hotel for the night and planned to explore the town the next day.

The following day we walked around Lincoln City, and it was the most gorgeous place. The air smelled sweet and so clean compared to LA. It looked like a painting, with all the pine trees leading right up to the ocean. We decided to move there. What I didn't know was that it rained for the rest of the year, nonstop!

We rented out my beloved Angeles Crest house. I really didn't like the idea of someone else living in my home, but we needed the money so we rented it to a group of musicians. I never met them. I never imagined that I was leaving this house for good, though. In the back of my mind, I always thought we would come back to it. I was wrong about that too. Soon we put all the money I had left into the Lincoln City house. I was getting sucked in deeper and deeper, my freedom increasingly caged.

IN OREGON I spent most of my days and nights by myself. I'd walk the cold beaches alone and eat dinner alone while sitting in a stinky rental unit with my dogs. It was a brutal move for me.

We had been living in Oregon for a few months when I heard that Joan Jett was playing at a club a hundred miles from Lincoln City.

"Let's go see Joan Jett play," I said. "I just want to see her and say hello to her."

We made the drive, and when we got there, I walked backstage to see Joan for the first time in fifteen years. She saw me, and I hugged her, but she didn't hug me back. As I tried to catch up with her, Joan looked over my shoulder and began talking to the person behind me. I was being ignored, and it pissed me off. I was hurt because I expected more of a greeting from her. But there was something deeper too, as if her coldness was confirming a fear I was unwilling to admit to myself: my old life, particularly my musical passion, was fading further and further out of reach.

I looked at my husband and said, "Let's get out of here."

We walked to the front of the house to wait for the show to start. We waited and waited, and then we heard she wasn't going on until 11:30. We had come a little early because I was hoping to hang with Joan, so now we had three hours to kill. We had some wine and got buzzed, further darkening my mood. I said to my husband, "If we eat, we will sober up enough to drive the hundred miles home." I ordered a burrito covered in sour cream, guacamole, and cheese. It was a big, juicy, messy burrito. But there was one problem; there weren't any knives or forks. I was dressed nicely and had my hair and makeup done.

I didn't want to get messy, so I asked the waitress for a knife and fork. She said, "There's some plastic utensils on that table over there."

I looked, but there weren't any knives. But I noticed the server was holding a bread knife in her hand. *Perfect.*

I asked her, "Can I use your bread knife?"

She said, "No. You can't use this."

"Please. I'll just cut up my burrito and give it right back to you."

Somehow words must have gotten turned around or misunderstood, because she answered by calling me a bitch. I sat there confused for about five minutes as my blood started to boil.

"Bitch?" I kept saying. "She thinks I'm a bitch? If she wants a bitch, she's got one now."

Just then she walked past our table. I picked up the entire plate of burrito, sour cream, guacamole, cheese, and salsa and flung it onto the back of her neck. It splattered on the wall and in her hair. She started to cry.

My husband had ordered a plate of nachos with the works on them: chicken, sour cream, cheese, jalapeños, and so on. I asked him, "Are you gonna eat those?"

He said, "Well, I guess not." So I picked up the plate, stood up, and looked around the room.

Everyone in the restaurant yelled at me: "NO!"

I looked back, replied "Yes!," then threw the nachos against the wall. As the nachos exploded, we sat back down and looked at each other.

My husband said, "Well, I guess we'd better leave now."

"I guess so," I agreed.

"Hold on to the back of my jeans and don't let go."

"Okay," I said.

I never saw Joan's show, though I don't think I missed much. And yet that still goes down as one of my favorite nights in Oregon. That should tell you how much fun Oregon was for me. My only "rock-and-roll moment" involved a burrito.

YEAH, I HATED living in Lincoln City. First of all, it seemed that the day we first saw the town was one of the only days of the year it didn't rain. When we moved there, the clouds rolled in and never fucking parted. Second, I was realizing more and more just how unhappy I was becoming. I stopped listening to music completely. I didn't feel in control of my life. I was growing resentful of my marriage, because it had taken me away from the people and things I had known all my life and loved the most.

To occupy myself, we bought two horses. Unfortunately I couldn't ride often because it rained constantly, but I would go down to the stables and groom them. When there was a rare decent day, I would go for long horseback rides. My favorite horse was an Arabian named Ziggy. He was like a hot rod: fast as fuck. I loved Ziggy. Our other horse was Bonnie, an Appaloosa; she had a giant tumor on the side of her leg. We had the tumor removed and tested for cancer. Turns out the horse didn't have cancer, but she did kick me and almost broke my knee once, so I didn't ride her after that. My horses were my distraction because I missed my California home so much.

The decision was made to have kids. I had been on birth control for more than eighteen years before this, and as soon as I went off the pill, I developed a cyst in my uterus. Every time I had sex it was painful. I saw the doctor and she told me the cyst was the size of a grapefruit, and I would have to slowly wean myself off the pills, which worked, thankfully. Once I was off the pills, however, I still wasn't getting pregnant. My depression deepened.

AFTER THREE MONTHS of living in Oregon, it was announced we were moving to Florida. That sounded okay by me. Anything to get out of that dreary place. The one thing that bothered me about leaving was having to sell my horses. I'm not one to purchase an animal and then walk away from it. When I have an animal, it's for life, so leaving Ziggy and Bonnie behind was difficult. When we sold them at a livestock auction, I had to ride the horses when they came for bidding. As soon as they announced Bonnie was a "kid-friendly" horse, she promptly slammed me against the wall. Fucking mares. It was as if she was saying, *Get the hell out of town.*

We drove to the Southeast in two twenty-six-foot-long trucks, one towing a Porsche and the other hauling a Cadillac. We had left Lincoln City immediately after packing up the truck, at one A.M., not exactly an ideal time to begin a cross-country trip. We got lost in Portland, about a hundred miles inland from Lincoln City. We finally found the freeway at dawn. I was getting tired, but we didn't stop.

"I'm towing a twenty-six-foot truck full of stuff, with a Cadillac Coupe de Ville, and I'm falling asleep. I need to stop to sleep," I said into the walkie-talkie. *Nope.* Apparently we needed to get to Florida by a certain time or another buyer would get to the house we had our eye on before us.

I was livid. But I shut up and kept following my husband.

Once we were in Panama City Beach, Florida, we got the project house and building began again. Two weeks later, in October 1995, Hurricane Opal hit and ripped the roof off and scooped out the sand from underneath the foundation. The ocean came through the windows since it was a beachfront property. The National Guard declared the city a disaster area. Septic tanks, pools, and downed electrical wires were all over the place. My neighbor found one of my dog's squeakie toys five blocks from our house. Even the road was gone. The house was largely destroyed, but we got money from the insurance company to rebuild. The total damages from Hurricane Opal were over $5 billion and it hit the East Coast hard.

As terrible as it was, that natural disaster was the perfect welcome to my life in Florida. Unfortunately, unlike Opal, my personal storm didn't blow over in a day. In the years that followed, I would be swept further from the things that made me who I am: Lita Ford.

Within every hurricane, though, they say there's an "eye" at the center, a place of peace amid the chaos swirling around. Finding it would be my lifeline.

TWO AND A half years of marriage went by, and I couldn't get pregnant. I researched female fertility, seeking a solution. I went so far as to have my amalgam dental fillings—old fillings can contain mercury—taken out of my teeth, hoping that was the answer. I still didn't get pregnant, and, after years of trying, I figured I never would have a child, and anyway, I was afraid I wouldn't know what to do. Kids don't come with a manual, and they don't have six strings. You can't hit pause or mute, and there's no standby switch. Yet for some reason, children seemed to be drawn to me throughout my life. I always would take time to talk to kids and hang out with them whenever they were around. I felt like we could relate to each other somehow; maybe it's true that rock and rollers are kids who never saw much point in "growing up." But as for being a mother myself, by the summer of 1996 I eventually figured it just wasn't in the cards.

Then for some reason I kept needing to pee while we were at Disney World that September. I avoided one particular ride with a steep, sudden drop—I didn't know why; it just didn't seem like a good idea.

Later that night, we went out to eat with our old real-estate agents, Vicki and Denis, who were visiting from Oregon. The Indian food made me sick, which never happens. At three o'clock in the morning, I sat up in bed. I didn't feel so good. It hit me in a flash—I was pregnant. I knew it. I didn't have to take a test. I just knew.

When I went home and took that pregnancy test, sure enough, it was positive. *Oh my God, my parents are both gone. How can I raise a child without the help of my parents?* I had no real family members close by or friends who could help me. No one to talk to.

By the grace of God, my neighbors on either side of me, Lynne and Kelly, happened to both become pregnant as well, and the three of us drew close. It was like we had the same milkman. We all took long walks on the beach every day and supported one another through the process. I read a lot of books on pregnancy and how to be a great mother. I set a high bar for myself: I wanted to be just like my mom. This was my main priority. For the first time since I left music, I had a focus. I did everything the doctor told me to do during the pregnancy. I didn't drink liquor or any caffeine; I religiously took prenatal vitamins.

During my pregnancy I actually saw what my baby would look like as a toddler—a beautiful boy—in a dream. He was so clear to me: blond with blue eyes, a beautiful face, and light skin. When he was a toddler, he looked exactly as I saw him in my dream.

I HAD NO complications until the last trimester, when I started bleeding. The doctors couldn't figure out where the blood was coming from, so they put me on bed rest and told me to lie low for the last three months. At this time I was thirty-eight, which is a little on the older side to be having your first child. But I had heard that older parents make better parents, and that was true in my case. I was meant to be a mom when I was thirty-eight, no sooner.

Around that time, I received a phone call from my aunt Rosetta, my mother's oldest sister, from Italy, and she really wanted me to come and see her. She lived in the heart of Rome. The city had built up around their tiny apartment. The language barrier was so thick between us that without a translator, I couldn't understand what the problem was and why the rush to all of a sudden go see her. She was sad I couldn't fly because of my pregnancy. Soon after that phone call, I was devastated when she passed during the last trimester of my pregnancy. Then I understood. If I had known she was sick, I would have gone to Rome anyway, despite the bleeding.

I went into labor with James on May 13, my wedding anniversary. When the time came, I started bleeding badly and I got really scared. One of my husband's workers drove me to the hospital, which was on the other side of town. I sat on a black towel all the way there, humiliated that I was sharing this experience with a stranger.

I was in labor for twelve hours, and I went to sleep until the doctor came in and said, "You are not dilating. We are going to have to cut you."

"A C-section?" I asked.

"Yes."

"No," I said. "I want to do it naturally."

"You are bleeding. You can lose the baby now if we don't take him out right away."

I couldn't argue with that, so I agreed to the C-section. The doctor took me into another room to prep me for surgery. They put a sheet over me and prepped an epidural; I was completely numb from the waist down as the doctor began to cut me open. Then I felt the weight of the baby lifting off my chest. Suddenly I could breathe, which I hadn't been able to do for months prior. James was screaming, as any healthy baby does.

The doctor said, "Man, he is loud!"

He was so fucking loud that I thought, *Oh God, another lead singer!* I fell in love instantly.

JAMES LENARD GILLETTE was born on May 13, 1997. A Taurus. He weighed six pounds, ten ounces. I gave him his middle name in honor of my father—the grandfather he would never get to meet. I was sad Dad wasn't there to see his grandson enter the family. When James came into my life, I finally understood the meaning of true, unconditional love. He was my one and only focus. My reason for being. After three long, dark years, a ray of love and happiness now lit up my life.

I would sing "Sweet Baby James" by James Taylor as I held him in my arms every night. "There is a young cowboy who lives on the range . . . Rock-a-bye, sweet baby James." He would always fall asleep in my arms while I sang. I hadn't known it, but I had been waiting thirty-eight years to meet my sweet baby James.

James changed my life. I took him everywhere with me. I bought a jogging stroller and immediately got to work discovering what it means to be a mother. We went to the zoo. We watched all the children's TV shows together. I never once fed him jarred baby food, only the fresh-cooked food I put in a food processor, with no preservatives or formula. I consistently tried to meet the standard my parents had set.

Damn if I wasn't proud too! And so when *People* magazine asked to include James in an article along with Richie Sambora and Heather Locklear's child, I got excited about the idea of introducing the world to this beautiful boy—after all, he was rock royalty, the son of the "Queen of Heavy Metal." However, the decision was made to decline the request. My universe quickly shrank back to just James and me.

When James was about nine months old, we moved again. I was exhausted with building and moving. I thought, *Can't we just buy a house and move in? I don't want to build another house.* Well, soon we were moving into our new home on the bay in Panama City in 1998. I would stand in the kitchen of our new house and hold James while singing to him. I had no real friends nearby, and of course no family members close by.

I WAS STILL holding on to bits and pieces of my music career, trying to maintain connections I wanted to keep. Dina Weisman was representing me as a manager for certain things that would come up. My old guitar tech, Tom Perme, was her boyfriend. Dina was my friend and I trusted her: I had known her since the beginning of my solo career. We met in the women's bathroom in the Long Beach Arena when I asked if anyone had a pair of pliers because I was trying to pull up my jeans, which were very tight. I had put them on by lying on the bed and sucking in my gut, but the bathroom at the arena didn't have a bed so there was no way I could zip them back up without a pair of pliers. She put a pair of pliers in my hand and said, "I do. How many girls do you know who carry a pair of pliers in their purse?"

"Really? What do you do?"

"Your guitar tech is my boyfriend." We remained friends for many years after that. It was Dina who gave me my first bottle of black nail polish. I had never seen it before.

I had Dina arrange a meeting with Kenny Laguna and Joan Jett in 1998 because I wanted to write a song with Joan. Kenny ended up coming out to Panama City, but he didn't bring Joan with him like Dina and I were expecting. We went out to dinner, but it ended up becoming a nonmeeting because Joan wasn't there. There was no resolution and nothing came out of it except Kenny saying that he thought it was a good idea. There were no efforts made on his behalf or ours. I don't think he wanted to work with us, and we didn't want to work with him. We didn't trust him.

After the meeting, he left, and I didn't hear from him again until about six months later when, early in 1999, Kenny arranged a conference call with me, Joan, Cherie Currie, and Sandy West to discuss the possibility of putting the Runaways back together. Joan hadn't had a hit record in a while, and Kenny was also Cherie's manager at this point.

In the week leading up to the conference call, I had spoken to Sandy and Cherie but not to Joan. I was wary of talking with Joan after she'd given me the brush-off at the Portland gig. The phone rang. It was Kenny, who had Cherie on the line as well. They dialed in Sandy. Cherie was overly nice and friendly. Sandy was happy and her usual self, and I told them about having James.

Joan was the last person to get dialed in. I was expecting her to be happy to hear from everyone after so many years. But when she came on the phone, she sounded like someone had just woken her up from a stone-cold sleep and shoved the phone in her face. It didn't seem like she knew who she was talking to, or that she had even been prepped for this call. She didn't say hello to anyone or ask how anyone was; she seemed miserable to me. I thought to myself, *Whoa, this is not gonna happen.* I apologized to everyone. "I'm so sorry, but I have to hang up now."

Cherie said, "No, no, no, Lita! Please don't hang up!"

Sandy chimed in, "Joan's just tired."

"If that's tired, then I definitely don't want any part of this. I'm sorry, but I can't do this." I hung up, and that was the end of the conference call. I don't know what had happened in the twenty years since the Runaways days, but this was not the same Joan I once knew. I was disgusted with her attitude. That's what did it for me.

In the Runaways, Joan and I had never argued, and when we parted ways, I had a lot of respect for her, like a sister. Perhaps Kenny looked at it as a competition, although I was never out to compete with Joan. I wonder if he saw me as a threat even though Joan and I have two completely different audiences.

In the days that followed the conference call, I got a call from Sandy, who was trying to convince me to get back together again. I told her, "Why don't you move on with your life, Sandy? You're so talented. You're Sandy West. You could join anybody's band. It doesn't have to be the Runaways."

Cherie also called and tried to convince me. I used the excuse of just having James, and I also knew the music scene was fucked up, so I told her that I wasn't going to do it.

Regardless, 1999 was not the right time to release a Runaways album or have a Runaways tour. If we couldn't be respectful of one another over a simple conference call, we would not have made it through one day of rehearsal, let alone an entire tour.

MEANWHILE THE YEARS slipped by.

By the time we moved out of Florida in 2001, we owned an apartment complex, a whole bunch of smaller houses, and two waterfront properties. I remember the year well because of the lead-up to the year 2000. My household was obsessed with Y2K fears: nuclear war, financial meltdown, planes falling from the sky, collapse of civilization, and so on. Insanity. Supplies began appearing: massive amounts of powdered eggs, condensed milk, wheat, beans, rice, flour, sugar, tampons, mouthwash, toothpaste, water jugs that stacked up to the ceiling; a $20,000 generator; hundreds of ten-pound buckets with food ingredients in them. It didn't end there. We had stocked up on shavers, antibiotics, and medicine. It invaded my space and consciousness such that I started to believe it too. We were going to die! My baby was going to die! A countdown-to-Y2K digital clock was installed in the home office. Every time I walked by the room, I could see the seconds ticking away on that damn clock.

The night before Y2K I was convinced we wouldn't wake up the next morning. Our house had been so wound-up the entire year! I was so scared. I snuck away to bed silently, crawling into the bottom bunk in the guest room with baby James. As crazy as it sounds, I pinned baby James against the wall with my body in case I could protect him from the nuclear blast.

Much to my surprise, the next morning we all woke up. I looked at baby James. He was sleeping. I looked at my arms. They were still there. I opened the drapes. Nothing was burned. I got up and went into the office to look at the clock that was counting down to the apocalypse. It was past Y2K by a few hours. I turned on the TV and nothing was blown up. The news showed Times Square and people who went to parties, like any New Year's celebration.

I was so fucking angry. We ate freeze-dried food for years to come. Which sucked.

I GREW CONCERNED about James being an only child. I wanted to have another baby so if anything ever happened to me, my children would have each other. But I was already forty-two. I had been seeing a doctor who was the same age and had just had a child herself. The doctor told me, "It is very rare, and you most likely will never get pregnant at this age. Do you want some fertility pills?"

"No," I said. "Shit, I don't want quintuplets. If it is meant to be, it will be."

"Give it three months and if nothing happens, come back and we'll see what other options are available," the doctor said.

At the end of the three months, I took a pregnancy test: it was positive. It took me years to get pregnant with James. I was in disbelief because of my age; I would be forty-two years old and delivering my second child.

Rocco was born on June 27, 2001. A Cancer. He weighed seven pounds, two ounces. I saw Rocco in my dreams just as I'd seen James years before. He was a little darker than his older brother, with brown eyes, brown hair, and olive skin. Sure enough, that is exactly what he looked like when he came out of me. "Like my mother," I said the first time I held him. He lit up my life. Once again, I wished my parents could be there to see these two miracles, but I knew they were watching from somewhere. James was such a great big brother. He would help me with diapers, baby clothes, and anything else I asked for. They were the loves of my life. It seemed my life was complete with these two beautiful boys.

And then my husband announced we were moving yet again. This time to an island in the Caribbean. He went ahead of us, leaving me to take care of a newborn, a four-year-old, and a blind dachshund (my beloved Chili Dog). We sold all ten of our properties, including the house we lived in. One day the furniture was emptied out. I looked at my two little sons, and I had no choice but to follow him. I didn't want to go, but there was no way I was going to take my sons away from their father. Before we moved, everything we owned was put into storage lockers, including all my guitars, except one electric and one acoustic.

We had just three suitcases as we boarded the plane for the islands on August 16, 2001. The anniversary of my mother's death. A bad sign.

CHAPTER 14

THE ASYLUM

No one seems to hear me now,

As though my words were all blacked out.

And written on the walls of the Asylum.

—"The Asylum"
(Written by Lita Ford and Michael Dan Ehmig)

WE MOVED TO THE BERMUDA TRIANGLE—LITERALLY *AND* METAPHORICALLY.
More precisely: Turks and Caicos, a chain of islands that's approximately
seven hundred miles off the coast of Miami. For the first year and a half,
we lived on the main island, Providenciales, called "Provo" by the locals,
where the population is about ten thousand people. In that time, we
moved our household six times. Provo at least had a few resorts, a school,
a grocery store, a doctor—that is, some signs of life.

My first order of business was to get James into a school. He knew his
basic school skills, and I had already taught him to write. But I wanted to
get him into a school so he could make friends. James went to the Ash-
croft School for first grade and the first half of second grade; it was filthy.
When James would come home from school, we had this huge container
where we would dump the dirt from his shoes, just to see how much we
could collect. His fingernails would be dirty, and his face would be beet
red from the heat. How does a child focus on doing schoolwork in that
kind of heat? I went to the school one day to see how James was doing

and I didn't recognize him because of how red his face was. I asked if the school had fans and they said no. They would do physical education at one o'clock in the afternoon, the hottest time of the day. I tried to get them to change the time of the class, but they wouldn't do that, either. I started pulling him out of school for the afternoons, since all he would be missing is running laps around the school for an hour in the hottest sun of the day.

My husband became interested in purchasing a deserted stretch of oceanfront property on North Caicos, an undeveloped island twelve miles from Provo. Was it beautiful? Sure. But there was almost nothing there but mosquitoes, flamingos, crabs, cockroaches, island rats, and bushes. The mosquitoes were turbocharged, like jumbo jets. There was no water, electricity, roads, medical facilities, mailboxes, FedEx, restaurants, grocery stores. Forget Walmart or Starbucks. It was all sugar-white sandy beaches and mangroves where the hammerhead sharks gave birth to their young. They were indeed healthy ocean waters. But the beach was as desolate a place as you could imagine—if you need help, think of *Robinson Crusoe* or *Cast Away*. It would have been wonderful for two weeks out of every summer, but it was not where I wanted to raise the boys. On that stretch of coastline there was *nothing*. No children to play with, no normal human society or culture.

The only hint of civilization nearby was a small community of shacks in the middle of the island and one shitty, broken-down school that was a thirty-minute drive on a poorly maintained road. There were no computers or air conditioning; on a Caribbean island it is too unbearably hot for there not to be air conditioning or even ceiling fans! Our house was bigger than the school was. What kind of credentials did the teachers have? I would have died before I let James, and eventually Rocco, rely on that place for their education.

Meanwhile construction began on our new home—actually two mansions right next to each other. My husband and the Piergiovanni family, his Jehovah's Witness business partners who would become our next-door neighbors in North Caicos, employed more than one hundred Haitians and "belongers," as the locals were called. One house would be ours, and the other was the Piergiovannis'. The Piergiovannis did most of the manual labor. They were big lumberjack-style people who lived their lives studying the Bible and building. Not my type of hang!

I didn't go to see what they were doing until the foundations had already been poured for these two massive, three-level mansions. When the boat pulled up to the property, I almost passed out. I was under the impression we would at least have some privacy in this god-forsaken place. Nope. The two foundations were poured not more than forty feet away from each other.

"Oh great," I said to my neighbor, "we'll be able to pass each other the oregano."

I was not happy. I think the feeling was mutual; the devout Piergiovannis probably thought I was the Antichrist because I was a rocker chick. Well, that doesn't make me bad, ladies and gentlemen. I'm not antisocial, either: I just didn't understand the logic of living forty feet away from anyone when there was an entire fucking island at our disposal. It defeated the whole purpose of moving to such an out-of-the-way place.

Needless to say, I dreaded the day when I would have to move into that house, but the foundation was already poured.

WHILE THE HOMES were being built, I heard that Dee Snider from Twisted Sister was on the main island at one of the resorts with his family. We had a rental there we were living in, while we waited to relocate to North Caicos. I'd known Dee since 1984, when Twisted Sister played with the Lita Ford band. They were so supportive of a chick on guitar, and they'd always be cheering me on. Dee as a front man was just incredible, packed full of energy with a terrific voice and equally great attitude. He was also a very loyal husband and father, and I loved that about him. I felt like he was a big brother to me, looking out for me and offering words of advice and encouragement. I thought Dee and his wife, Suzette, might like to meet my boys, who were growing up so beautifully. I also couldn't wait to see a familiar face.

It was a thrill. The Sniders and my family became friends immediately. Dee has a daughter who is the same age as James, and they got along well. They were both little rocker kids. Dee's daughter wanted to be a lead singer like her father and James wanted to play guitar like me. To anyone who saw me or talked to me, it looked like I had one big happy family. I firmly hid the fact that I was miserable, living in such an isolated, dirty, and lonely place, away from everyone and everything I had once known.

We took Dee and Suzette over to show them our future outpost on North Caicos, which by this time had all three levels in place. We went up to the top floor of the house, where you had a view of nothing but ocean as far as the eye could see. Not even a single boat cruising by. It was breathtaking, but also you could sense the isolation. I looked at Dee's face and could tell what he was thinking. *How is Lita going to last here with the boys? No school. No doctors. No friends. No music.* Dee seemed to be a little in shock. "Okay," he kept saying in between deep breaths. "Okay."

I felt sad. But, hey, it sure was a pretty view.

The next morning, we said our good-byes to Dee and his family. He returned to the world I had left behind, while I awaited sentencing on Alcatraz, a.k.a. North Caicos.

IT TOOK TWO years to finish both houses. They were built like a bank vault—or a prison cell, depending on your perspective. According to the contractors, our mansion could withstand "450-mile-per-hour winds." It was cold inside, with granite floors and countertops. To me it looked like an asylum with balconies.

I was scared to death to move to North Caicos for many reasons. It was even more remote than Provo. My children's well-being concerned me the most. There was only one doctor on the main island in Provo. He was the guy you went to if you had the flu or a bad cut, but if you needed emergency attention, you had to be airlifted into Miami.

Moving to North Caicos would make urgent medical treatment even more of an issue. Risking my personal well-being was one thing, but when you've got two young kids, that's not a chance any mother wants to take. I went so far as to stock up on EpiPens, antibiotics, and other first aid items. Because we would be living in such a remote place, I needed some kind of reassurance, no matter how small, that I could buy twenty to thirty minutes of time in case something happened to us, like a shark bite or a boating accident.

I also had a tutor set up for the kids on North Caicos. When the day rolled around for her to come over for her first visit, though, she never showed. Later that afternoon she called and apologized, explaining that her car had broken down. This was not unusual since the roads there were so bad. She said she would be there at the same time the following day, but again, she didn't show up. She was my only chance at finding a tutor on North Caicos who could teach second grade, and she proved to be unreliable. Finally that good old saying came to mind again: "If you want something done right, do it yourself." So I decided to homeschool the boys myself. I had no choice but to put them through the Lita Ford School. Still, I was livid, as this was not my idea of life, and I had no clue where to start. I had been in a rock band since I was sixteen years old—I wasn't a teacher. No one had hated school more than me. There were no school supplies on the island or books of any kind, and more important, I wanted the kids to have friends their own age and be in a school for that reason.

I started doing my research, trying to figure out how the hell I was going to make this work. I finally found a respected curriculum on the mainland, the Calvert School, from Canada, that I really liked. It made learning fun and was the easiest to understand. If this was going to be our reality, I wanted it to be as fun and educational for the boys as possible.

Homeschooling was life-changing for me, as it turned out, and brought me even closer to my kids. Every morning my sons and I and the dogs would get up and walk the beach. The boys would run, swim, exercise, and hunt for shells. I remember looking at their little footprints in the sand. My kids' footprints and mine were the only ones on the beach—that's how deserted it was. They'd find some conch shells that were as big as basketballs. We'd head back to the house and the boys would jump into the pool to rinse off the sand and salt from the beach, and then we'd have breakfast. I'd make a fresh homemade breakfast of eggs, waffles from fresh ground wheat, or French toast, a breakfast fit for a king, and then we would get to work on school. James, Rocco, and I would all sit at a huge antique round table and do schoolwork every morning. I taught James his times tables, how to read, and how to write cursive and printed words. I would put on an educational CD for Rocco to keep him occupied while I taught James, and then we would switch. I was teaching two different grades at the same time and it was hard work. After lunch, we went back to work again till about three or four in the afternoon before heading out to go fishing—I had taught the boys to fish, the same way my father had taught me.

At night before bed we would read dictionaries and encyclopedias. James would also read storybooks to Rocco and me. We had all the Dr. Seuss titles and heaps of other books. My favorite book was *Are You My Mother?* I taught the boys a lot. We would have music lessons too. James recorded his first song at age seven. It was called "Destruction" and was inspired by a particularly messy day in our house after three meals and a full day of activities.

Between homeschooling the boys, cooking, making bread, picking vegetables from the garden, and cleaning a five-bedroom, six-bathroom, ten-thousand-square-foot house filled with sand, I was fucking exhausted. I felt like Cinderella, stuck in her wicked stepmother's house. We were living like the fucking Amish. I loved being with my boys, but I felt trapped living in that house and being on that island. I barely watched TV because half the time the satellite was blocked by a massive cloud in the sky and wouldn't work. I didn't keep up with music. At night, I would often fall asleep in the top bunk of James's bed while we were watching a movie. Before dozing off I'd look out the porthole-shaped window in his room. I'd fix my gaze on the brightest star, just like I had as a teenager in the back of that station wagon when the Runaways were on tour. There it was. That same star still followed me wherever I went. But I could never really relax. The only joy or pleasure I had during those years on the island was being with my kids. They were my world. I'd lie in bed praying my kids would grow up and live a happy and healthy life, and that they'd always be my best friends. Given the isolated life we were living, who else were we supposed to be friends with?

I MISSED THE music industry so much, and it made me sad my kids had no connection to the world I loved. For the first time since I had moved to Florida, I started listening to music again. For fun, I decided to teach James and Rocco about the "School of Rock." I started with the first letter of the alphabet: A is for AC/DC or Alice Cooper, B is for Black Sabbath, and so on. We did that for every letter of the alphabet and the boys would ask me to tell them stories about the bands, since I had met them all at some point in my career. I'd always have something to tell them about the bands we were learning about. I told them about MTV, and how I'd wait all week to watch Don Kirshner's *Rock Concert,* wondering, *Who will the guest of the week be?* I'd go online and we would look up the songs for whatever group or artist we were studying, and go over the guitar solos. We had a hell of a lot of fun doing it. I would talk to James about touring, explaining how to warm up for a show, and then how to cool down. I'd tell Rocco about charisma and stage presence.

One day my son James said to me, "Mom, for everything that happens, you have a song."

He was right: whenever anything happened around the house, I'd sing an appropriate verse or part of whichever song came to mind. "Yes, James," I replied, "life is a song. Music makes the world go round." Doing the School of Rock was therapeutic for me, and it was special to share with the boys. But it was a Band-Aid over a hole in my heart. If music made the world go round, I ached to contribute my note.

JAMES AND ROCCO were introduced to UFC/MMA fighting at the most competitive level possible as they grew older. Seriously. They began practicing the Gracie form of Brazilian jujitsu, which is regarded by many to be the fiercest school of the martial art—and the most lethal, if used the wrong way. The school's founder, Hélio Gracie, "insisted that fights should only be decided by submission or loss of consciousness." Does this sound kid-friendly? Well, my family became acquainted with the Gracie family (their ranks include Rorion Gracie, a cofounder of Ultimate Fighting Championship) and their Miami-based protégés, the Valente brothers. According to their own website (graciemiami.com), the "Valente Brothers is [sic] the official representation of Grandmaster Hélio Gracie in Florida. Professors Pedro, Gui and Joaquim Valente started training directly under the Grandmaster at the age of 2 years old and were his loyal disciples." If language like "loyal disciples" sounds fanatical to you, I'd say you're probably on the right track.

Soon we were in too deep. In fact, the Valente brothers were asked to be our boys' godfathers. My husband got their logo—of a triangle chokehold—tattooed on his stomach. Yes, I thought it was freaky. I began to fear I was losing my boys to this madness.

Grandmaster Hélio Gracie, the founder of Gracie Brazilian jujitsu, is worshipped among Brazilian jujitsu enthusiasts. It was a total way of life that extended far beyond the fighting mat, from how you thought to what you ate. Hélio Gracie had stomach issues, so he created a restrictive diet to heal himself, which later became well known and used by Gracie trainers like the Valentes. He called it "the Gracie diet." Chocolate or candy was out of the question. Cake—only vanilla—was allowed once a year. If the boys ate chocolate, they got a mark against them in jujitsu, which meant they wouldn't get their belts at the next ceremony. I was thinking, *This is crazy. The boys need to be able to have a childhood. Let them eat a fucking M&M.* They didn't have any stomach issues, so why would they need to follow the Gracie diet? We bought them a fighting cage and put in a home gym that was full of exercise equipment: rowing machine, VersaClimber, weights, and an inclined rock wall. A child with an eight-pound vest on doing this kind of climbing wasn't my idea of healthy exercise. Olympic champion Howard Davis Jr. was hired to teach James and Rocco to box.

This is beginning to sound nuts, right? If you have any doubts, type "Rocco Gillette" into YouTube and see for yourself: there's a video of my precious seven-year-old son sparring with a gold-medal-winning boxer; it has more than fifteen thousand views. The boys also were put into Russian judo classes to teach them to kick and learn throws.

Believe me, I just wanted them to be children, free to do and act as kids would: eat chocolate, be carefree, have friends, and be happy and healthy. James and Rocco would end up in tears after each intense workout. They were only little boys; this was something they should not have had to stress about night and day. They weren't the only ones who stressed. I did too.

I OFTEN GET asked about the tattoos on my arms, and I've never really had the opportunity to explain why I got them in the first place. I'm sure a lot of people believe they were something I chose to do on my own, without anyone else's input, but that's certainly not the case.

The first tattoo I got done was the skull with "Gillette" across it, on my left arm. It was a four-hour job. The tattoo artist, Christian, asked me discreetly, "You don't really want this tattoo, do you?"

He could see I was sick to my stomach over it.

"No, I don't."

"Do you want me to do it anyway?"

"Yeah."

Grin and bear it, Lita, I thought to myself.

In my eyes, "Gillette" represented my boys. I was okay with that.

That wasn't enough. I ended up with a second tattoo, with the cross and Roman numerals that spell out May 13, 1994—our wedding anniversary—on my right arm. My son James was born on May 13, 1997, so in my eyes I looked at it as his birthday instead of as our anniversary.

Over the tailbone of my lower back, I have a tattoo that reads MY HUSBAND. Finally, I broke down and got my husband's first name tattooed down my forearm. I felt like I had been branded.

I WAS BECOMING a shadow of who I once was.

I fell asleep on the couch one night and woke up gasping for air, almost as if I was underwater. It was hard to breathe, and my heart was racing in my chest, like I had just missed a flight. What I really wanted to do was run to the door so I could get outside into the open air, but I would have set off the alarm system. The keypad was in the master bedroom in the closet. *I'm trapped*, I realized. I never kept alcohol in the house, but we had had some company over that night—a rare occurrence—and they had brought over some red wine, so I poured half a glass, thinking it would ease the anxiety. It didn't. It made my heart pound even faster. Now I was really panicking.

I managed to make it to Rocco's room, which was empty, because there had been a leak onto the bamboo flooring. It had become moldy and made me worry, so I made him sleep in James's top bunk some nights. This was one of those nights. I sat there from ten P.M. till about four A.M., paralyzed. I wanted to get to a paper and a pen to write my children a note. I felt as though I was having a heart attack and was seized with a powerful desire to compose a final message to my children. But I couldn't raise my arms; I thought that if I moved, I would die. All I could think about was my boys.

Who is going to take care of them once I'm gone? What's going to happen to them?

It wasn't until ten A.M. that morning that I was able to settle down enough to emerge from the room. I grabbed the Mayo Clinic's *Family Health Encyclopedia* that I kept around for emergencies and starting reading. I wanted to know what had happened to me. I realized I had experienced a panic attack. Living on this island was really starting to destroy me, and the feelings of loneliness, being trapped, and being isolated had taken their toll physically, not just psychologically.

What's going to happen to me?

It became clear to me, finally: I needed to get away from my marriage and off that damn island. I needed to do something that made me feel like Lita again. I didn't have the answers yet, but I had a mission. I had to save myself and my boys.

THE FIRST STEP was to get a toehold back in the United States. I started pushing the idea of buying a house in Miami. The boys frequently were traveling there anyway for jujitsu training. It took me three years, but we finally bought a place in Miami. I thought I was one step closer to freedom, but I was wrong.

We would go back and forth between the islands and Miami, but I wanted to figure out a way to keep us in Florida more. James was eleven now, and Rocco was seven. I got involved in a school talent show for some friends of ours. I put together the kids to sing "We Will Rock You." I hung out in the background and borrowed a gold-top Les Paul to play during the show. We named the band "Kids Row." I made them costumes and we had a lot of fun. A couple of the boys who James and Rocco did jujitsu with were a part of the group. Each kid had a verse to sing. James had so much fun with the Kids Row project that I decided to buy him the gold-top Les Paul I had used for the talent show for his eleventh birthday. He showed a natural inclination for playing guitar, and I figured that even if it sat in his room for a while, if he wanted to play it, he could, instead of playing one of "Mommy's guitars." Most of my guitars were in storage.

Working with the boys on Kids Row spurred my hunger to make music. In 2009, I released a record called *Wicked Wonderland*. Or at least it was packaged as a "Lita Ford album." Here's what *All Music Guide* had to say about it:

> It's an album with explicit sexual content, examining S&M,
> bondage, power exchanges, and all manner of kink and crave
> in lyrics, words, and sleeve images. Ford wrote all of these

songs with her co-producers Greg Hampton and Gillette. Gillette is also either a duet partner or backing vocalist on every track here.

Take a look at the credits list if you want to figure out who had artistic control. As for the "S&M, bondage, power exchanges, and all manner of kink," when I look back at photos or video footage of the tour on the Internet, it makes me sick to my stomach.

All I will say is, this wasn't a Lita Ford album.

Let me state for the record: I disown *Wicked Wonderland*.

IN THE MONTHS that followed the release of *Wicked Wonderland,* my husband declared, "There's no money in the music industry." He said, "If we want to make some money, why don't we do a reality show."

I thought it had the potential to be cool, but we had to be realistic. We needed professional management, unlike the *Wicked Wonderland* experience.

We called Morey Management, who had represented Miley Cyrus, and much to our surprise, they got on a plane and flew to Florida to meet us. I made them pasta and served red wine. We showed them the house and they got to meet our boys. They flew back to Los Angeles and thought that they could work with us. We had a manager. *Awesome!* They helped us find an agent, and we started shopping for a reality show. It took months, but the Gersh Agency finally landed us a contract with TLC.

They drew up an agreement and sent it to us. The way it was worded bothered me. It didn't say "Lita Ford" anywhere on the contract. "They're signing us because this is Lita Ford's family. Not for any other reason." I was confused. A couple of months passed, and the contract issue still bothered me. I hadn't spoken to our managers since they had been at our house. It pissed me off that I was in the dark about how I was going to be portrayed. I would be damned if I was going to be presented as a broken-down Cinderella on national television. I wouldn't let it happen. I needed the truth, and I knew the only way to get it was to find it myself.

I told my husband, "I'm going to get on a plane to meet the TLC gang. I also want to talk to Jim Morey and Bobby Collin," the company's top executives.

When I walked in to meet with the TLC people, they were thrilled to see me. I was shocked because of what I had been told about them before I left for LA. I sat down with the director from TLC, a couple of the main writers, and the vice president of TLC and had a great conversation. They had some exciting ideas. Morey Management sent me over to a songwriter so that we could write some songs for the show. We wrote two really great songs. One was going to be the title track for our reality TV show. The kids were also going to make an album as a Jonas Brothers–type group. We would have had a reality TV show, and the kids would have had their own album. I think it would have been successful.

After that I made more trips to Los Angeles. I was getting more confident and asserting my independence; it was as if being back in LA had awoken me from a nightmare.

The spell was broken. But life's never simple. The path ahead of me would be as dark and challenging as anything that had come before.

I made the two last flights to LA by myself. For only the third time in seventeen years of marriage, I was alone—without the boys or my husband.

When I was in Los Angeles, my cell phone broke, and so I walked into a Sprint store to buy a new phone. The salesman said, "Lita Ford?"

I said, "Yes, that's me." It felt good to hear someone say my real name after so many years of not hearing it. They hooked me up with a brand-new phone, listed under my own name. It might sound like a small thing to most people, but it felt like an important step in reclaiming my identity and freedom.

For more than a decade I had done the best I could to endure the way I was living, but I knew staying in my marriage would have been the death of me, emotionally and spiritually. It was time for Lita Ford to return.

I flew home to Florida eleven hours earlier than originally sched-uled. I landed in Fort Lauderdale, rented a car, drove to my attorneys' office, and filed divorce papers. I had bravely crossed the point of no return—but I didn't understand how devastating the fallout would be. What happened next was pure heartbreak. I succeeded in gaining my independence, yet I would lose the most precious part of my life.

I PAID THE ultimate price for my freedom.

When I filed for divorce in 2010, I lost my boys. Suddenly they would not speak to me or visit me. It was a complete transformation from my social, lively, and colorful boys. Their neighbor, who is a respected attorney, witnessed the change in them too. She came out of her house one day, said hello, and the boys ran back inside the house. This wasn't some stranger; we used to go to her house often to ride horses and play with her animals. Now the boys wouldn't speak to her, either. It seemed unreal that the sons I had poured all my love and life into could turn against me.

In retrospect, I have deep sympathy for them. Breaking away from my marriage was the hardest thing I'd ever done—but I was able to draw on enough life experience to finally understand the situation I was in wasn't right. My kids were not so lucky. They knew nothing else. In fact, their primary contact with the outside world—extreme martial arts—seemingly reinforced their home environment, proudly promoting the virtue of being "loyal disciples." (Readers may be inter-ested to learn that "Control" is the third tenet of the "Gracie Triangle.") By leaving the family, I was now a disloyal outsider. It seemed as if I was being shunned.

I have chosen not to detail the divorce proceedings here. Ultimately, the only fact that matters is that I became disconnected from my dar-lings. It's hurt me beyond measure. And unfortunately it seems that if you pay the right attorneys the right amount of money, the courts turn a blind eye and allow parents to be cut out of their children's lives. It's called parental alienation.

For a time I moved into an apartment nearby my boys, hoping to reconnect with them. I had a sleeping bag, a pillow, my suitcase, and my two dogs who slept at my feet. The apartment complex I was staying in was full of kids. Every time one of them would be close by, the dogs would get all excited, thinking it was James and Rocco.

No one will ever know the emotional pain I experienced. I want James and Rocco—and the rest of the world—to know it is not their fault. They are children—*my* children.

SHORTLY AFTER I escaped from my horrible situation, I went in to get my soon-to-be-ex-husband's name removed from my forearm. I had them black it out because it would have taken two and a half years for them to burn off that name, and I wasn't going to wait. I had waited long enough to escape from my life with him. I let it heal for about three months and then went to get it blacked out again, and this time I had them add the red lining to the black widow symbol as well as the script BLACK WIDOW right below it. I had survived a miserable hell, and now I had the battle scars to prove it.

LOST AND ALONE, I turned to the only thing that could give me solace: music. During the divorce proceedings I started playing guitar again and writing songs. Working again and doing shows kept me busy and my mind off the horrible things that were going on. I got involved with David Fishof's Rock and Roll Fantasy Camp. It's such a rewarding feeling to get a group of five strangers who have never played together into a room and watch them grow into a band in just four days. Sometimes they come in nervous or scared, but I always remember what Mike Chapman told me in a preproduction meeting decades ago when he saw my hands shaking. "Lita, if you weren't scared, I'd be nervous, because being scared means you care."

To see fans care that much about playing their instruments with me is a humbling experience. Sometimes you get a camper who isn't as cooperative. At one particular camp, I had one girl in my group who came in, sat down, and crossed her arms. She looked miserable. I said to her, "Stand up."

"I don't want to stand up."

"Okay. Well, we have to write a song, so let's all write a song."

She said, "I don't want to write a song about sex, drugs, or rock and roll."

"Well, why are you here?" I asked her.

I suggested writing a song called "Agony," because she looked like she was in agony being there. We got started and all of a sudden, she started singing and totally sang the shit out of it. The issues she was having in her life at the time had made her angry, but I saw her channel all of that into our group's song. It was so rewarding to see her get off that chair!

At one of the Rock and Roll Fantasy Camps, I reconnected with guitarist Gary Hoey. We had met years before, but had never really had the opportunity to know each other well. We exchanged information, and sometime after that, Gary called me and said, "Lita, I have a studio in my house, and if you ever want to record here, you're more than welcome to." It would be about a year into the divorce ordeal before I took Gary up on his offer and headed to New Hampshire. I thought that getting out of the scene and studios in LA and into a very peaceful place in the woods—which had a soothing, calming vibe—would do me some good. Gary's studio had a very homey feel to it. We allowed ourselves to feel that the music was right, because when you're alone like that, I think you really come to more of the truth in your work.

When Gary and I started working together musically, we were finishing each other's sentences. We had many of the same influences, so when we connected, it was effortless. The first song we wrote and recorded was "Branded," which was about the tattoos I had gotten while I was married. There were times when I would play a solo and Gary would say, "Wow, that's awesome"; then he'd add something, and I'd say, "Woah!" Gary's guitar parts complemented mine. The next song we wrote was "Love to Hate You," which would turn out to be the happiest song on what would become the *Living Like a Runaway* album. We traded off licks and guitar parts in that song because as a duet, it felt right doing it that way. In "A Song to Slit Your Wrists By," I played the first part of the guitar solo and then handed the guitar to Gary, and he played the second half. It got to the point that when we'd play back the songs, I couldn't tell whether some parts were mine or Gary's! That's how connected we were musically.

When I went back to Gary Hoey's house for the second time, we wrote "The Mask" and "The Asylum." After working with Gary, I felt like I had just had the best sex of my life, through music: it was a creative thrill I hadn't felt in sixteen years. I loved it.

Some nights, I'd say, "I'm not going to play guitar on this," and he'd say, "Lita, you *have* to play guitar on this." He knew as well as I did that I had to make this the best thing I had ever done. "My" previous album, *Wicked Wonderland,* had damaged my credibility in the industry to such an extent that I needed to reset everyone's expectations.

Sometimes we'd get started recording, and I'd ask to begin from the top.

"Sorry, can I do that again?"

Gary responded, "Lita, you can do a hundred takes if you want. You're the artist."

Slowly I gained confidence in myself after not playing or being in the studio for so long. After a decade and a half away, I had to rediscover who Lita was, and Gary brought that out of me.

It was such a different, positive feeling compared to the awful emotions I was dealing with during the divorce. It may have saved my life.

I WAS EXPERIENCING extreme highs writing with Michael Dan Ehmig and Gary Hoey, and profound lows because I'd had to deal with the horrible feelings about my relationship with James and Rocco. Gary and his beautiful wife, Nicole, and their kids were a godsend in my life. He took me into his studio and his family welcomed me into their home, and I was able to dump all the pain I was going through into my music. They were so wonderful to me. Nicole would make me blueberries, yogurt, and granola for breakfast, whatever she could get me to eat. My mind was always on my kids so I didn't feel like eating much. It was usually coffee and that was it. She kept trying to be my home cook and take good care of me. One night, I helped Nicole make dinner. I showed her how to make the pasta sauce my mom had taught me to make all those years ago. It was so much fun. While we were working, Gary would call into the house—which was steps away from the studio—and Nicole would copy down notes and put them in a neat order so that I could use them for my lead vocals. I never wanted to leave. It felt like I was home. I fell in love with their children, who were the same ages as my boys, and they adored my dogs.

I went back to Gary's many times, and each visit, we'd get into the groove of writing songs. I would lay down a vocal, then Gary and I would put in the rest. Then we'd play the song back to Nicole and the kids. If Nicole wasn't in tears, or someone in the room wasn't in tears, or the teenage friends that Alison had over didn't like it, then we'd record it again. It always helped us out to hear the ideas that Nicole had. She was honest and would give input as to whether something was too slow, too much, not enough. She was as much a part of the record as Gary and I were.

When we would get stuck on ideas, I'd call Michael Dan and say something like "I have a song idea about an angel but it's become about the devil." A few seconds later he'd sing a line like "Love don't come easy for a lonely soul like me. . . . I find myself in trouble on a road to misery. . . . I try to do the right thing but I'm easily misled. . . . I'm drawn to the dark side . . . and the devil in my head," and I would be like, "What the hell?! Yes! That's brilliant!" If I didn't know him as well as I do, I don't think that I would have been able to write the album the way we did.

Michael Dan and Gary Hoey and his family saw me through the entire record when a lot of people would have turned their backs on me and said, "No, I don't want to work with Lita. She's too eighties." At this point I had been out of the music scene for twenty years. When

I returned, I had no idea where the music culture was, since we never listened to the latest music on the island. I played what I wanted and not whatever was the flavor of the month. Just to make life easier, I didn't start listening to music (other than my own) when I lived in LA. As far as I was concerned, I'd earned my right to play whatever the fuck I wanted to play. Which was exactly what I did.

IN BETWEEN WRITING sessions, I would go back to Florida to meet with attorneys, go to court, and, most of all, to see my boys. I did that for almost a year as I wrote what would become my next album. I wished James and Rocco could have come up to New Hampshire to play in the snow with Gary's kids. My children had never experienced winter. I wanted to take them so badly, but the alienation continued: I was unable to speak to the boys on the phone or even e-mail or text. I was blocked on Facebook. All communication was denied. This was *not* court ordered.

From my perspective, the legal system didn't care about my kids. My ex was allowed to take the children "fishing" to a country where US laws do not apply. A place I knew they'd never come back from. If they do, I sure won't be told about it. The record was handed in to the label the same day my divorce was made final in February 2012. I came out of it with a good amount of money, but it should have been *a lot* more considering the millions of dollars' worth of land we owned. But I just wanted to be free of my ex-husband, and I wanted the whole process to stop torturing the kids, so I accepted the shitty deal. The only thing I truly wanted was my children, and with the boys acting the way they were, it had become painfully clear I was going to lose my sweet baby James and Rocco. I took the reduced sum of money, signed the settlement, and got on with my life.

To be clear: I would give up all the money in the world to be able to hold my boys in my arms.

CHAPTER 15

LIVING LIKE A RUNAWAY

Run baby run.

—"LIVING LIKE A RUNAWAY"
(WRITTEN BY LITA FORD AND MICHAEL DAN EHMIG)

EVERY NIGHT I WOULD GOOGLE "LITA FORD" ON MY LAPTOP, SITTING AT the office chair. I would look at my old videos and listen to my old interviews, trying to recover my identity. Whoever that person was, "Lita Ford," I missed her. I wanted her back! I would see clothes I used to wear, people I used to know, things I used to do, guitars I used to play, things that made me remember who I was. A Grammy-nominated artist. I would sit there deep into the night, transfixed by old videos. I hadn't been that person in such a long time. Each night I studied images on the Internet, and I slowly started to remember who I was.

After the divorce was final, I moved back to California because I consider it my home. My parents are buried there, my aunts, uncles, and cousins live there, and it's where I started my career. LA had changed so much over the years that I had no idea where to look for a home. I was shell-shocked. I got a place in a temporary housing complex back at the good ol' Oakwoods and decided I would stay there until the tour for the album started. One night in my apartment in LA, I was on the phone with Michael Dan. I explained my living situation to him and he said, "Lita, you *are* living like a runaway." With that we had an album title: *Living Like a Runaway.*

When people ask me, "Lita, what really happened those fifteen years you were gone from the music scene?," I tell them to listen to *Living Like a Runaway.* The songs tell the story of my life during those painful, isolated, horrible years, but they also tell the story of how I survived some of the most tragic events of my life.

I WROTE A song on the new album called "Mother" for my kids. It's dedicated to them. Their photograph is on the record beside the lyrics. When I first brought the idea to Gary, I knew it could come out one of two ways—really great or really cheesy. We tried it, and it turned out beautiful! We got tears of approval from Nicole, and we knew we had stumbled across something special. When I played that solo, it would be the same heartrending emotions I had when I played the solo for "Lisa." Gary stayed up late adding some beautiful little subtleties. All those years later, it was as if I had come full circle from "Lisa." I wrote a song about *my* mother, and now I had written a song for my own children, as *their* mother.

The song explains parental alienation because I want my boys to know what happened. Pouring the pain from losing my boys into my new record wasn't enough. I've found that there are so many people all over the world who are going through parental alienation. In every country, in every state we are being ripped off, and the legal system is using our children to do so. It's become one of the main causes I have dedicated my time to, not just for me and my boys but for all the mothers and fathers out there who have experienced it. My heart goes out to all parents and children who have had to suffer this pain beyond measure. It's one of the reasons I made the video for "Mother." The fact that most of our legal system, family law, judges, politicians, and so on allow it to happen is absolutely gross. In my opinion, they are the true criminals who should be put in jail for allowing parental alienation to happen in our family law systems. I take comfort in the fact that truth always prevails in the end, and one day my boys will come find me.

In the meantime, I will never stop fighting for them.

To my sons, James and Rocco: I want you to know I've tried calling you, texting you, writing you letters, sending messages on Facebook and to your martial-arts schools, and using any other form of communication possible to reach you. Every message seems to have been intercepted. You are the true loves of my life.

I BELIEVE ANGELS helped me through the difficult period when I was writing *Living Like a Runaway*. Like the time a handwritten note my mother wrote before she died fell out of a box of old magazines that had been sent to me from the islands. It was written on an old Sheraton Hotel notepad. It must have been from a tour we were on in the 1980s. It read: "I shall love you always, Mother." That note is at the end of the "Mother" video. I decided to just leave everything in God's hands, because I trusted he would always work out the situation. My managers knew it, Michael Dan knew it, and Gary knew it. After escaping such a hell, angels were watching over me.

I was still with Morey Management, and Bobby Collin had gotten me a licensing deal with SPV Records, which was the best I could do at the time given how much *Wicked Wonderland* had diminished my credibility in the industry. My management helped me put together a team of people, including business managers and a booking agency that landed me a spot on the Rock of Ages tour opening for my old buddies Def Leppard and for Poison. It was a godsend.

Living Like a Runaway was released the day before the tour started. The response was amazing. Loudwire.com hit the nail on the head: "The deeply personal album shows [Lita Ford] at her most vulnerable and honest point as an artist." My hometown paper, the *Los Angeles Times*, wrote, "After 11 years of semi-exile on a Caribbean island and a harrowing divorce, and just in time for '80s-metal nostalgia and Runaways revivalism, the mother of all metal is back"; "much of *Living*

Like a Runaway is about what Ford went through. That channeling of energy gives the album a powerful visceral charge." *Guitar World* hailed *Living Like a Runaway* as "one of the best rock albums of the year" and recognized it as my "true comeback album," in a dig at *Wicked Wonderland*. Many other reviewers noted the contrast to my previous record. *Rolling Stone* wrote: "2009's nü metal-inspired *Wicked Wonderland* left many of [Lita Ford's] hardcore fans befuddled. So the former Runaways guitarist recorded an album much more in line with her earlier efforts." "Ford strips away some of the conceptual and electronic mayhem that made the last album so confusing," wrote *All Music*, concluding, "fans will be relieved and thrilled to hear her return to form." Nobody was more relieved or thrilled than I was—and the fans couldn't have been more amazing on that tour.

I hired Mitch Perry to play guitar and Marty O'Brien to play bass. I had known Mitch for years—he was like a brother—but I had never met Marty. I did some research on Marty and really, really liked him as a person. Plus, he was a badass bass player. My drummer was later replaced by the great Bobby Rock. We sounded like rolling thunder.

Salt Lake City was our first show, and we went to play before ecstatic sold-out crowds in forty cities. Seeing the fans, my family, and my musician friends again was such a beautiful feeling and also helped me to remember who I am. It was like I had just woken up from a bad dream. People I hadn't talked to in years or had been kept from talking to: my former keyboard player, my ex-boyfriend, some old friends and family. Now I have a lot of these people back in my life, and it's wonderful. I found out a few had passed away, which was sickening to hear, because at the time of their deaths I was not able to show affection or share memories. I had to bury my feelings. But not anymore.

The tour lasted four months, and it gave me the strength and the confidence to know that I could rise again. Things were looking good for me career-wise, but just like when my father died, I felt like I was trading something really bad happening in my life for something really great.

ON ONE OF our days off during the Def Leppard–Poison tour, we decided to play a little club in San Antonio, Texas. I had a powerful band that was extremely loud and ballsy, but I couldn't hear my vocals over the band because there were no floor wedges in the monitor system, and we were not on in-ears. I had a fever and a sore throat that night and thought, *I can't scream over my band*. I started pacing across the stage. Back and forth, back and forth. I was so mad I thought about throwing my Marshall amp head across the stage. Instead I jumped off the front of the stage and started walking through the audience. I didn't really know where I was going, I just knew that I had to get to a place in the room where I could hear my vocals. As I was pushing my way through the crowd, all of a sudden I bumped into the bar. It was covered with everyone's drinks, so I swept my arm across the bar, pushing everyone's drinks to the floor and clearing a space for me to jump up and stand on it. My sound man at the time, Tom, looked at me and smiled and gave me the nod of approval to go ahead. Awesome! Dugie, my tech, grabbed my mic stand, my set list, and my guitar off the stage and brought them over to me. I strapped on my guitar and looked down at the bartender and ordered a vodka on the rocks. At that point I was standing across the room from my band, who were still onstage. I finished the entire show standing on the bar. Not bad! After the show, Dugie said to me, "Well, there's one for the books." One of the many adventures of coming back into the music industry, I guess. The audience loved it.

AS THE END of the tour's celebration with Def Leppard and Poison, I broke down and drank some Irish whiskey with Joe Elliott. Their band and crew have a game you play where you take a rinse-and-spit paper cup, fill it with Irish whiskey, drink a shot, throw the cup in the air, then watch it drop. If it lands upside down you have to drink another shot. If it lands right side up, you are done and win the game. Well, I remember our guitarist, Mitch Perry, walking into the room and saying, "When I was in here a few minutes ago there were only two cups on the floor. Now there's eighteen." Ah, yeah, Mitch. Jeez. I hadn't noticed.

Anyway. I gave Joe a hug good-bye and made my way to my dressing room, where I said my good-byes to Rick Allen. What a wonderful man he is. Rick and the entire crew: Phil, his wife, Helen—they were such wonderful human beings as well as insanely great musicians. The real deal, no doubt.

I started walking back to my bus to ride eight hours home. It's a good thing I left when I did, because the whiskey was creeping up on me. I climbed into the bus, went into the restroom, and sat on the toilet. All of a sudden the bus began to move, and so did my head. My manager, Bobby, said to me, "Are you okay? Can I get you anything?" I said, "Ah, yeah! Stop this bus from moving!" Oh, no. I hadn't had that much to drink in years. I was in for the night of my life.

I started vomiting, trying to aim in the toilet and not spill any on my leather pants. I was able to get them off, in this little cramped bathroom on the bus, and Bobby handed me a trash can to throw up in. Every ten to fifteen minutes or so my manager would get the trash can and dump it out the bus door as we were moving down the freeway. I puked in between emptying buckets and I puked between my legs into the toilet while I sat on it. Just like in the old days. Things seemed to be completely back to normal.

The next morning I called Joe Elliott and told him I woke up in someone's bunk. Joe said, "Really, no shit. I woke up at six o'clock this morning facedown in the front lounge of the bus." If you know Joe Elliott, he never, ever hangs out in the front lounge: he always took the back lounge for himself. He said he didn't know where he was. I told Joe it took me thirty minutes to figure out whose bunk I was in. Then I looked out and saw, in perfect order, a bottle of water, a trash can for puking, a box of tissues, a Sprite, a ginger ale, and a wet towel, neatly folded. I finally realized I was in my own bunk and that Bobby had laid everything out in the utmost order. Bobby saved my life that night. Everyone else went to bed and left me alone. Bobby treated me like I was his daughter, which meant the world to me. How he emptied those trash cans full of Irish whiskey vomit was beyond me, but he did. That's a real brave manager. I was grateful for the help. However, poor Joe had to play a show that night in Santa Barbara, California. I don't know how he did it. I bet he was in great pain.

BOBBY HAD CALLED Kenny Laguna to arrange a dinner for Joan Jett and me. I had been in and out of the Long Island, New York, area so many times and was never able to hook up with Joan. Bad timing, I guess. Despite our rocky road, I was excited to see her. When I arrived in New York City, I called her and said, "I'm here!"

Joan said, "I'll meet you around the corner." She had picked a little Italian place.

"Call me when you're ten minutes out and I'll walk over."

"Okay."

I hung up and started to get cleaned up after a long five-hour flight. Forty-five minutes later, the phone rang.

"We're about ten minutes out. We'll see you in ten."

I said, "'We'? Who is 'we'?"

Joan and Kenny, of course.

I choked. *Really. Kenny?* I thought, *Oh shit—couldn't she go anywhere without Kenny?* I would never take Bobby to a girls'-night-out dinner, nor would Bobby want to go with me. Bobby was a little perturbed that Kenny was there and he was in LA. Either way, I needed a date ASAP!

I went downstairs to the lobby where the guys were rolling in from Los Angeles for David Fishof's Rock and Roll Fantasy Camp event. I saw my dear friend Rudy Sarzo just arriving. I went up behind him and said, "Rudy!" He jumped out of his skin.

I said, "I'm so sorry. What are you doing?"

"Nothing, why?"

"I need your help."

"Okay. For what?"

I told him I was stuck for a date, that Joan was coming to meet me for dinner in ten minutes, that she was bringing Kenny with her, and that I needed him to be my date for the night.

"Oh, cool. Yeah, no problem. Let me go upstairs and clean up, drop off my bass and luggage, and I'll be right down."

"Okay. Hurry up," I said.

"Don't worry, I will."

Sure enough, thank God for Rudy. He was the perfect date.

It was perfect timing for a Runaways reunion. Unfortunately, Sandy had lost her battle with lung cancer and passed away in 2006. We all missed her and knew that it would be next to impossible to replace such an awesome drummer and a huge part of what made up the Runaways. But thankfully the rest of us were still capable of kicking ass. I wanted to ask Joan, "Why don't we get the Runaways back together? NOW!" I had e-mailed Joan that very question a month prior to this dinner, but she didn't acknowledge my e-mail, nor did she bring it up at all during dinner. She completely ignored my Runaways question, which blew my mind. I couldn't raise it in front of Kenny because it was about the girls in the band. Not him. It was supposed to be our decision, not Kenny's. The only problem was that now, the timing was ideal. Not 1999. Now! Timing is everything. It was one of those things where it's now or never. Fans were asking for the Runaways. Demanding the Runaways!

As I was saying good-bye to Joan, she reached into her pocket and took out a Sharkfin guitar pick that said JOAN JETT on it. She said, "Do you remember these?" Those were the picks I used in the Runaways, before I received the home plate pick from Ritchie Blackmore. I had turned Joan on to Sharkfin picks in the early Runaways days. "I still use them," she said. That warmed my heart a bit. She never mentioned the Runaways that night. And I felt that, with Kenny sitting there, it was impossible to talk. Still, it was good to see Joan. It only took thirty years.

She drove off with Kenny, and I went into the hotel with Rudy. Rudy was a total gentleman, and I thanked him. He knew what was going down and had tried to help as best he could. We said good night, then went to our separate rooms to get ready for the camp the next day in NYC.

IN THE MONTHS that followed, I spoke to Joan a couple more times. She still didn't bring up the Runaways. One time she e-mailed me Cherie's contact information. Cherie had asked Joan to give it to me. So I decided to call Cherie.

"*Liiiiiii-taaaaa!*" she screamed when she answered the phone. That put a huge smile on my face. We ended up having dinner together, and we talked about our ex-husbands and our children. I told her about my ordeal with the boys. I recall being shocked and upset when Cherie said, "Well, Lita, maybe you were just meant to suffer in life!" What a horrible thing to say to someone! I said, "Cherie, can you imagine if your ex took your kids away?"

She said, "Oh no! I'd curl up and die!"

Cherie's son is a handsome and talented redhead. She and her ex-husband are best friends. "I wish me and my ex could be like that," I said to Cherie. "You are so lucky. You have your son too. You don't realize how lucky you are."

She said, "Yes, I do. I count my blessings every day." That night, I realized Cherie and I had never really gotten to know each other while we were in the Runaways. Kim had put together the band with five teenage girls who didn't know one another. It was like going to class in a school with girls you don't know: not everyone in the classroom gets along with each other. Cherie and I are very different people. But Cherie and I did a couple of photo sessions together, and we sang a Christmas song together.

WHEN YOU FLY as often as I do, you're bound to have run-ins with airport security. We must have about thirty of the TSA's "Notice of Baggage Inspection" flyers in each guitar case. These are the calling cards they leave in your luggage to let you know they've rummaged through your stuff. My tech Dugie lays them down on the guitar, so when the TSA person opens the case, they know we're wise to them. Once, Dugie opened a case and there was a note from the TSA saying, "I suppose you think this is funny." Yeah, actually it is! I've got a long-running grudge against the TSA because they snapped the headstock off my red Warlock. Dugie was the one who had to break the news to me. Needless to say, I was upset that they had broken one of my prized possessions.

We were coming back from Sturgis after our show in 2013. That weekend 750,000 bikers had come through town, and ninety bands played. There were people selling stuff everywhere: souvenirs, hand-made items, you name it. There were people running around naked. Little old men wearing nothing but a cock ring. Later that night, I came by again and those same old men were wearing hoodies. Little old men in hoodies and cock rings. A great combo.

I met one man who was selling all kinds of items out of his van on the side of the road. He showed me some switchblades. They were so badass! I bought one and he wrapped it up for me. I got to my hotel and threw it into my makeup bag. I put my huge makeup bag into the suitcase I was checking and flew back to LA. I got home, unpacked my stuff, and forgot about the switchblade.

A couple of days later we left for yet another show and this time I threw my makeup bag in my carry-on. We got to LAX and I put my purse through the metal detector. The lady working the conveyor belt called a police officer over. I thought I had left a bottle of water in my purse.

"I left water in there, didn't I?"

"No, ma'am."

They called a couple more officers over. There were about five after all was said and done. I thought, *Boy, I sure have a lot of police officer fans here at LAX.*

My tour manager was asking what was going on but was being kept away from me. When I saw him panic, I knew then that something was wrong.

"What is it? What did I do?"

"Do you realize you have a switchblade in your purse?"

Oh fuck, the switchblade! I had forgotten all about it. It was still in the box.

I explained that I had been playing at Sturgis, the biker festival, that I was a rock musician, and that I had forgotten I'd thrown it into my makeup bag.

Another officer came over and said, "I need your driver's license. I'm going to run your license and if ANYTHING AT ALL comes up, you're going straight to jail."

"Fine, run it."

I knew it was going to come up clean so I wasn't worried. The officer came back and said, "I ran it, it's clean. I'm going to write you up for a misdemeanor."

I was trying to further explain myself, and the officer shoved the ticket in my face and said, "Explain it to the judge on your court date." I put my tail between my legs and wandered off with our tour manager to board the plane.

My business manager had to hire a criminal defense attorney to make sure this switchblade incident didn't turn into something bigger than it was, because they could have put me on a no-fly list and sunk my ability to tour. The day I was scheduled to appear in court I got stuck in LA rush-hour traffic. Great. I called my attorney who was close to the courthouse and asked her to show up in my absence. Before I knew it, the judge was on the phone. He had apparently googled me, and said, "I looked you up, I see what you do, I know who you are, I get it." Whew! What a cool dude! The charge was dropped. Another travel story that ended up a lot better than it could have. I'm convinced I have angels watching over me every day of my life.

CHRISTMAS 2013 ROLLED around, and to keep myself from going crazy without my sons, James and Rocco, in my life, I wrote and recorded a Christmas single with my dear friend Rodger Carter. Rodger played drums, and we recorded it at his studio, the Dog House. Cherie would end up singing the song with me as a duet. I said to her, "This is a song that will come out and be played every year." Cherie and I are just becoming comfortable around each other again. But we had a blast in the studio together, laughing a lot. What a big difference from our Runaways studio sessions. My dear friend Gene Kirkland took pictures while we recorded.

Shortly after the Christmas single was released, I found out that I was going to be receiving *Guitar Player* magazine's Certified Guitar Legend Award. I was so happy. I heard I had won the award when I was on tour and on my way to South America. I couldn't wait to get back to accept it.

This was something I'd waited almost an entire lifetime to achieve: to be recognized for my abilities as a guitarist. I had traveled a long, hard road to hear such praise from an awesome but male-dominated guitar-slinging magazine. Mike Molenda from *Guitar Player* had acknowledged the work I had done through the years, and also the fact that I'm still standing tall after four decades in the industry. Mike and Cherie Currie presented me with the award at the Sunset Strip's Whisky A Go Go on March 24, 2014, at a benefit show for multiple sclerosis. Although an MS benefit wasn't the first place I would have chosen to accept the award, it was still one of the highlights of my life. Thank you, Mike Molenda and *Guitar Player* magazine, for making my year and my life complete. It's something I will take to my grave, when it's "my time."

CHERIE ASKED ME to go along with her and her son, Jake, to visit Kim Fowley, who had been diagnosed with cancer. Kim had written four songs for Cherie and was too weak to travel outside of his home. When he saw me, Kim said, "You look like your mother." If you knew my mother, that was a compliment.

I said, "Thank you. She was a lovely lady."

"Yes, she was," Kim said, remembering that my mother had died from cancer. Kim wrote some songs for Cherie, and later he wrote a song for me that will be on my next album. It's got deep lyrics: something I'd never heard Kim write before.

By this time, Kim had developed several types of cancer and had a lot of health issues. I was worried for him. We stayed in touch by phone and e-mail, especially when the *Guardians of the Galaxy* movie soundtrack came out and used "Cherry Bomb." The song finally reached No. 1 and was nominated for a Grammy—thirty-seven years after it was first released, the Runaways had a platinum record! I also told Kim about my boys.

I told Kim, "I don't think I would be who I am today if not for Kim Fowley." He discovered me. Plucked me out of Long Beach and created the Runaways. He was the mastermind, the creator of the Runaways. Not Lita Ford. Not Joan Jett. Not Kari Krome. Not Cherie Currie. Not Jackie Fox. Kim Fowley: that's who single-handedly changed the face of rock and roll with an all-girl teenage jailbait rock group. Several months after this meeting Kim lost his battle with cancer. I was glad that I got to thank him for the Runaways. I didn't like seeing Kim sick, and I don't want to remember him like that. Cherie went on to record the songs he wrote for her, though the engineer they used did a funky job with dangling mics and bad recordings. Cherie's son, Jake, was left to fix it up on his own. The kid did a real good job. To put a twist on her versions of some Runaways songs she asked me to sing a duet with her. I was happy to. It was fun to reconnect with Cherie—and Kim—in that way.

WHEN EDDIE TRUNK first started *That Metal Show* on VH1 Classic, I had recently been a guest on his radio show. I was just coming back into the music business after my hiatus, and he wanted me on his new pilot for the TV show. I agreed and was on the very first episode. Eddie has always been a great supporter, and I've been back on his show several times. He also made me the first female musical guest. That meant I got to shred some licks as we led into commercial breaks or segments in the show. I had a blast doing it, and it was a pleasure to be back on the set.

Later that same year, in August 2014, Eddie turned fifty on the day we played a huge rock festival in Montana. Eddie was the host, so when it was time for the set, we played a couple of songs before I called him out onstage and had the crowd of thousands sing him "Happy Birthday." We had a crew member from the festival bring out the cake we had ordered for him and Marty O'Brien, my bass player, captured it all on his GoPro camera. It was a great moment for me and for Eddie.

Being on the road with my new band has brought many great new memories, but with all the traveling, there are also bound to be horror stories about lost baggage, missed flights, and even lost band members. I was playing this big club in Salt Lake City and the hotel we were staying at was about two doors down. Bobby Rock, my drummer, prefers to spend as little time at the gig as possible because he finds it draining. At this particular venue, he ended up using his hotel room as an extended backstage area because it was so close to the gig. The venue had an odd setup because the backstage area and the stage were completely separate—the stage was upstairs. The elevator was manually operated, so unless someone was in it to operate it, it didn't work. When it was showtime, Marty, Mitch, and I found ourselves waiting for Bobby. The intro was playing and he was nowhere to be found. Dugie got on the phone.

"Where the fuck are you?"

"I'm downstairs! Come get me! I can't get the elevator to come down and there is no other way for me to get into the venue from here!" He had left with more than enough time to get there, but had gotten stuck in this weird "holding area" for fifteen minutes while we searched for him and he tried to call us. Dugie goes down to get Bobby and he literally got to his drum kit right after the intro to our set had already played. It was one of the strangest *Spinal Tap* moments in both of our careers, and believe me, there have been many.

THE BAND AND I were going to be playing the Monsters of Rock cruise in 2015. We all packed up and flew across the country to Tampa, Florida, to play a show, then flew to Fort Lauderdale early the next morning to catch the ship. I was told to wait in an area with some fans who were having trouble boarding the ship. At first I was confused.

"Well, your passport is good, but your green card is two and a half months expired."

I thought to myself, *When I got my green card, they told me it was good for ten years.* After 9/11, anyone who is not an American citizen can only have a passport and a green card for no longer than ten years. I assumed my green card expired when my passport did. I was wrong.

"You can't get on the ship."

The lady helping me tried calling immigration, but all it did was alert them that my green card had expired and I was really in trouble. I had shows coming up in Canada and was worried. All the fans walking by were saying, "Rock on! Can't wait to see you rock out, Lita!"

I was thinking, *Maybe not.*

I waited five hours. Everyone else had boarded the ship at this point. Bobby and Pilgrim, my tour manager, were by my side, but everyone had done everything they could. Larry Moran is a great promoter and he helped tremendously, but the rules are the rules, and I wasn't getting on the ship.

The lady who was helping me then turned to me and said, "One last thing. We cannot leave the dock until we find your luggage."

I'm waiting, knowing I'm not getting on the ship, with Bobby sitting next to me while we wait for my luggage. The lady came back and told me, "I'm sorry, Lita, we can't find your luggage."

Things were off to a bad start. Bobby, realizing there was nothing more he could do and figuring he could work with the promoters once the cruise departed, boarded the ship.

I was in Miami, stranded, with no luggage. Awesome!

One of the promoters decided he wasn't going on the cruise, and he drove me to a nearby hotel. As we were pulling out of the terminal, I heard someone yelling, "Wait, wait! We found your suitcase. Pilgrim found it!" It had been sitting on a baggage cart and he happened to see it as he walked by. They put my luggage into the cab and off we went—my band on the ship and me headed to some hotel. Great.

When we got to the hotel, I called a friend of mine I hadn't talked to in ages and said, "Rudy, I need a yacht, a helicopter, or a private plane."

"Okay, baby, speak to me."

"I gotta catch a cruise ship in the Caribbean. I have to play a show."

Shortly after he hung up to see what he could do, he called me back and said, "I can fly you in a helicopter."

I would be flown to an island. Once I got to the island, I would still have to catch a boat to the other private island where the ship would be docking. Well, I figured it was better than nothing. I waited for another phone call to find out when the helicopter would be coming for me. Then I get some bad news: there was a wind storm so my friend couldn't fly the helicopter. Scratch that idea.

Rudy's sister Diana called me the next morning and said, "I might be able to get you a ninety-eight yacht. Let me see what I can do." But it turned out her connection who owned the yacht was out of town. Great. He was also the guy who had a private plane. I was shit out of luck.

Diana also happens to be an immigration attorney, so she called the immigration office for me. Turns out the guy who worked there had a crush on her and she begged him to get me an extension on my green card.

She called me and asked, "You have any eight-by-tens?"

"Um, yeah. Why?"

She starts to rattle off a list of names for me to personalize the 8 x 10s with, for pretty much everyone in the immigration office. I was there for about an hour signing photos, and by the time I left, I was able to board a flight from Miami to Nassau.

When I landed, I finally got ahold of Bobby, my manager.

"Bobby, I'm in Nassau."

"The ship docks at eight A.M. tomorrow morning."

That night, I had to stay in a hotel on the opposite side of the island, because all the other hotels had no vacancy. It was a piece-of-shit, run-down hotel, and the mosquitoes were horrible. I walked to get bug spray and covered myself in it before I went to bed. I just kept thinking to myself, *Just make it through the night. At seven A.M. you're outta here.*

The next morning, I asked the woman at the hotel how to get to where the ships dock.

"You have to take bus. On the 25." So there I was, with my suitcase, standing at the bus stop.

I boarded the bus and looked around. People going to work, school kids, you name it. Me, this rocked-out blonde, on the local bus headed toward the cruise ship pier. The driver put my suitcase at the back and with the wheels on the ground. Every time he'd put the brakes on, my suitcase would come flying forward, and when he pressed the gas, it would roll backward. The door on the bus didn't close properly so every time he'd hang a left, the door would open, and every time he hung a right, the door would close. Rush-hour traffic in the Bahamas. Gotta love it.

When we got to the stop, I didn't see any ships anywhere.

"You have to walk through the straw market. Keep walking that way," the bus driver said to me, gesturing. I should have known it wasn't going to be as easy as just getting off the bus and walking a few steps. I started walking and then got a text message: it was Bobby. "I see land."

I looked up and saw a ship in the distance. I was thrilled!

I got to the gate and the security guard there said, "I have a list of names here of people who are allowed to pass through, and your name isn't on it."

"You gotta be kidding me!"

Because of the green card issue, my name hadn't been added to the list of passengers who could board from other ports. But my green card was now up to date, so what was the problem? The promoter worked on getting me past the security guard. "Find a place to chill out. This is going to take a couple of hours." Right. Island time. How could I forget? I found a Starbucks. Yes! I went to hang out there until finally I was able to get on the ship.

Come hell or high water, I was going to be on that ship. I wasn't going to let my band down. When I arrived, they couldn't believe their eyes. They were thrilled to see me. Bobby Rock told me that people had come up to him at the buffet and said things like, "We heard. We're so sorry." Almost like there had been a death in the family. Marty O'Brien said he just wandered around for three days with no purpose. Every corner he'd turn people would ask him, "Is Lita going to make it? I heard that she's flying to an island with a helicopter and catching a speedboat, is that true?" It was like we were in a James Bond movie.

I had finally made it on the ship, and that morning they made a ship-wide announcement: "Ladies and gentleman, the Queen has arrived. The Queen is on the ship!" The last day of the cruise, Wendy Dio hosted a special cancer fund-raiser gala and when I walked into the place, the entire room shouted "Liiittaaaaa!" Everyone was so happy to see me, and it warmed my heart, especially after the crazy journey I had been on to get there.

But most of our performance slots had been given to other bands, so we had to play in a midday slot on the last day. I was hoping to play later, but it wasn't possible. The passengers were so drunk by the time we hit the stage that when I asked them if they could clap along to "Kiss Me Deadly," most of them had a hard time doing it. All I saw was a sea of sunburns and hangovers. Right after we were done with our set, a huge storm cloud came in and it started to rain. Had we played a later time slot, the rain would have forced our set to be cut short. There were those angels, looking out for me again.

BEFORE LEAVING FOR the Monsters of Rock cruise, I caught a black widow spider in my house. I trapped it in a Tupperware container and took it to rehearsal. Marty took the Tupperware container and put it on top of his bass rig.

"Marty, what are you going to do with that spider? Give me the container."

Marty and Bobby were convinced that the spider was dead. They got a kick out of the fact that a black widow spider had made its way to my house, of all places. It is the symbol I have used since the beginning of my solo career—one that I consciously chose because I knew that having come out of the Runaways, I could devour the boys of the music industry, no problem. I was ready to take on the world.

"Those things don't die that easily," I said. "Trust me, it's still alive."

We stood there and debated what to do with it. Flush it down the toilet? No, it would come back up and bite me in the ass, I thought. I wasn't about to step on it. Marty decided to take it home with him. The next day, he sent me an e-mail telling me he had gone to a crafts store and bought a kit to make a paperweight out of the black widow. At least it was out of my house.

At the next rehearsal, he came in and said, "Lita, you're never going to believe it! I had the spider in the container, and when I was getting ready to make it into a paperweight, my friend was holding the container and she said, 'Marty, this thing is still alive!' I couldn't believe my eyes!"

"I told you, Marty!" I said.

"Well, that goes to show, when Lita Ford tells you a black widow isn't dead, don't doubt her."

I thought that was the end of the black widow fiasco. After the cruise, I flew from Florida to Detroit to do a signing at a horror convention. I flew home three days later, looking forward to relaxing after a week of chasing cruise ships, city buses, and immigration offices. I walked into my house, put down my stuff, and walked over to my bedroom. It was all dark, and I walked toward my window to open the drapes, only to see this huge black ball hanging from the window screen, outside the sliding glass window.

"Oh dear God! Don't tell me it's another black widow spider!"

I went into the kitchen, grabbed another Tupperware container, and went outside to catch it. I wasn't sure what kind of spider it was, but I caught it. Sure enough, it had the red hourglass symbol on it. Another black widow! I walked into the kitchen and saw another one crawling out from behind the fridge. I looked in the hallway and found another one there. I needed to get the fuck out of that house! I went to a hotel and called my business manager, who contacted the exterminator. They promised to come the next day to try to get rid of the infestation. I was told that it would take seventy-two hours to kill them all. I stayed at the hotel and didn't come back for three days. When I walked in, I saw one spider on the floor and used a Tupperware container to catch it. Don't tell me they were still here?! It was the last spider I saw, but it was in the Tupperware container and wouldn't die. I ended up taking Marty's advice and put it in the freezer overnight. It was dead the next morning.

Maybe the black widow spiders *had* thought I was their queen. I couldn't help but smile about what Marty had said when I had brought that first spider to rehearsal: "Lita, they probably saw your jumpsuits with the red hourglass on them and thought, 'Yeah, man, this place is the shit! Let's hang out here!'"

I'VE COME A long way since the days when I would sit and stare at the stars and pray for God to help me and make me a better guitar player. Although I still do gaze at those stars, it's now for other reasons, and I ask God to help guide my children. I pray that one day soon the family court system will pay for the crimes they commit on a daily basis against the innocent children of the country. They are a disgrace to God and to the Constitution they stand behind. I think there is a special place in hell for the ones who have inflicted mental and emotional pain on children and their loving family members.

For years I have put my blood, sweat, tears, pain, sex, love, laughter, and heartache into paving the way for others. I put up with doors being slammed in my face, being turned down by many executives because I was female, and getting mind-fucked, financially and musically, by the assholes of the world. I was told what to do and what not to do, when all I wanted to do was be LITA and follow my dreams.

Here I am, fortysome odd years later, and the front row of most every concert is now lined with women. Women who want to rock, and play hard, sexy rock and roll, and the men who support these women are not afraid to step forward and show their loyalty. It's a beautiful thing. The rock world has evolved into a universal language that's no longer just for the testosterone-driven. The path is carved, and now it's free and clear for anyone who wants to walk it. The wonderful men who were the main musical influences in my life and helped to shape me as a guitarist, performer, and singer helped me become a charismatic leader in the male-driven world of heavy metal music. I truly believe I was put here on this earth as an only child, with the support of my incredible mother and father, and after going through the Runaways school-of-rock-and-roll college, to become an icon for those who weren't able to cross that line yet. Now they know they can.

As for me, I will go to my grave with the title "The Queen of Heavy Metal."

Why?

Because I am!

"Living Like a Runaway"

WRITTEN BY **LITA FORD** AND **MICHAEL DAN EHMIG**

I was running crazy, I was running wild.
Living on the edge, yeah, I was living in style.
My hands start shaking like the streets of Hollywood.
And my mind was wasted, I still did the best I could.

One day I left town with just the shirt on my back.
And a guitar on my shoulder, yeah, I wasn't coming back.
I had to break the spell that my heart was under
So I rolled out of town on wheels of thunder.
And I still remember what my mama said. She said:

Run baby run, cross New York City
Run baby run, through the streets of LA
Run baby run, yeah, you can't slow down.
You can never stay when you're living like a runaway.

I remember when I was seventeen, riding in the back of a black limousine.
I used to stare at the stars, and ask for God to please guide me
In the right direction. I didn't know where I was going.
I didn't know where I was gonna stay.
All I knew I was going far, far away.
And it still feels like yesterday, when he said:

Run baby run, cross New York City
Run baby run, through the streets of LA
Run baby run, yeah, you can't slow down.
And you can never stay when you're living like a runaway.

I left each town with a wink and a kiss, that maybe I'll be back real soon.
A lot of memories from fans like you, people that made my dreams come true.
And I can still hear them saying:

Run baby run, cross New York City
Run baby run, through the streets of LA
Run baby run, yeah, you can't slow down.
And you can never stay when you're living like a runaway.

ACKNOWLEDGMENTS

THANK YOU TO PETER HUBBARD AND EVERYONE AT HARPERCOLLINS, FOR your patience, trust, and belief in this book and for always having my back. To Bobby Collin, Jim Morey, Kyle Whitney, and everyone at the Morey Management Group: I asked to write a book, and they delivered HarperCollins. Along with Jeff Silberman from Folio Literary Management, together we made it all happen!

To everyone at King, Holmes, Paterno, and Soriano LLP, especially Peter Paterno, Harold Papineau, and Marjorie Garcia.

To Amir Malek from Glass/Malek: I wouldn't have made it so far without you. Special thanks to your staff and for all you do for me.

To Jon Freeman at Freeman Promotions: The fun has just begun. LOL. You've done an amazing job ever since we met. Now it's time to do it again. I have a list for you . . .

To my kick-ass band: Marty O'Brien, Bobby Rock, and Patrick Kennison. When you've got rolling thunder like these guys in your band, you'd better thank God and hope your face doesn't melt!

To my tech Kevin (Dugie) Dugan: We all love the Dugster. You are the number one road tech of all time.

ACKNOWLEDGMENTS

To Michael Dan Ehmig, my favorite songwriter whose friendship is as close as friendships get. Michael is the best lyricist on the planet, and together with Gary Hoey, producer on *Living Like a Runaway*, we had a blast! I talk to Michael a lot, and he keeps me grounded. So did recording *Living Like a Runaway* with Gary. It was a huge undertaking; I spent approximately four days at a time at Gary and his wife Nicole's place. We'd write songs with Michael on the phone and Gary and I in his studio. Nicole would be cooking, and their kids, Ian and Alison, would hang out and talk with my dogs. I loved them so much, because I was losing my kids and Ian and Alison were so wonderful—and the same age as my boys too. I felt my kids through Ian's and Alison's hearts. They knew it, and it was good. My God, a gift from God again! In *so* many ways.

To my sons' road dogs, Churro and Rascal: two four-legged, faithful, five-pound dogs.

To fireman Michael Tassaug, who was the only one there at times when I had no money or food.

To Robyn Melvin and everyone at the Hard Rock Cafe in Hollywood, Florida, my own personal SWAT team and my home away from home. My dear friends, they took in me and my children, fed us, and treated me like royalty.

To Kim Fowley: There are times when I think I wouldn't still be in the music business if not for you. Even though you want everyone to think you're one of the most frightening people in the world, you're the exact opposite. You actually have a heart. RIP Kim. Thank you for the gift you've given me.

To Chris Kizska, my partner in crime: You're a daredevil, and we make a good team. Thanks for always having my back.

To Kristine Johnson, my awesome neighbor: Thank you for being real. You saved me by letting me stash my guitars at your house.

Thanks to my endorsing companies: B.C. Rich Guitars, Marshall Amplification, Taylor Guitars, Dunlop, Dean Markley Strings, Peterson Strobe Tuners, Majik Box Custom Pedals and Electronics, Seymour Duncan, Monster, Taurus pedals, and to I.C.O.N., Lovecraft Leather, and Rockwood Saloon.

ACKNOWLEDGMENTS

It seems like God has been listening to me a lot lately. When I was asking myself "Who the hell understands what it's like to be Lita Ford enough to help me write this book?," the answer had to be a gift from God. Out of the blue, when I needed her most, God drops this little Italian rock-and-roll chick from Toronto, Canada, into my lap, who seems to know more about me than I know about myself. Thank you, God, and thank you, Martina Fasano, for being my cowriter.

From Martina Fasano: Thank you to my husband, Rocco; my daughter, Emily; and my parents for all your love and support; and to Lita for the opportunity to help her write the story of her life.

★ ★ ★

For more information about Parental Alienation and Kids First Parental Alienation Awareness, please go to www.kidsfirstpaa.org.

In addition to Parental Alienation awareness, I am also a proud supporter of cancer research, and pray that one day a cure for this horrible disease will be found.

And, for rock and roll that will melt your face off, please go to www.litafordonline.com.